HOW LONG? HOW LONG?

HOW LONG? HOW LONG?

African-American

Women

in the Struggle

for Civil Rights

BELINDA ROBNETT

Oxford University Press
New York   Oxford

Oxford University Press

Oxford   New York
Athens   Auckland   Bangkok   Bogotá   Buenos Aires
Calcutta   Cape Town   Dar es Salaam   Delhi   Florence   Hong Kong
Istanbul   Karachi   Kuala Lumpur   Madrid   Melbourne   Mexico City
Mumbai   Nairobi   Paris   São Paulo   Singapore   Taipei   Tokyo   Toronto   Warsaw

and associated companies in
Berlin   Ibadan

Copyright © 1997 by Oxford University Press, Inc.

First published in 1997 by Oxford University Press, Inc.
198 Madison Avenue, New York, New York 10016

First issued as an Oxford University Press paperback, 1999

Oxford is a registered trademark of Oxford University Press

Library of Congress Cataloging-in-Publication Data
Robnett, Belinda.   1956–
How long? How long?   :   African-American women in the struggle for
civil rights   /   Belinda Robnett.
p.   cm.
Includes bibliograpical references and index.
ISBN-13 978-0-19-511490-4; 978-0-19-511491-1 (pbk.)
ISBN 0-19-511490-6; 0-19-511491-4 (pbk.)
1. Afro-American women civil rights workers—History—20th century.
2. Afro-American—Civil rights—History—20th century.
3. Civil rights movements—United States—History—20th century.
4. Sex role—United States—History—20th century.   5.   Man-woman
relationships—United States—History—20th century.   I.   Title.
E185.61.R685   1997
305.48'896073'009045—dc21   97-2263

7 9 8 6

Printed in the United States of America
on acid-free paper

For my parents
Ozie and Novelette Robnett, whose hard work, support,
and love set me on a positive life course.

For my husband,
Neal, for standing by my side and helping
me keep my head above water.

For my sons,
David and Jonah, who are a constant source of joy.

"The Black female is assaulted in her tender years by all those common forces of nature at the same time that she is caught in the tripartite crossfire of masculine prejudice, white illogical hate and Black lack of power."

From *I Know Why the Caged Bird Sings*
by Maya Angelou, p. 265.

"You may write me down in history
With your bitter, twisted lies,
You may trod me in the very dirt
But still, like dust, I'll rise.

Leaving behind nights of terror and fear
I rise
Into a daybreak that's wondrously clear
I rise.
Bringing the gifts that my ancestors gave,
I am the dream and the hope of the slave.
I rise.
I rise.
I rise."

From *And Still I Rise*,
by Maya Angelou.

Acknowledgments

THERE ARE MANY PEOPLE without whom I could have never completed this book. First and foremost, I want to thank the activists who so graciously gave of themselves and their time to provide me with their powerful and thoughtful stories. For many, recalling the trials and tribulations in their struggle for freedom and justice was a source of both joy and pain. To all of you, I offer my appreciation for your openness, honesty, and trust.

I also wish to extend my gratitude to Diane Ware and the staff at the Martin Luther King, Jr. Center for Non-Violent Social Change; to the staff supervising the Civil Rights Documentation Project at the Moorland Spingarn Research Center at Howard University; and to the Boston University staff who provided access to the Martin Luther King, Jr. Papers. Although I requested numerous files, all who helped were kind and patient. A special thank-you is offered to Marymal Dryden, Georgia State University, and civil rights activists Reginald Robinson, Cleve Sellers, and Jack Chatfield, who were kind enough to assist me in locating the women activists.

Funding and in some cases leave time, without which this project could not have been completed, were provided by the Rackham Dissertation Grant, University of Michigan; American Sociological Association Minority Dissertation Fellowship, which was funded jointly by the Association of Black Sociologists and the Society of Women Sociologists; Center for the Continuing Education of

Women Scholarship, University of Michigan; Program on Conflict Management Alternatives Dissertation Grant, University of Michigan; the Wellesley College Mary McEwen Schimke Dissertation Scholarship; the University of California, Davis, Pre-Doctoral Fellowship; the Program on Economy, Justice & Society, University of California, Davis; and the Faculty Research Grant, Faculty Development Grant, the Murals Program, and the Humanities Institute Fellowship, University of California, Davis.

A project of this magnitude required the help of many graduate and undergraduate assistants. For their hard work, I thank undergraduates April Harris, Lael Washington, Carrie Goehring, Ghazi Wossne, and Lynn Matsuzaki. The support and assistance of graduate students Kimberly Meadows, Lara Gary, Lalia Kiburi, and Molly Cate sustained me during moments when I felt overwhelmed by the project and all of my other commitments. Lara provided excellent editorial assistance in a timely and professional manner. Lalia not only assisted with the interviewing but offered moral support as well. I am deeply grateful for their unwavering help and support. Throughout the writing process, Molly was of special help. She read the entire manuscript several times, offered editorial suggestions, and let me know when certain parts just weren't clear enough. She has also been a friend who constantly offered her opinion that the book is not only important but terrific. Bless you Molly!

Numerous mentors assisted me from the early days, when it was just a dissertation proposal, through its final stages. I especially thank Aldon Morris and Mayer Zald who, early on, had faith in my "fishing expedition." I am also indebted to Renee Anspach for her encouragement and helpful insights, and Edith Lewis for her intellectual reflections. In an earlier version, both Myra Marx Ferree and Verta Taylor were kind enough to provide extensive comments, even though we had not met. Verta Taylor, more than anyone else, has continued to mentor me, to shore me up when I am down, and to read the entire manuscript even while writing her own book. I am deeply grateful to her and to Michael Schwartz, whose intellectual challenges stimulated new ideas and insights. Their guidance, as well as David Meyer's, pushed me to expand my theoretical ideas. I am equally indebted to the anonymous reviewers who read, guided, and commented on a portion of this study that was published in the American Journal of Sociology. Reviewer A, in particular, set me on the right course—one which led to the development of many ideas for this book.

Along the way, colleagues from both the Sociology Department and the Women's Studies Program at the University of California, Davis, offered me tremendous encouragement. I especially want to thank Judy Stacey, Fred Block, Lyn Lofland, and John Hall for their suggestions and support at various stages in the development of this book. I also want to thank Judith Newton and Linda Morris, as well as the Women's Studies faculty for believing in the project. And, during my darkest moments, my friend and colleague, Vicki Burbank, provided moral support for which I was and am, grateful.

I am equally indebted to MaryBeth Branigan and the entire editorial staff at Oxford who were not only competent, but helpful. I especially want to thank my editor, Thomas LeBien, whose enthusiasm for and commitment to the book served to buttress my energy level as I revised the manuscript.

Last, but not least, I would like to thank a few of my Compton Unified School District teachers who inspired me along the way. I offer my appreciation to my third-grade Mark Twain Elementary School teacher, Mrs. Peters, who encouraged discovery and an appreciation for new ideas. Both Mr. Watkins and Mr. Grubbs, my Vanguard Junior High School history teachers, taught me to question "history as fact," the latter assigning me a thought-provoking book entitled *The Way It's Supposed to Be*, which, as I recall, questioned mainstream beliefs about the capabilities of African Americans. Thanks to these dedicated teachers, our curriculum included black history; and their love of teaching stimulated my interest.

Without the support of all those listed, I could not have completed this project. To all, a heartfelt thanks.

Contents

HOW LONG? HOW LONG?

Introduction

THIS BOOK WAS INSPIRED by childhood memories of the civil rights movement. As a child growing up in South Central Los Angeles, I was fortunate to attend schools in Compton, California, where Black people were the principals and teachers. This experience provided me with a sense of pride and an understanding of my Black heritage and community. Within this context, I was aware of the struggle for freedom and can still recall the emotional feelings sweeping over me while listening to Martin Luther King's speeches on the television.

My family had long endured the struggles against racism; my father's family is still in possession of my great-great grandmother's freedom papers. My father grew up poor but managed to obtain a college education through the G.I. Bill. But his bachelor's degree in biochemistry did not translate into a better job until after the civil rights movement. He, as well as many of my educated aunts and uncles, survived by taking any job he could get. My father, for example, was employed as a cafeteria bus boy, and my aunt worked in the post office. In the late 1950s and the early 1960s, it was not unusual to find Black people with PH.D.s working in the post office.

I can still recall the many sacrifices my parents made for our survival. Equally vivid are the memories of a family vacation in the South and my parent's fear when we made a wrong turn onto a backwoods road in Texas. Lynchings, rapes, and murders on such roads were prevalent at that time, and the fear did not subside

3

until we reached our destination. This fear, coupled with the memory of the FOR WHITES ONLY signs on the bathrooms and water fountains, remains as a powerful image from my youth. My interest in the civil rights movement is, therefore, both personal and academic.

Encouraged by my history teachers Mr. Watkins and Mr. Grubbs, I became an avid reader of Black history while at Vanguard Junior High School, and this personal interest has, quite naturally, extended into my academic work. While reading numerous accounts of the movement, I was struck by the paucity of information provided on the activities of women. I recalled watching footage of those attacked by dogs, water hoses, and batons. Women, it seemed, were suffering alongside men and sometimes children. I wondered who they were and why they had been so excluded by historians and other academicians in movement accounts.

I thought of my grandmothers, mother, and aunts who struggled along side my grandfathers, father, and uncles. This book is inspired by the struggles of these women and the realization that they (and I) needed to know more about our Black heroines. I wanted to know more about their work and struggles within the movement, and this I thought could only serve to strengthen us and our community. Ironically, this quest for a deeper knowledge and understanding of African-American women's activities in civil rights organizations has led to several personal, methodological, and, therefore, political dilemmas.

African-American women's activities within the movement cannot be accurately evaluated using today's standards and expectations of gender equity. Yet, as I analyzed the data, it was clear that women could not simply be added in a genderless fashion to an account of civil rights activities. Although race, class, gender, and culture shaped the organization of the movement, many of the women interviewed stated that they did not view gender relations as relevant to an account of their activities in the civil rights movement. Others stated that only after the women's movement did they think about their positions as women in the movement. A few African-American colleagues, both men and women, have blasted this project as inherently divisive to the African-American community and to any analysis of gender as a white woman's issue. Still others viewed the project as an attack on Dr. King and other notable Black male leaders. Given these reactions and the responses of many interviewees who stated that they wanted African-American men at the forefront of the movement, why would I, as an African-American woman academic, write about a nonissue or, even worse, a potentially divisive issue? Had I been coopted, brainwashed, or "Whitenized"?

These were serious accusations that deserved serious thought. This book could have been written in many ways that would avoid the eye of this storm. Yet avoidance would have been a disservice to the African-American community. A gendered analysis of movement activities provides a much needed understanding of leadership within African-American communities in particular and mixed-sex social movements in general. In many ways, the critics are correct: gender is and was a nonissue. The struggle for survival superseded and supersedes any preoccupation with gendered relations. This does not, however, mean that gendered relations do not exist within the African-American community, nor does it mean that they are unimportant.

Historically, Black women have supported women's rights. At the same time, women's rights activists such as Harriet Tubman, Sojourner Truth, Frances E. W. Harper, Ida B. Wells, and Mary Church Terrell were no less committed to the freedom of Black people as a whole. They, like African-American women today, have been challenged to analyze the positions of women within the context of Black existence in America. It is no secret that the contemporary women's movement has alienated women of color, as did the women's suffrage movement before it. Yet we cannot allow this alienation to blind us from analyses and issues that are of concern to African-American women.

Patricia Hill Collins, bell hooks, Angela Davis, Barbara Christiansen, Alice Walker, and other African-American women scholars and writers have challenged us to develop our own analyses for our own needs. When I initially conceived of this book, I intended to write about African-American women's leadership in the movement. Soon, however, I realized that to adequately tell the story, I needed to include the activities of men as well. While a great deal has been written about men, and only recently the story about Black women activists has begun to emerge,[1] all previous accounts lack a sense of the interactivity of relationships: the symbiosis on the one hand and the conflict on the other. Instead, we have separate accounts, and the readers are left to imagine the interactions. For this reason, a holistic story of the movement needs to be told from the perspective of the women within it.

Margaret Somers and Gloria Gibson[2] have recently challenged social scientists to use what they term "conceptual narrativity," which moves away from the simple representational use of narratives to a "new, historically and empirically based, narrativist understanding of social action and social agency—one that is temporal, relational, and cultural, as well as institutional, material, and macro-structural."[3] This approach allows one to avoid the pitfalls of essentializing categories such as race, class, gender, and African-American culture. The complex process of identity formation builds within each person a unique constellation formed from experiences thematically linked to broader social structures ranging in size from small subcultures to large-scale signifiers such as class or gender. The narratives of civil rights movement activists describe different identities and processes of constructing such identities. Women participants differed not only from men but from each other on the axes of race, class, and a multiplicity of other, more subtle signifiers of identity formation. How, then, was I to reconstruct a history, a story primarily about African-American women in the civil rights movement without essentializing their identities? Given that I have criticized other accounts of the movement as leaving women out, for reductively using the term "activist" to mean male, would I not be just as guilty if I were to treat African-American women's experiences as though they all sprang from the same head, from "the" African-American woman of the Deep South in the 1950s and 60s? To avoid this quandary, I rely upon the narratives to express the identities of the actors in question and define their own social locations.

This book, then, is written from a "womanist"/black feminist perspective as defined by both Alice Walker and Chikwenye Okonjo Ogunyemi. According to Elsa Brown, Walker and Okonjo have defined womanism as "a consciousness that incorporates racial, cultural, sexual, national, economic and political considerations. As Ogunyemi explains, 'black womanism is a philosophy' that concerns itself both with the sexual equality in the black community and 'with the world power structure that subjugates' both blacks and women. 'Its ideal is for black unity where every black person has a modicum of power and so can be a brother or a sister or a father or a mother to the other. . . . [I]ts aim is the dynamism of wholeness and self-healing."[4]

According to Alice Walker, "Womanism is to feminism as purple is to lavender."[5]

This story, while written from the perspective of women in the movement, includes men. It is an account of Black women's participation in the civil rights movement in the context of the larger story of movement mobilization, which necessarily includes men. Retelling the story of the civil rights movement from this particular standpoint provides the African-American community with a new understanding of how the movement succeeded and especially how important the symbiotic and sometimes conflictual relationship between men and women was, and is, to the African-American community. It is a story that includes formal leaders, but emphasizes giving voices and names to unsung heroines—those often nameless "others" who led in myriad ways.

No honest and holistic account of the civil rights movement can or should exclude men. The civil rights movement was the struggle of a people, of grandfathers and grandmothers, of brothers and sisters, of husbands and wives. Very few of the conversations I had with my women interviewees excluded talk of men activists. Much of the movement was organized around a gendered division of labor, vital to movement success, which had and has important implications for any future movements within our community. We as African-Americans have looked to men in general, and religious men in particular, as our formal and legitimate leaders. Yet 60 percent of our children live in woman-headed households. While it is true that African-American men are deeply endangered as a group, it is also true that Black male youth are being raised primarily by their mothers or other extended female kin; those voices are not heard in our mainstream political arenas. No account of our history is adequate without inclusion of us all.

This study evokes a sense of our community in the 1950s and 60s, a community in which men and women struggled together for change. We also gain an appreciation of the social relations that shaped women's actions within the movement. Women's leadership existed, but it was circumscribed by community and societal norms. Furthermore, these limitations on women's leadership status have important implications for our community's struggle today.

Through a sociohistorical analysis of women participants in seven civil rights movement organizations—the National Association for the Advancement of Colored People; the Congress of Racial Equality; the Women's Political Council of Montgomery, Alabama; the Montgomery Improvement Association; the Southern Christian Leadership Conference; the Student Non-Violent Coordinating Committee; and the Mississippi Freedom Democratic Party—and interviews with the women themselves, this book examines the nature of women's interactions with male leaders and the contributions of women's leadership to the success of the civil rights movement.[6]

Chapter 1, "Rethinking Social Movement Theory: Race, Class, Gender, and Culture," critiques social movement theories in the context of this retelling of the civil rights movement. This chapter is rather dense, so readers more interested in a history of women's activism may choose to skim this chapter for an understanding of terms used throughout the text. For others, this chapter argues that the explanatory power of existing social movement theories is compromised when any component concept inadequately reflects the substance of real cases. This chapter investigates such deficiencies in the specific areas of movement mobilization and the conceptualization of race, class, gender, and culture.

Six core concepts central to various movement mobilization theories, and often treated singularly by movement scholars, are of particular concern here. These are: (1) political opportunity structures, meaning that the permeability of state political and economic structures and institutions to outside challenges change over time and for a variety of reasons; (2) solidarity, that group cohesion does not develop through formal leadership alone, but requires grassroots leaders as well; (3) identity formation, that not all African-Americans were predisposed to join the movement and that grassroots leaders were essential for individual identity transformation; (4) leadership formation, that leadership is complex and its development is predetermined by race, class, gender, and cultural constructs; (5) movement sector organization, which is equally shaped by race, class, gender, and cultural constructs; and (6) emotionality, rationality, spontaneity, and planned activities, all of which contributed to the success of the civil rights movement. The fragmentary treatments of such concepts commonly miss the dialectical and interactive complexities of these forces.

This chapter provides a critique of the common use of rational choice models (i.e., that most activities are planned and that rational actions are the only ones of consequence) to underpin resource mobilization theory and its variants. It is clear from this study that spontaneity and emotionally charged decision making were crucial mobilization strategies used in the civil rights movement right alongside rational planning and leadership decision making.

Finally, gendered hierarchy and racial and class constraints, in addition to Black cultural norms, shaped the structures of the civil rights movement and defined the nature of activist participation. Moreover, these created a particular substructure of leadership that became a critical recruitment and mobilizing force for the movement. In other words, race, class, gender, and culture were significant determinants of who became a formal leader and in what context others participated in the movement.

Chapter 2, "Exclusion, Empowerment, and Partnership: Race Gender Relations," begins with women participants' views of gender relations in the civil rights movement as a means of keeping the reader grounded in the gendered social mores of the 1950s and 60s, when issues of gender equity were ignored. It is always difficult for a researcher to evaluate a period of time in which women's rights or gender equity were rarely topics of discussion. It would be simplistic indeed to discuss sexism in the civil rights movement, *post hoc*. Of greater analytic significance, however, is the notion that the gendered interactions created a particular context in which women participated. Although it is beyond the scope of this book, I provide a brief discussion of the historical context of Black women's participation in social movements. It clearly illustrates that Black women have always been active in the fight for racial, as well as gender, equality and that Black women have often found themselves awkwardly positioned between the two struggles. Yet this positioning did not deter their participation or impede it. Rather, women continued to act as leaders in many different ways. This participation preceded and led into the civil rights movement.

The civil rights movement, just as scholar Verta Taylor has characterized the women's movement, developed on a continuum.[7] It did not begin in 1954 with the Montgomery bus boycott, but rather emerged from a period of abeyance. Activity prior to the Montgomery bus boycott included the efforts of women who later influenced the ideology and strategies of the civil rights movement in important ways. Moreover, this legacy of activism affected the ways in which women participated and viewed their participation in the civil rights movement.

Chapter 3, "Women and the Escalation of the Civil Rights Movement," builds on these arguments. Here I discuss the ways in which the Montgomery bus boycott developed out of a continuous history of women's challenges to segregated transportation and that this method of resistance was not new or unique. Rather, as these actions escalated they suddenly became visible to the American mainstream; movement activism intensified owing to hard-won, favorable developments in federal legislation and court rulings, as Doug McAdam has argued.[8] Moreover, this chapter explores the pivotal positions of grassroots leaders (or "bridge leaders"). Leadership formation is complex, and this chapter illustrates the ways in which race, class, gender, and culture provided the basis for a particular division of labor in the civil rights movement. Additionally, this chapter demonstrates that movements mobilize leaders as much as leaders mobilize movements.

Finally, and most important, this chapter makes clear that spontaneity and emotion stimulated grassroots support for the boycott. Women, it is argued, could empathize with the humiliation suffered on the buses. It was their emotional responses to inequality that provided the impetus for their initiation of and participation in the boycott. Given the context of their lives, their anger and humiliation served as the basis for not only spontaneous acts of rebellion but also their strategic and planned activities.

In Chapter 4, "Sustaining the Momentum of the Movement," I discuss the ways in which bridge leadership was the primary domain of Black women's leadership. This chapter vividly discusses women's participation in life-threatening activities aimed at breaking down racial barriers. It is a chapter fraught with emotion and fear born of the extreme conditions of oppression and subjugation. Yet it is clear that women, despite the enormous risks, continued to lead, propelled by anger over injustices and a deep need for racial equality.

Chapter 5, "Sowing the Seeds of Mass Mobilization," argues that women with the capabilities to become formal leaders were often excluded and their energies personally directed into the "free spaces" of the movement. In this way, women with extensive mobilizing skills built the base upon which the entire movement rested. Miss Ella Baker's keen understanding of the need to build a movement from the ground up led to her insistence that the Southern Christian Leadership Conference adopt an educational program that would draw the masses to the movement. Septima Clark, an ex-school teacher and longtime activist, developed an approach and technique: a pedagogy of the oppressed that drew upon the daily experiences of individuals and, in a dialectical fashion, forged a bridge between the prefigurative politics of individual experience and the politics of the movement.

Chapter 6, "Bridging Students to the Movement," recounts the development of the Student Non-Violent Coordinating Committee (SNCC) and its ideologies in historical context. I establish that Miss Ella Baker was one of the most important figures in the civil rights movement and that her ideological bent developed out of the Harlem Renaissance. Baker's notions of a participatory democracy governed SNCC and provided a permanent belief in the development and mobilization of community leaders. SNCC, as a bridging organization, and its bridge leader became critical grassroots mobilizers, often acting spontaneously to sustain the momentum of the movement.

In Chapter 7, "Race, Class, and Culture Matter," I critique scholarly accounts of the movement that emphasize the relationships between African-American men and White women in the movement.[9] I argue that: (1) these previous studies are nonrepresentative of the full spectrum of gendered relations in the movement, since they focus upon Freedom Summer volunteers who were not part of the main cadre within SNCC participants; (2) previous research had not analyzed the majority of relationships within SNCC, those between Black men and Black women; (3) the majority of relationships between Black and White participants were positive; and (4) Black women and White women's experiences in SNCC were, because of race, class, and culture, not identical.

In Chapter 8, "Bringing the Movement Home to Small Cities and Rural Communities," I conclude that while Black male formal leaders contributed significantly to the movement, Black female indigenous bridge leaders provided a particular type of leadership that was critical to the movement's successful mobilization of rural communities and small cities. Given the lack of media resources and the realistic fear of reprisals, most of those in these communities would not have joined the movement otherwise. It was the work of indigenous bridge leaders, many of whom were Black women, that led to the successful identity transformation and shared solidarity with the movement.

Chapter 9, "Cooperation and Conflict in the Civil Rights Movement," provides a macrosocial as well as microsocial account of some overlooked elements of social movements. This chapter provides a cohesive analysis of the relationships, operational differences, and conflictual interactions between formal and bridge organizations. Distinct philosophical, organizational, and structural differences contributed substantially to their divergent roles in the overall movement and their subsequent dissension. In addition, these distinctly different kinds of organizations each harbored both formal and bridge leaders.

The micro analysis conceives of leadership conflicts as complex, but explains them through an analysis of gender and class, as well as by the competing goals which necessarily developed between male formal leaders and women bridge and formal leaders. Both bridge and formal leaders were accountable to local communities and constituents, while male formal leaders were also accountable to state officials, from whom they sought concessions. This divergence in accountability created a division in the mobilization tactics of these leaders. While male formal leaders acted in ways that reassured the state and the public that the movement and its actions were rational or planned and therefore worthy of backing, female bridge and formal leaders often acted to sustain movement mobilizations when plans went awry or when the state threatened sanctions.

Chapter 10, "The Movement Unravels From the Bottom," chronicles the destruction of the bridging tier within the movement sector. This chapter illustrates that, while primary male formal leaders were compelled to compromise with political elites, their decisions, which gained them greater credibility and further state concessions, served to undermine the morale of the bridging tier within the movement. The negative consequences of SNCC's demise included the loss of a bridge between rural communities and the movement, the collapse of "free spaces" where women's leadership most often flourished, and the beginning of the decline of the civil rights movement.

In the final chapter, "Theoretical Conclusions," I argue the following: (1) African-American women participated as leaders in the movement, not just as organizers, as previous scholars suggest; (2) women's leadership most often took the form of bridge leadership, which served to mobilize and sustain the movement; (3) emotion and spontaneity were central to the success of the movement, and the strategic use of emotion is not enough to mobilize the masses; (4) the civil rights movement was won because of a division of labor between primary formal organizations and bridging organizations; (5) ideology is central to the development of organizational forms and mobilizing structures; (6) while primary formal organizations must adhere to normative organizational forms to succeed, bridging organizations are more successful if they develop inclusive and empowering alternative models; (7) there needs to be an expansion of political opportunity models to include analyses of a variety of participants and organizations within the movement sector. I argue that opportunities and outcomes are perceived variously by participants based upon their social location, and cultural norms that dictate race, class, and gender templates of organization. Moreover, I argue that political opportunities, charismatic leaders, and resources are not enough to sustain or even mobilize a movement. With the demise of SNCC as a consensus-building, anti-hierarchical organization dedicated to empowering local communities to lead themselves, the base upon which the movement was built began to erode. The root of its demise was a shift in ideology and philosophy that was antithetical to the teachings of Ella Baker and Septima Clark. With the rise of Black nationalism came the imposition of hierarchy and the reinstitutionalization of gender and class norms. It is not the case that the Black Power movement was negative in its entirety. To the contrary, it created a positive base for racial identity and pride. However, its ideology created a narrowing of participation options.

The *Epilogue* questions the direction of our current mobilization efforts, and argues for the development of a bridging tier that seeks to build local leadership and to empower all segments of the African-American community.

ONE

Rethinking Social Movement Theory

Race, Class, Gender, and Culture

THIS WOMANIST/BLACK FEMINIST retelling of the story of the civil rights movement contributes significantly to our understanding not only of the civil rights
movement but of social movements in general. It is evident that social movements
are complex and many diverse theories have developed to explain them. This book
brings to light some connections between these competing ideas.

One of the earliest social movement theories—collective behavior theory—
concluded that movements were irrational, spontaneous events that tended to
emerge from shared grievances and collective frustration. This model has increasingly lost favor, and many social movement scholars have turned their attention
to the more rational components of a movement.[1] Resource mobilization theory
posits that, while grievances and frustrations may spark collective action, resources
are most critical for shaping those grievances into a viable social movement. Movements cannot occur without money, persons with free time, and other such pragmatic elements. This framework disavows the strategic significance of emotions
and the spontaneous. Social movements, resource mobilization theorists claim,
develop through rational, planned activity as do organizations that maintain the
status quo. Moreover, activists behave in ways similar to actors in ordinary organizations.[2]

The political process variant of this model adds the notion that movements,
while emerging from rational choices and dependent upon resources, require po-

litical opportunity.[3] That is, the state (i.e., its economy and institutions) must be open to challenges or the incipient movement would be crushed. Both resource mobilization theory and its political process variant emphasize structure, strategies, and institutions.

Conversely, new social movements theory, more popular in Europe, stresses the internal dynamics of social movements, focusing upon the need to develop movement cultures, or shared attitudes about society, and movement identities, or personal transformations of potential movement followers. Scholars with this emphasis suggest that, in the past, these forms of movement work were less necessary because movements such as the French Revolution attracted individuals with similar social backgrounds and experiences, while new social movements center on issues that do not necessarily draw upon a constituency with shared social characteristics and experiences; for example, the peace movement. Others add that developing movement culture and identity are difficult, even when participants are all women or of the same race.[4]

Recently, within these theoretical frameworks there has been a new wave of social movement work that emphasizes micromobilization. These theorists analyze the processes by which consensus is formed and action is mobilized. As Klandermans notes, structures alone cannot mobilize individuals to act.[5] Potential constituents must be convinced of the credibility and legitimacy of participation. They must be persuaded to act. Research has centered on discerning the processes necessary for persuading adherents and potential constituents to join a movement. Snow and his colleagues outline four social psychological processes central to the recruitment process.[6]

Frame bridging involves providing those already predisposed to one's cause with information sufficient to induce them to join the movement. The process of *frame amplification* rests on the compatibility of the movement's values and beliefs with those of the potential constituents, emphasizing efforts to convince individuals that their participation is crucial and that the movement's goals can be achieved. *Frame extension* occurs when movement adherents cast a wider recruitment net, incorporating concerns not originally part of the movement's goals but valuable as a means of expanding support. Finally, *frame transformation* is the process whereby individually held frames are altered, entirely or in part, to achieve consensus with the movement's goals.

The above brief discussion of recent theoretical disputes regarding the impetus for and nature of movement mobilization introduces the arena in which the research presented here is situated, and provides the basis for my contention that these movement theories are not as incompatible as they seem. Scholarly dialogue, while valuable, has largely centered on arguing the supremacy of one set of constructs over another, obscuring the need to deepen our understanding of the concepts and assumptions within them.

One approach to the study of social movements that has the potential for a more complete understanding of the movement is *identity*, in both the collective and individual senses of the word. The social location of an individual in relation to society and the movement provides a means of understanding movement mobilization. This leads to the questions of how movements cultivate collective identities and how this translates into collective actions. As Melucci, in Johnston and Klandermans's *Social Movements and Culture*, notes, the field of social movements suffers from a dualism between the actors and systems. Rather, what is most important is to analyze the system of relations between a set of actors and the larger system of relations. He further notes that even establishing one's difference, as a group, establishes one's belonging in the system. Moreover, he conceives of *collective identity* as a "system of tensions" and gives the example of the strain between competing branches of the women's movement in Italy.[7] Melucci sees much of the dispute among theorists as rooted in the dualism of either focusing on actors or on systems but not on the interaction. This, he contends, has led to a reification of the movement in terms of the one aspect that the researcher has studied. The totality of the movement is viewed from one perspective or the other.

I agree with Melucci, but I also believe that his conceptualization of the actor component of the dyad in terms of collective actors (or the group) in relation to society does not solve all of our problems. His conceptualization of collective actors can also be extended to include differences within groups of collective actors. In other words, the notion of a "system of tensions" may also be conceived in micro terms. While collective actors, as a group, are constituted within a larger system of relations, individual actors are also situated relationally within the group of collective actors, the movement system, and the larger system. With this in mind it is important to analyze the movement from many different perspectives, and researchers must resist the urge to reify the movement from only one level of movement activity.

My work on this book has led me to the conclusion that many authors who seemingly disagree do so because "the movement" is reified from the level at which they have viewed the collective action. To avoid such a pitfall and provide a means for a more integrated understanding of social movements, researchers need to analyze a movement on several relational levels. These levels should include the relations between the individual in a collective and the collective; between the individual in a collective and society; between a collective and competing collectives; and between the collective and society—that is, the state and other institutions—with an eye on the individual actors within them. This book provides the seeds of what such an analysis might look like, and argues that such an approach suggests social movement theories are not as incompatible as they seem.

The present study addresses these issues by focusing on three salient areas of research that I contend have received scant attention: social location and movement identity formation; definitions of leadership; especially in light of a reevaluation of emotion in movements; and the dialectical, rather than linear flow of movement momentum.

In sum, a holistic theory ought to move from the emotional-internal motivations discussed by collective behaviorists to the various interfaces with external and presumably more rational concerns over resources and political opportunities. Although new social movement theorists emphasize the internal maintenance of social movements, including the importance of culture and identity, they do not provide us with an understanding of the strategic uses of emotion for micromobilization and group solidarity. Moreover, we know neither who nor how these tasks are performed. The womanist/black feminist perspective leads to a clearer understanding of the social construction of "who does what for the movement and why."

Social Location and Identity

The significance of the social location of movement carriers within gender-integrated movement organizations (or movements with men and women participants) has generally been neglected. Although identity is discussed in the context of developing collective identity, group consciousness, and solidarity,[8] an analysis of who is likely to succeed at the bridging, amplifying, extending, and transforming techniques needed to persuade potential constituents to join the movement has been neglected. Consequently, the significance of "who" is doing what type of micromobilization for the movement is left unanalyzed. We do not yet fully understand how mobilization takes place in day-to-day community work, and we do not know who is likely to do such work.

Recently, scholars have begun to examine the differential experiences of men and women activists.[9] McAdam, for example, has discussed the importance of deconstructing the experiences of movement participants. He found significant gender differences in the recruitment processes of white male and female participants in the Student Non-Violent Coordinating Committee, a civil rights movement organization. Such a study provides support for the notion that participants are not a monolithic group. Thus it is equally important to analyze the ways that race, class, gender,[10] and culture determine different movement experiences.

Indeed, scholars of "new" social movements emphasize the need to analyze movement groups whose solidarity does not emerge from shared cultural and/or racial experiences.[11] The contention that collective identity is important only to the study of new social movements is limiting and problematic.[12] The notion that collective identity is more important for movements that are, for example, non-ethnic and interracial assumes a uniform experience within racial and ethnic groups. It does not take into consideration differences based upon class and gender. Scholars of new social movements would, therefore, assume that the collective identity of African-American participants in the civil rights movement was non-problematic. Rather, just as John Lofland, in *Social Movements and Culture*, charts movement cultures in terms of degrees, I contend that shared collective identities might also be considered in such a fashion. The degree of overlap between one's personal identity might be charted in relation to the movement's or movement organization's constructed collective identity.

As recent cultural theorists have argued, race cannot be essentialized.[13] Craig Calhoun argues that 'Black' is not a settled, pretheoretical or prepolitical position from which to grasp practical affairs or achieve knowledge."[14] The cry against essentialism has been, of course, most vehemently expressed by feminists of color who object to the limited construction of "woman" to mean a White, middle-class woman residing in the United States of America. To truly understand the construction of identities in the civil rights movement requires discarding the belief that identities and solidarities in the movement were not problematic simply because it was a Black movement and most of the participants were Black.

Dyson challenges the notion of an essentialized African-American culture:

> Of course, I don't mean that there is not distinct black cultural characteristics that persist over space and time, but these features of black life are the products of the historical and social construction of racial identity. . . . These distinct features of black life nuance and shape black cultural expression, from the preaching of Martin Luther King to the singing of Gladys Knight. They do not, however, form the basis of a black racial or cultural essence. Nor do they indicate that *the* meaning of blackness will be expressed in a quality or characteristic without which a person, act, or practice no longer qualifies as black. Rigid racial essentialism must be opposed. (emphasis in original)[15]

One of the fundamental confusions about identity formation in the civil rights movement is a failure to distinguish personal identity from its development into political identity and discourse. The personal meaning of Black political discourse for an educated Black in the civil rights movement would differ from its personal meaning for a poor, illiterate Black sharecropper. The movement, while centered on emancipation rather than identity formation, found itself grappling with the task of forming shared political identities, but could not do so without cultivating change in personal identities as well. One could argue that the distinction between personal identity and political identity is irrelevant since the manifestation of a shared political identity and discourse sufficient for mobilization is all that is required. Yet ignoring the distinction obscures critical differences among movement participants that strengthened the ability to mobilize the movement and ultimately contributed to a decline in its momentum.

In the civil rights movement, the signifier was race, but race, as Stuart Hall has argued, has many meanings, and the construction of its meaning into an objective political discourse does not translate into a static political identity shared by all.[16] Rather, its final manifestation is an overlap between one's personal identity and the cultivated political identity of the movement. Political identities, as well as personal ones, are in constant flux and are subject to shifts in form and discourse as that political identity intersects with other discourses. The subject "Blackness" is not a sufficient signifier to cultivate movement participation. If this were so, far more African-Americans would have joined the Black Power movement. Instead it was the fact that their personal identities, as Black, did not coincide or sufficiently overlap with "Blackness" as defined by that movement.

Studying the civil rights movement with an eye on the social constructs of race, class, gender, and culture leads to the conclusion that the development and sustenance of a collective identity within the civil rights movement was anything but nonproblematic. Not all African-Americans were eager to join the movement or even knew about the movement. Particularly in rural pockets of the South, any media coverage portrayed the movement as Communist backed. Many rural African Americans believed that the "outsiders" who were stirring up trouble in their communities were going to get them killed.

This meant that broad-based appeals by formal leaders were not enough to mobilize the movement. Each person needed to be convinced to join the movement, and the conversion process required individualized and location-specific methods of recruitment. Individuals needed to overcome their doubts and fears and be persuaded to risk their lives for the movement. Mobilization, therefore, required one-on-one grassroots organizing that became the foundation upon which the movement gained recruits and momentum. And often, formal leaders were not the grassroots purveyors of the movement's message.

Gendered hierarchy and racial and class constraints, in addition to Black cultural norms, shaped the structures of the civil rights movement and defined the nature of activist participation, including those leaders in the grassroots sector. Moreover, these constructs created a particular substructure of leadership that became a critical recruitment and mobilizing force for the movement. In other words, race, class, gender, and culture were significant determinants of who became a formal leader and in what context others participated in the movement.

Reconceptualizing Leadership

To understand the complexity of these negotiated relationships, it is important to first examine the necessary components of mobilization activity. A primary resource for mobilization activity, whether inside or outside of a social movement organization, is leadership. Recent scholarly research on the civil rights movement, most notably Morris, has transformed conceptions of movement leadership from a focus on outside benefactors and elites to indigenous resources. Morris argues that the Black church provided the institutional base of the movement from which leaders, participants, financial support, and a means of dispensing protest information emanated. This reconceptualization of movement leadership has shifted the focus of movement activity away from exogenous factors and placed an emphasis on indigenous activities.[17] Although Morris's analysis provides greater insight into the interworkings of community-based mobilization activities, his focus is on the formal or hierarchical and visible leadership, namely the clergy. While he does acknowledge the participation of other grassroots organizers, he does so only within the context of their relationship to the clergy. Thus, the clergy are viewed as leaders and everyone else is viewed as an organizer or follower. His account has focused on the indigenous clergy as the primary resource for leadership within the church structure and therefore, the movement.

My research findings are consonant with Payne's conclusions, drawn from his local study of Mississippi activism, that the clergy did not always lead the masses to act; rather grassroots participants within both organizations and local communities provided the door-to-door mobilization necessary to recruit followers.[18] Unlike Morris, Payne does not treat these participants as anonymous rank-and-file members of the church and social movement organizations, but instead provides colorful descriptions of their courage and participation.[19]

His analysis, much like mine, while acknowledging the church as the institutional base of the movement, emphasizes the indigenous base of the movement and its corresponding grassroots leadership. While the church was often a tool for providing the organization's leaders with connections to the rural leadership, it was not always the institutional church networks that provided the mobilization necessary to develop a rural base of support for movement organizations. In other words, individuals decided to participate in movement activities and capitalized on their community leadership status to mobilize their communities. Churches, or the preexisting institutional networks, were but one of the tools utilized by both rural leaders and the movement organizations. The focus on the male clergy as mobilizers has been driven by visibility and narrowly defined conceptions of power—that is, titled positions.

Traditionally, researchers have focused on those who make the organization's decisions regarding tactics, goals, and strategies. In the case of the civil rights movement, ministers became the formal leaders for the press as well as for the masses. *Formal leaders* may be defined as those with titled positions within a primary movement organization—that is, one that is recognized nationally. They usually provide the press statements and are responsible for decision making regarding organizational tactics, goals, and strategies. Though the press, scholars, and the public may view these few as the movement's leaders, such a view obscures the importance of participants who may display leadership at the grassroots.

In this book, the narrowly defined conceptions of leadership, which have included only the most visible actors within a singular hierarchical model of organizational leadership, are expanded. Similarly, Sacks, in her study of union organizing, discusses the role of *centerwomen*, or those "who were key actors in network formation and consciousness shaping."[20] As Sacks notes, many of the women she studied operated as leaders but rarely accepted the title as such. They preferred to stay behind the scenes. Moreover, through her study, her own *a priori* notions of what constituted leadership were challenged. Like most scholars, she had conceived of those in leadership as those who hold titled positions, have power over the group's members, make decisions on behalf of the organization, and are perceived by the public and the state as leaders. Sacks has challenged these definitions of leadership, suggesting that they are too narrow.[21]

Similarly, in my study I used the women's understandings of who the leaders were and their own definitions of what they felt constituted leadership. Activist Victoria Gray provides a response typical of my interviewees:

> They [Ella Baker and Septima Clark, both activists who will be discussed in detail later] were both leaders. . . . In the sense of that effectiveness, of the loyalty of those who work with and around them. It was a lot to do with a kind of loyalty and influence that you are able to elicit from the people around you.[22]

She further suggested that it didn't matter whether leadership was exhibited at the local or international level; what counted was the presence of the aforementioned personal qualities. According to Gray and a number of other respondents, what defines a leader is not his or her position in terms of titles or recognition by the state, public, or international community, but the ability to influence others and to gain the loyalty of followers.

Feminist scholars, of course, have been challenging the basic approaches and theoretical underpinnings of analyses of political participation.[23] They suggest that a top-down standpoint toward political participation necessarily excludes women and ignores their significant contributions. In contrast, several studies of women's organizations have analyzed organizational hierarchies in terms of their forms of power and leadership.[24] Other feminists writing about women's organizations have approached the study of social movements through an examination of women's networks[25] or their separate communities of organization within a movement.[26] All of these studies suggest that analyses of women's participation are essential not only for the study of women's groups but also for a clearer understanding of the ways in which women participate in gender-integrated organizations and movements. Moreover, this leads us to reformulate our ideas about the needs of social movements and about how movements succeed at recruiting, mobilizing, and sustaining support for their cause. In this book, I argue that a substantial proportion of the processes of recruitment, mobilization, and sustenance were performed by African-American women as bridge leaders in the civil rights movement.

Defining Bridge Leadership

Gender was a defining construct of power relations and shaped the structure of the movement.[27] Men and women clearly had differential access to structural and institutional power. Dr. King, for example, had access to the primary institutional hierarchy, or formal leadership, track of the Black church. For most women, the ladder up to a position of formal leadership and power within a movement organization did not exist. Instead, women held positions of power based on their community work or extraordinary activism within the movement, not from their position in the church hierarchy. Within this context, it is important to deconstruct leadership activities from their imbeddedness in institutional hierarchies and structures. In the civil rights movement, many so-called grassroots followers or organizers operated as what I term *Bridge Leaders* who utilized frame bridging, amplification, extension, and transformation[28] to foster ties between the social movement and the community; and between prefigurative strategies (aimed at individual change, identity, and consciousness) and political strategies (aimed at organizational tactics designed to challenge existing relationships with the state and other societal institutions).[29] Indeed, the activities of bridge leaders in the civil rights movement were the stepping stones necessary for potential constituents and adherents to cross formidable barriers between their personal lives and the political life of civil rights movement organizations. Bridge leaders were able to cross the boundaries between the public life of a movement organization and the private spheres of adherents and potential constituents.

One's position as a bridge leader was socially constructed and largely determined by one's race, class, gender, and culture. Only by studying women was I able to discover this important area of leadership within social movements. Women constituted a large portion of those in this category of leadership and were underrepresented in the formal leadership sector even though their rates of participation exceeded those of men.[30] Bridge leaders were not always women, but it was the most accessible and acceptable form of leadership available to them. In general, women were excluded as formal leaders because of their sex, but this did not deter their leadership efforts in the movement. Women were not simply organizers within the civil rights movement; as bridge leaders they were critical mobilizers of civil rights activities. Gender, which operated as a construct of exclusion, produced a particular context in which women participated. This gendered power structure served to strengthen the informal tier of leadership, thus providing a strong mobilizing force within the grassroots sector.

Women as bridge leaders may be characterized as follows:

1. They become bridge leaders not because they lack leadership experience, but rather because of a social construct of exclusion.
2. They sometimes initiate organizations, do the groundwork, and when this is true, are more visible before an organization is formalized.[31]
3. They operate in the movement's or organization's free spaces, thus making connections that cannot be made by formal leaders.
4. They employ a one-on-one interactive style of leadership for mobilization and recruitment.
5. They have greater leadership mobility in nonhierarchical structures and institutions.
6. They act as a movement organization's formal leadership during moments of crisis, often catapulted by spontaneous and emotional events.
7. They are more closely bound to the wishes and desires of the constituency because, unlike formal leaders, they do not need legitimacy with the state.
8. They tend to advocate more radical or nontraditional tactics and strategies because, unlike formal leaders, they do not need the legitimacy with the state.
9. They can hold a formal leadership position in a social movement organization but be considered outside the circle of formal leaders within the social movement sector (or among all of the movement organizations).
10. They may be formal leaders at the local level, but within movement organizations or within the movement sector, they are excluded from the primary formal leadership tier.

This defines the general contours of all bridge leaders. Yet there were four different types that are distinguishable from one another.

Several women who were professional organizers were not privy to the formal leaders' inner circle, as were men of their status. Rather, because of their gender, they could obtain power and high status only as bridge leaders, which was usually the highest position attainable for women. These women, whom I term *professional bridge leaders*, may be distinguished from their sisters, the *community bridge leaders*, the *indigenous bridge leaders*, and the *mainstream bridge leaders*. Professional bridge leaders had significant civil rights experience prior to the rise of movement activism. They often held positions with primary formal organizations and generally had worked with more than one civil rights group. Their vision of movement mobilization extended to concerns beyond the local level. Had they not been part of a group excluded from formal leadership, they undoubtedly would have served as formal leaders, professional organizers, or part of the inner circle. Community bridge leaders worked primarily through a specific movement organization. Many were drawn to the movement because of their local civil rights experience. Prior to their civil rights organization participation, many of these women were formal leaders in their local communities. Because of their high status at the local level, or even state level, several of these women comprise a subset of community bridge leaders, *formal local community bridge leaders*. Within the movement organization or movement sector, however, they acted as community bridge leaders whose primary task was to bridge local communities to the movement. For these extraordinary women, this was the highest level of leadership attainable. Many community bridge leaders, because of their extraordinary courage and skills, often acted as formal leaders during moments of crisis, when formal and secondary leaders were unwilling or unable to do so. These leaders were often the decision makers during these temporary periods, which were characterized by spontaneous, emotional events when planned activities went awry. Most community bridge leaders were not formal local community bridge leaders, especially young women, but they operated in a similar fashion with less status and power. The indigenous bridge leaders often worked in concert with community bridge leaders, but many tended to float among the movement organizations, simultaneously working with them all. These women were often the community bridge leaders' contacts upon arrival in a local community. Sometimes indigenous bridge leaders had previous contact with a civil rights movement organization and were active, trusted women in their communities. These women generally had no formal position with a local organization, but were well known as solid, outspoken, and trustworthy individuals who often took the initiative during community crises. The mainstream bridge leaders were usually White women, and this was the highest position available to them in the movement. They generally worked alongside community bridge leaders, forging ties between mainstream White institutions and organizations and the movement.

How might bridge leadership be contrasted with formal leadership? The primary difference is that formal leaders possess institutional and organizational power. In contrast, bridge leaders make similar decisions except that their organizational and mobilization skills are performed within what Evans and Boyte term a "free space."[32] Such a free space might be defined as a niche that is not directly controlled by formal leaders or those in their inner circle. It is an unclaimed space that is nevertheless central to the development of the movement, since linkages are developed within it. Moreover, bridge leaders operate through one-on-one, community-based interaction. While formal leaders may also work in this manner, it is neither a sufficient nor an efficient means of mass mobilization. Someone needs to draw together the masses and to represent them at the national level. It is equally important to mobilize them through an interactive one-on-one approach. Both types of leadership are required, and neither the bridge leadership nor the formal leadership is more important than the other. Rather, the two operated in a dialectical relationship marked by symbiosis and conflict. All four types of bridge leaders operated in free spaces providing bridges that facilitated recruitment and mobilization. These four types of bridge leaders were not always mutually exclusive, with some women wearing several hats.

In all cases, women's power was largely derived from autonomous pioneering activities rather than through their titled or hierarchical position within the organization. For example, Ella Baker, a professional bridge leader, was a consultant to SNCC and the individual most responsible for its philosophy of "group centered leadership." Septima Clark, also a professional bridge leader, worked largely in the field going from rural community to rural community teaching citizenship education. She was not simply carrying out a program constructed by the male leadership. Rather, she designed her instructional materials and developed a means of communicating the message of the Southern Christian Leadership Conference to those in rural communities. Both women, though a part of their organizations, had control over their day-to-day activities. Through these activities they gained power and status. The central point here is that gender operated as an organizational construct that served to create a tier of leadership that operated in a free space relatively autonomous from the social movement organization.

Yet it is also true that not all men could rise to positions as formal leaders. Certainly gender was not the only organizational construct for exclusion within the movement. If a man lacked formal schooling or a college education, was White, was a nonminister or gay, any one of these social constructs served as markers for exclusion from a formal position of power within movement organizations. This suggests that even all-male or all-female groups may have constructs that serve as exclusionary criteria. However, in the case of the civil rights movement, one needed to be a man to gain a formal and powerful leadership position or even to become part of the inner circle. Although many men also worked as bridge leaders, such limiting characteristics did not preclude their inclusion in the inner circle. Often, those excluded were quite close to the formal leaders as either professional organizers or as, what I term, secondary leaders.

Professional organizers often included men who had been activists for some time, participating over the years in many civil rights organizations. They worked to advise formal leaders on strategies and tactics, generally at the national and state level. *Secondary leaders* were part of the inner circle. They were generally drawn into the movement from their positions as formal leaders in local communities. In movement organizations, they became the link between bridge leaders and formal leaders, facilitating and articulating the needs and desires of one to the other. While their treatment in this text is often cursory, their relationship as mediators between bridge and formal leaders is significant to movement recruitment and mobilization and is briefly discussed in later chapters. For now, it is important to note that if secondary leaders do not successfully mediate between bridge and formal leaders—that is, persuade formal leaders to comply with or to strike a compromise with the viewpoints of bridge leaders—the mobilization and sustenance of the movement is jeopardized. Primary formal leaders, secondary formal leaders, and bridge leaders were all critical actors in mobilizing and sustaining the movement.

The lack of analysis of the complexity of movement leadership has led to several problems in theory development. Aside from the fact that race, class, gender, and culture shape who does what for the movement, analyses of only formal leaders and their organizations have led to an oversimplified understanding of the internal dynamics and structure of specific movement organizations, as well as among movement organizations in the overall movement sector. Correspondingly, social movement theory has suffered from overemphasis on political opportunities, rationality, and the planned nature of movement activities. Moreover, the acknowledgment of bridge leaders has led to my conclusion that emotion and spontaneity were central elements in the formation and sustenance of movement mobilization, though such elements were not exclusive to that tier of leadership. The following sections highlight these issues.

The Movement Sector: Centralized Power, Primary and Secondary Formal Organizations, and Bridge Organizations

Conflicts between bridge and formal leaders often arose over a duality of focus. The former were primarily concerned with a specific grassroots constituency, while the latter were concerned with the organization's credibility, image, and relationship with the state. This is not to suggest that King and the other male leaders were unconcerned with their grassroots constituencies; rather, their decisions were made with an eye to optimizing political and legal outcomes. McAdam and Piven and Cloward argue that central to the development of a civil rights movement is a cognitive change in consciousness.[33] Granted, as Morris notes, Dr. King sought to transform the religion of the Black masses to that of a newfound activism, and his speeches inspired individuals to participate in the movement,[34] but as I have argued, it was the bridge leaders who provided the local community members with the day-to-day lessons on self-empowerment.

A central point here is that, because of the centralization of power among the educated male ministers, women's leadership was primarily channeled into the bridge leadership tier. This channeling of leadership resources had two effects. First, it tended to channel strong leadership potential into an area that may otherwise be more supportive of the upper echelons of leadership, since support would mean moving into more important positions. Second, this conflict can be considered gendered and classed.

From a structural and organizational perspective, women lacked positional power within the movement sector or among all the movement organizations as a whole. Morris has emphasized the decentralized nature of the Southern Christian Leadership Conference (SCLC), the organization recognized and legitimated by the state as the primary formal civil rights movement organization.[35] Morris points out that the SCLC was not a single organization but consisted of several affiliates that possessed the power to make their own decisions. The SCLC, based in Atlanta and for which King was president, was a coordinating body and a source of charismatic leadership. Morris emphasizes the unified efforts of the ministers to support the leadership of King.

Women were not privy to this fraternal order of minister-led leadership. Within this context SCLC, though structurally decentralized, operated with a centralized core—that is, the power was centralized. Though Dr. King did not directly control the operations of every affiliate organization or other movement organizations, his influence among ministers and formal leaders of other organizations was striking. King had gained legitimacy and credibility among the movement organizations as well as with the state.

Using Gamson's concept of centralized power structures,[36] it is apparent that Dr. King was a central figure around which the movement sector revolved and through which it was identified. In applying Gamson's perspective, it is clear that while the structure was decentralized, power relations were not. It is true that these movement organizations were relatively autonomous—that is, they had the freedom to decide whether or not to support King's collective action efforts—but from a gender and class perspective, the power relations were not decentralized at all. Taken as a whole, it is evident that power within and across the groups centered on the ministers.

Although numerous researchers have dealt with the differences in centralization versus decentralization of power in social movement organizations, none has provided a gender and class analysis. For example, Piven and Cloward and Jenkins and Eckert have noted the importance of centralization in the implementation of direct action.[37] Gamson has stressed the importance of centralized power for preventing debilitating factionalism.[38] Zald and Ash found that decentralized organizations were more effective for mobilizing grassroots participation than were bureaucratic structures, owing to their concentration on personal transformation. Though Zald and Ash have looked more directly at power, this too has been from a structural perspective, showing the ways that a bureaucratic structure reinforces hierarchical centralized power relations in which there is little autonomy.[39] Thus far, arguments have tended to focus on the structural level, and it is in this sense that Morris has argued for the SCLC as decentralized. We must consider the centralization of power relations per se, rather than as merely an aspect of structure. This is much easier to see from the stance of a gender and class analysis. Within this context, the SCLC's power was centralized, and it was women who were largely excluded from this domain.

Gusfield argues that leaders experience role-set conflicts because they must focus their attention in two conflicting directions. First, they represent and are symbolic of the movement in the eyes of the media and the public. Second, they must face inward as "negotiator and communicator between the environment and the internal" organization.[40] In the first function, the leader is an articulator who "must be prepared to meet halfway the publics and the organizations of the total society." As mobilizer "the leader act[s] to maintain the movement's sense of a unique mission by upholding the doctrines and convictions which differentiate it from the behavior it is attempting to change."[41] He posits that in many organizations there is a strain between these two roles when they are the responsibility of centralized leadership.

Gusfield's framework can be modified and extended in several ways. First, movements may be analyzed in terms of organizational types in relation to one another. There were three distinct types of organizations within the civil rights movement sector: (1) *The primary formal organization*, newly emerged during the peak of political opportunity, has a direct, legitimate link to and a dialectical relationship with the state and its authorities, often moderating its agenda to gain concessions, while the state will often grant concessions in the face of increased activism. This organization more than any other represents the movement to the media, public, and state. Its legitimacy is measured by the extent to which its activities can be perceived as rational and planned. (2) *Secondary formal organizations* are viewed as legitimate but not at the forefront of current movement activities. These organizations have usually existed for years and have remained in abeyance until the momentum of the movement increases and they attach themselves to the primary formal organization or offer complementary and supplementary services. (3) *Bridge organizations* operate to empower the masses by teaching indigenous groups how to help themselves. They often have the least centralized leadership because once a community is organized, they leave, leaving the organization and power in the hands of local leaders. The tactics, strategies, and activities of these organizations are born of the wishes of those whom they seek to empower. Bridge organizations have the least credibility with the state because their activities are as likely to be planned as they are to emerge spontaneously and emotionally during crises, branding them as nonrational.

Each of these forms of movement sector organizations has its own internal structure. Primary formal organizations and secondary formal organizations have the most similarities, each containing a primary formal leader, secondary formal leaders, and bridge leaders. Clearly, within the civil rights movement sector, the SCLC held the premier, state legitimated position as the formal movement organization and its head, Dr. King, held the status of the formal leader of the movement. Both the primary leader and primary organization focus on: (1) creating bonds between the organization and the larger, White society, especially through the media and various political alliances; (2) national level mobilization, utilizing such tactics as marches, rallies, and speeches; (3) linkages and coalitions with other movement organizations, particularly the secondary formal organizations; and (4) linkages to local organizations, recruiting formal local leadership into the movement's secondary tier, primarily ministers and other Black male local formal leaders.

Secondary formal organizations, such as the NAACP and CORE, and their leaders, Roy Wilkins and James Farmer, respectively, mobilized their affiliates and formed ties with the primary formal organization and its leaders. Their movement activities often filled a void that the primary formal organization and its leadership could not or would not fill. For example, the NAACP concentrated its energies on legal activities, while CORE concentrated on northern sit-ins and interracial Freedom Rides throughout the South.

Bridge organizations contain clusters of formal and secondary leaders, as well as bridge leaders, giving structure a somewhat different shape. The formal leaders of bridge organizations bind the loosely structured groups together, bringing a sense of continuity, purpose, and loosely defined goals to the organization. They are usually grudgingly acknowledged by both the primary and the secondary formal organizations and the leaders of each. The central tasks of bridge organizations and bridge leaders are (1) links between the organization and the Black community; (2) local grassroots organizing—that is, door-to-door or workshop training; and (3) links with the indigenous local leadership, often bypassing formal local leaders who may be more resistant to their entry. Formal leaders of bridge organizations act as bridges to other movement sector organizations while maintaining linkages to local community leadership. The relationships between primary and secondary organizations and bridge organizations are tenuous, and the former are careful to maintain a distance from the bridge organizations. When the activities of bridge organizations are positive, the primary organization can proclaim its involvement and often steal the limelight. Conversely, when the activities are perceived as negative, the primary organization can distance itself and deny any involvement.

This division in leadership helped to mitigate the strains and difficulties outlined by Gusfield, as well as by Zald and Ash. The success or failure of a movement with centralized power relations may depend largely upon the extent to which the bridge organizations and bridge leadership in the primary and secondary movement organizations can act to "maximize personal transformations . . . mobilize grassroots participation and insur[e] group maintenance."[42]

In all of the organizations discussed, other than SNCC because of its nonhierarchical decentralized nature,[43] gender stratification tended to define the secondary leadership tier. This tier consisted primarily of men who, because of social constraints or personal attributes, were unable to rise to primary formal leadership positions. They were, however, included in the overarching fraternal leadership order connecting primary and secondary organizations. Primary formal leaders of the secondary and bridge organizations had much to gain by maintaining their allegiance to this fraternal order. These leaders, such as Bob Moses, James Forman, and James Farmer, needed the legitimacy conferred by the primary organization and its leader in order to take part in negotiations with the state. Only in this way could they and their organizations be viewed as significant actors in movement politics. Women in any bridge leadership position could never have been accepted as primary formal leaders within the movement sector. For this reason, their loyalties were not divided; their allegiance could remain with their constituency.

This typology serves to illustrate the complexities of the internal organization and dynamics of social movement organizations, as well as the relationships of movement organizations within the movement sector. These relationships have important implications for social movement theory.

Social Movement Theories

Bridge Leaders, Formal Leaders, and the State

As noted above, explanations of movement activities often compete. In the case of the civil rights movement, one account, Doug McAdam's political process model, emphasizes changes in political opportunity structures that led to cognitive changes regarding the feasibility of collective action.[44] While McAdam places theoretical emphasis on expanding political opportunities and the resultant cognitive liberation leading to collective action, Morris deemphasizes political opportunity, placing greater weight on preexisting indigenous organizations, such as the Black church, and on deliberate rational planning by leaders.[45] These two seemingly conflicting theoretical positions are not as incompatible as they seem when one examines, chronologically, the role of the state and civil rights legislation in relation to formal and bridge leaders.

Since 1945, attempts had been made in Congress to pass a law prohibiting the payment of a poll tax as a prerequisite to voting. This bill did not pass until 1964. In 1946, President Truman appointed a committee charged with determining the extent of civil rights violations, something President Roosevelt had refused to do. In 1948, Truman sent the committee's recommendations to Congress, requesting that they

> Establish a permanent commission on civil rights, a joint congressional committee on civil rights and a civil rights division in the justice department. Strengthen existing civil rights statues. Provide federal protection against lynching. Protect more adequately the right to vote. Set up a permanent fair employment practices commission. Prohibit discrimination in interstate transportation facilities.[46]

In July of the same year, President Truman issued two executive orders that called for desegregation of the armed forces by 1954, barred discrimination in the hiring of federal employees, and created a Fair Employment Board within the Civil Service Commission. Between 1948 and 1955, none of his other suggestions was able to pass both the House and the Senate.

In the meantime, the famous 1954 *Brown vs. the Board of Education of Topeka, Kansas* case was tried before the U.S. Supreme Court, resulting in the ruling that separate educational facilities for Blacks and Whites were inherently unequal. Still, the same year the court refused to hear a fair housing case.

In 1955, President Eisenhower's State of the Union message called for an end to civic-level, racial oppression. That same year, Eisenhower ordered a commission to counter discrimination in the federal government. Also, the Interstate Commerce Commission ordered an end to the segregation of passengers on trains and buses in interstate travel by January 1956.

In 1956 and 1957, both of Eisenhower's State of the Union messages called for congressional action on racial discrimination. In 1956, he requested that Congress create a bipartisan commission on civil rights. A year later, he urged passage of the Civil Rights Act, focused on voting rights, which had been proposed by his administration the previous year.

These governmental actions of the 1950s came as White civic leaders, aware of the growing significance of the Black vote, attempted to harness that potential; they were, in fact, responses to the long-term, steady pressure applied by the NAACP. Not coincidentally,

> the first meeting of what was to become the Southern Christian Leadership Conference was held in Atlanta on January 10 and 11, 1957. The title of this meeting, "Southern Negro Leaders Conference on Transportation and Integration" highlights the role the bus grievances played as a central organizing focus for the local movements and for the conference.[47]

Morris quite rightly points out that legislative or court actions do not create a movement. For activists, such positive motion at the state level does provide a sense of the feasibility of change and the inspiration of hope. That sense of "cognitive liberation," however, could only spread through community mobilization. Morris adds to our understanding with his focus on preexisting community mobilization and the evolution of its indigenous formal leaders. But his emphasis still provides only one, partial view of movement development.

The civil rights movement was a rebellion for mainstream inclusion and for equal access to social institutions. Therefore, formal Black leaders had to speak simultaneously to two opposing constituencies. While their fundamental intention was to speak for and act on behalf of all Black people, they understood that fulfilling those goals demanded that they persuade White leaders of the civic irrationality of racism and the democratic logic of desegregation. Seeking concessions from four successive administrations constrained formal Black leaders; the White body politic would have crushed the movement entirely. Formal leaders were not out of touch with the masses, but their adherence to their constituents' desires had to be balanced against that of the state's approval. Pushing the state too far could be disastrous. Their image had to be that of rational leaders in control of the activities to which they led their followers.

While formal leaders kept an eye on the state apparatus for opportunities and concessions, bridge leaders kept their hands on the pulse of the community. The goal of bridge leaders was to gain trust, to bridge the masses to the movement, and to act in accord with their constituents' desires. It was within this context that bridge leaders worked day to day with the people, unconcerned with the desires of the state. Feeling no need to compromise their vision, bridge leaders' actions were much less restricted, and this created different perspectives about the specific forms and strategies that these activists utilized to gain concessions. In other words, the acceptance and implementaion of particular "repertoires of contention" or methods of protest varied, depending upon the social location of the activist in the movement. While it is undoubtedly true, as scholars Charles Tilly and Sidney Tarrow argue, that new contenders adopt, alter, and extend upon the "repertoires of contention" of previous protest groups, it is also true that movement activists may be divided on the issues of which repertoires ought to be used and how. And one's decisions regarding their selection, alteration, and implementation rest squarely upon one's social location, both in the movement and in society.[48]

These factors necessarily created a degree of conflict between bridge leaders and formal leaders. Yet ironically, this conflict also contained a symbiosis that served to sustain and strengthen the momentum of the movement. When formal leaders were reluctant to act in a particular way, bridge leaders often acted in their stead. Likewise, affiliation with movement organizations and formal leaders gave legitimacy to the activities of bridge leaders.

Charismatic Leadership and Emotion

The kind of work done by bridge leaders was a characteristic consequence of their position, as determined by their social location in the movement. Many of their actions were spontaneous responses to planned activities gone awry and were motivated by the high emotions stirred up at such times. This truth requires a reconsideration of the ways in which social movement theories have depicted emotion and rationality in relation to leadership.

Max Weber, one of the founding fathers of sociology, discerned three forms of leadership: charismatic, traditional, and legal. Traditional authority is conferred by one's rank and status in society while legal authority is the legitimate use of force codified by law. These two types of authority are imbued with the position rather than with any personal characteristics of the individual. In contrast, charismatic authority remains independent of one's status or position, since power is derived from one's personal qualities. Weber believed that "true charisma" tends to be short-lived, emerging during moments of crisis when the emotionally charged masses look to some extraordinary individual to lead them. Followers generally perceive the charismatic leader as one embodying extraordinary capabilities, at times even a degree of supernatural power. The main point here is that, for Weber, the acceptability of emotion and spontaneity as leadership qualities was form-specific; these elements were not antithetical to leadership per se.

While to Weber charismatic authority develops outside of societal institutions and organizations, Morris has argued that, in the case of the civil rights movement, charisma developed within the most central of Black institutions, African-American Christianity. The Black church, he claims, demanded that ministers be charismatic and the majority of them "claimed to have been 'called' to the ministry by God."[49] Since ministerial charisma was rooted in the ultimate authority, church or movement members imbued these men with supernatural and extraordinary qualities. Thus, Black ministers were likely candidates as charismatic leaders.

Morris describes charisma as an outgrowth of the interactions between a minister and his followers, an interaction determined by the institution of the church and Black culture. Such an explanation necessarily precludes the emergence of women as charismatic leaders, since within the institutional context of the Black church and within the context of the culture, they could never be viewed as such. Yet the findings of my study suggest that women were indeed charismatic leaders, and in just the context that Weber describes.

We may begin by defining charisma in relational terms, as Morris does, rather than simply in terms of personal attributes. Borrowing scholar Richard Ellis's definition, charisma is "the effect one individual has on a group of other individuals. Without the effect, there is no charisma."[50] The purpose of charisma is "not simply behavioral change [as one would expect from traditional or legal authority, i.e. coercive power], but a conversion of individual values and beliefs."[51] This, of course, was what Weber had in mind when he wrote that charisma "manifests its revolutionary power from within, from a central metanoia [change] of the follower's attitudes."[52] According to Ellis, charismatic leadership can thus be defined in terms of the extent of the impact an actor has on the fundamental values and beliefs of other actors.[53]

Given this definition, I argue that women were, indeed, leaders in the civil rights movement. They emerged as short-term charismatic leaders during moments of crisis when people were emotionally charged by an incident. Women's leadership was accepted during these moments, and they made spontaneous decisions that took extraordinary courage. Women as bridge leaders did not gain their leadership positions through participation as traditional leaders within or outside of an institution, although some bridging activities fit the gendered division of labor traditionally found in Black churches. Rather, short-term charismatic leaders developed out of their interactions with followers in the cultural context of the movement.

Morris's error is to confound charisma arising within an organization and charisma emerging from a culturally ascribed position in society. As Wasielewski notes, "the analyses of both Weber and Toth (1968) implicitly point to emotions as the basis of charisma."[54] She continues: "Emotions are thus firmly based in a set of ordered understandings of the world; moreover, emotional responses to the world are often based on rational analysis."[55] Furthermore, cultural theory suggests "that the fundamental choice made by people, from which all other decisions derive, is the way of life they embrace. An individual's preferred culture operates as a decision rule, instructing the individual what to prefer and how to behave."[56] This is an inherently rational process, but not one divorced from emotion. Embedded in culture are hierarchies in which one's social position rests. These are, in turn, defined by the values society places on certain defining constructs, such as one's race, class, and gender.

Ministerial authority was rooted in church structure but emanated from Black cultural traditions. There were hundreds of charismatic Black ministers. Even when authority and charisma were jointly bestowed by the institution, they were not enough to catapult just "any" minister to formal leadership of an entire movement. Dr. King's emergence as "the charismatic leader of the civil rights movement" was decisively tied to his goodness of fit with a set of culturally prescribed attributes—as Black, as a man, as educated, and as a minister. Had any one of these constructs differed—his race, class, sex, or cultural status—he could not have led the movement. Thus, while the church served as the institution from which King's leadership emerged, it was the overarching cultural context—that is, beliefs about race, class, gender, and ministerial status—that defined his position in the movement.

Consequently, the cultural context also defined women's positions in the movement, thereby excluding them from formal leadership positions. This exclusion should not be taken to mean that women were neither charismatic nor leaders. Many of my respondents characterized women as charismatic and in much the same way Weber suggests. As Adam Seligman notes, according to Weber, "pure charisma is seen as a short-lived 'creative' force, erupting in times of 'mass emotion' and with unpredictable effect."[57] It was not the case that emotion and spontaneity were never a part of Dr. King's and other Black male formal leaders' decision making, only that they had to be concerned about the state. Their legitimacy in the eyes of the state depended on their appearance as legitimate, rational leaders.

Morris also confounds legitimacy and social constructs of power. As discussed, King's legitimacy and charisma emerged from his culturally prescribed, traditional authority as an educated male minister. Likewise, the legitimacy of women as bridge leaders emerged from their culturally prescribed, traditional status as community bridges to the church. Charisma, then, emerged for Dr. King from interactions with his followers, but these interactions were influenced by culturally prescribed social constructs (i.e. race, class, and gender) combined with his traditional authority position as a minister in the Black church. In stating Weber's position, Bendix notes:

> Charismatic leadership effects an "internal" revolution of experience, in contrast to the "external" revolution that occurs when, for example, people adapt themselves to a major change in legal rules without at the same time internalizing the ideas behind it. . . . Traditional rule is characteristically permanent, however temporary may be the power of an individual patriarchal master. Charismatic leadership, on the other hand, is the product of crisis and enthusiasm.[58]

Weber, as Hochschild notes, "posits a model of social action that is rational, while action based on emotion . . . is nonrational. . . . Surely emotion and sentiment are active ingredients in rational behavior as well."[59] It is clear that King's charismatic appeal, coupled with his social position as an educated man and a minister, led to mass support of his formal leadership position. In describing King's rise to power, Morris argues that charisma is a tool knowingly used by clergy to "stimulat[e], persuad[e], and influenc[e] crowds."[60] He elaborates:

> Students of charismatic leadership have persuasively argued that if individuals are to be recognized as charismatic leaders, they must personify, symbolize and articulate the goals, aspirations, and strivings of the group they aspire to lead. The ministers who were to become the charismatic leaders of the movement occupied strategic community positions which enabled them to become extremely familiar with the needs and aspirations of Blacks.[61]

The implication is that, at least for the formal leadership, charisma was a tool used in a planned, strategic, and rational manner by those in authority. Yet any discussion of the emotional use of charisma is neglected. Wasielewski, in analyzing the content of Dr. King's speeches and invoking Hochschild's use of emotion as a unit of exchange between leaders and followers, lends support to Morris's contention that charisma was rationally manipulated to move the masses. Yet unlike Morris, she emphasizes the emotional use of charisma as rationally manipulated, as a tool knowingly used to stir the masses.[62] Extending Hochschild's notion of framing rules, rules by which we "ascribe definitions or meaning to situations,"[63] which in turn define feeling rules, or rules which govern our subjective feelings and inform us of their appropriateness, Wasielewski develops three stages of charisma. She suggests that charisma is used when "problems arise when feeling rules mandate the display and experience of feelings individuals do not subjectively experience."[64] Charismatic leaders may then manipulate emotions to bring them in line with the movement's rational goals. This process includes evoking emotions, or tapping into the perspective of the potential constituent; revoking emotion, or "get[ting] followers to reassess the feelings they experience and the manner in which they display them; and reframing emotion, or "reshap[ing] their followers' interpretations of the world and their emotional reponses to it."[65]

However, I suggest that these emotional processes invoked by formal leaders were not always enough to move the masses to act. Throughout this text I argue that women bridge leaders, not just formal male leaders, as Morris describes above, often acted to "personify, symbolize, and articulate the goals, aspirations and strivings of the group they aspire[d] to lead." Moreover, they successfully used the processes of evoking, revoking, and reframing the emotions of potential constituents that served to recruit, mobilize, and sustain the masses. This form of charismatic leadership did not emanate from institutionalized training as a charismatic leader. Yet I argue that bridge leaders were often considered charismatic, and usage of such power manifested itself in planned, as well as in spontaneous, emotional and rational acts of leadership. In social movement literature, the terms *emotional* and *rational* are, of course, rarely found in combination. Yet as I will argue, emotion and spontaneity were as central to the formation and sustenance of movement mobilization as were rationality and planning.

Social Movement Literature: Emotion and Spontaneity

As already discussed, collective behavior theorists conceived of social movements as grievance-motivated, spontaneous events that were unplanned and irrational. Of course, later collective behavior theorists who began emphasizing the collectivity's normative nature still focused on shared grievances and frustrations. In an effort to refute such ideas, researchers, most notably McCarthy and Zald, developed a different conceptualization of movement activities that viewed grievances and frustrations as a societal constant and, therefore, insignificant causal factors of movement mobilization.[66] Rather, they emphasized the availability of resources, ignoring the specific cause of the movement. Their focus was upon the similarity of social movement activity to normal organizational activity, emphasizing the planned and rational nature of movement mobilization.

Both Morris and McAdam, in reformulating this model, stressed the importance of preexisting organizational structures for the development of the civil rights movement. They contend that such structures and organizations indicate a preexisting network, essential for planned, coordinated, rational movement activity. Drawing upon the work of Jo Freeman, Killian criticizes resource mobilization theory in general and Morris and McAdam in particular. He suggests that not all civil rights movement activities emanated from preexisting organizations and that many activities were spontaneous. He is careful to emphasize that calling actions spontaneous in no way implies that they are irrational. In his analysis of the Tallahassee, Florida, bus boycott of 1956, he provides a convincing argument that the boycott began as an unplanned event and that civil rights movement organizations emerged after its inception. This case, Killian concludes, establishes that not all civil rights movement activities were planned in advance, as is argued by McAdam and Morris. Rather, both spontaneity and planning are essential for successful movement momentum.[67]

Freeman calls for a reformulation of social movement theory to account for "both planned and spontaneous, leader-directed and grassroots" activities.[68] In an effort to address this problem, Killian develops a model that emphasizes the need for spontaneity in the early stages of a social movement and during periods of transition. He does not, however, develop a clear interactive conceptualization to account for these seemingly diametrically opposed conceptions of movement activities.

The root of this *problem* lies in several *problematic* assumptions. First is the still commonplace but false dichotomy maintained, in both scientific and mainstream cultures, between rationality and emotion.[69] While displaying calm rationality was an important tool used by formal leaders in order to maintain their legitimacy with the state, emotions certainly prevailed behind the scenes and, as discussed, were used to arouse the masses. Moreover, while bridge leaders displayed emotion more readily, it cannot be concluded that their behavior was any more irrational than formal leaders. Rather, the actions of bridge leaders were determined more closely by the event of the moment than by considerations of state approval. Thus, an action that may have been interpreted by the state, by nonparticipants, or even by formal leaders as irrational may have been an action emotionally charged, but nonetheless rationally calculated to produce a particular goal. Rationality, after all, does not have an objective reality. It is subject to individual interpretation.[70]

The second problem centers on the notion, still prevalent in social movement theory, that individual movement behavior must evince "self-interest," whatever that is, in order to be considered rational. While there may seem nothing wrong with such an assumption, in practice such a view tends to conflate emotion with irrationality. Rational choices, as conceptualized by social movement theorists, are only those choices that develop out of self-interest. Any decisions except clearly self-interested ones are thought to be irrational. Notions of the collective good or social ethics are not considered as bases for rational choices.

This utilitarian approach to social movements has, of course, been challenged extensively by social movement and other theorists.[71] In her argument against this approach, Jane Mansbridge states that "people often take account of both individual's interests and the common good when they decide what constitutes a 'benefit' that they want to maximize."[72] Moreover, as Taylor notes,

Feelings come into play in classical resource mobilization formulations only as affective ties that bind participants to challenging groups, and they are secondary to questions of strategic success in motivating activists.[73]

Taylor and others discuss emotions as an important organizing tool among already recruited participants.[74] They emphasize emotional aspects of commitment and the development of cultural climates as critical to the sustenance of social movements. Yet these and other critics of rational choice models have not developed a sufficiently interactive model of social movements.[75]

Rosenthal and Schwartz also support the notion that emotion and spontaneity are central, not irrational, aspects of movement mobilization. Moreover, they argue that grassroots groups through face-to-face interactions and emotionally charged and spontaneous events are often the "growth sector of social movements" and "play a crucial role in developing movement direction."[76]

To their credit, new social movement theorists[77] and feminist theorists[78] have also questioned the neglect of emotion in resource mobilization theory. They have turned the question, instead, to the relationship of the self to the community. Their research centers on consciousness, identity transformation, and solidarity as strategies for movement formation, mobilization, and sustenance. Within this context, I argue that emotion is central to the transformation of individual identities. It is emotion that creates the movement culture and persuades individuals to risk their lives for the movement. In other words, emotion becomes the conduit through which self-interest moves toward consonance with collective interest. Emotion, in this sense, becomes the catalyst through which individual transformations emerge, new ideas are embraced, and actions are undertaken that are against one's own self-interest, such as risking one's life for the movement.

Conclusion

Through an examination of the interactions of bridge and formal leaders, later chapters of this book will illustrate the interactive nature of spontaneous and planned activities, as well as the importance of emotion in social movement mobilization, calling into question the need to polarize these concepts. Moreover, I argue that bridge leaders are important agents of spontaneous activities and emotional appeals during moments of crisis when formal leaders either fail or are unable to lead.

Finally, the theoretical treatment of movement mobilization has focused primarily on the recruitment of potential followers and their subsequent mobilization, and given short shrift to the dialectical relationships *among* movement leaders and *between* movement leaders and followers. Consequently, movement mobilization is conceptualized as taking place in a linear fashion in which leaders begin movements and mobilize the masses. As later discussion illustrates, formal leaders are often mobilized by the masses they will eventually come to lead.

I have suggested that movement organizations also share relationships that, while not the primary focus of this book, create a particular context in which movement actors participate. In later chapters, the significance of the position of specific movement organizations and the actors within them, in relation to the movement sector as it interacts with the state, will be illustrated. It will become clear that in certain situations, the power of bridge organizations and bridge leaders to represent the constituency is significantly weakened.

Moreover, I have argued that political opportunities, resources, and a shared race were not enough to mobilize the masses to act. Rather, specialized appeals were needed to persuade individuals to join the movement, and these appeals took the form of one-on-one organizing that became the foundation of movement recruitment, mobilization and sustenance. This critical movement work was done by a special tier of leadership—bridge leaders—that developed through the exclusion of women, those without formal education or a college degree, gays, and non-Blacks from formal leadership. The effect of this exclusion was the creation of an extraordinary tier of bridge leaders, often charismatic women who bridged individual, prefigurative politics to the politics of the movement. Central to this process were spontaneity and emotionality, both of which contributed to individual transformations from self-interested identities to consonantal collective identities.

In this chapter, I have discussed the ways in which analyses of race, class, gender, and culture enrich our understanding of social movements. Studying identity, I argue, provides the nexus from which to understand the dialectical relationships between the individual within a collective and the collective, between the individual in a collective and society, between a collective and competing collectives, and between the collective and society—that is, the state and other institutions—with an eye upon the individual actors within them.

Gender, race, class, and culture were significant factors in the success of the civil rights movement. The strong tier of bridge leadership, where women most often flourished, provided a powerful resource for movement recruitment and mobilization. Moreover, as the following chapters illustrate, the partnership between Black men and women, as formal and bridge leaders, respectively, was constantly negotiated in an effort to provide freedom for the Black community as a whole.

TWO

Exclusion, Empowerment, and Partnership

Race Gender Relations

THE CIVIL RIGHTS MOVEMENT is best understood as part of a continuous history of resistance by both Black men and Black women. There have been untold numbers of Black heroes and heroines who have risked and given their lives for the freedom of their people. This struggle for survival is at the heart of Black consciousness. Yet the accepted historical record filters out the accomplishments of Black women with accounts of women's history as largely about White women. Even in the case of the civil rights movement, White women's participation has received more attention than that of Black women, despite the fact that the latter participated in greater numbers.[1] On the other hand, Black history has generally focused on the efforts and accomplishments of Black men.[2] Moreover, throughout history, Black women have had to divide their loyalties between the causes of women and that of their race, the latter often taking precedence. For this reason, issues of gender could never be divorced from issues of racism and racial oppression. Therefore, any story of Black women's movement participation must also be a story of the Black struggle, which includes the sons, husbands, and fathers of these courageous women.

Black Women Activists Speak Out: Empowered, Not Oppressed

Most of the women civil rights activists interviewed, in telling me their stories, included the courageous acts of men and women, and did not perceive their actions as having been limited by male domination. For most, the civil rights movement has remained in their memories as a special and unique period in history, one which evoked memories of cooperation, love, fear, accomplishment, and empowerment. All of the women considered their participation liberating because, for the first time in their lives, they could participate openly in organizations targeting the extreme oppression of their people in America. Any level of participation in such an endeavor was a form of empowerment. The fact that men held the offices or overt power was not perceived as the critical issue. Rather, men just as women were admired for their courage and skills. Bernice Johnson Reagon, an active participant in the Student Non-Violent Coordinating Committee, provides an insightful summary of many women's feelings about their participation in the movement.

One of the things that happened to me through SNCC was [that] my whole world was expanded in terms of what I could do as a person. I'm describing an unleashing of my potential as an empowered human being. I never experienced being held back. I only experienced being challenged and searching within myself to see if I had the courage to do what came up in my mind. And I think if you talked to a lot of people who participated in the movement, who were in SNCC, you find women describing themselves being pushed in ways they had never experienced before.

I am saying we were all, men and women, products of our time. So it's not about how the men were versus how the women were. . . . The ideas about what women should do and what men should do showed up in the civil rights movement among men and women, and none of those ideas, whether they were carried by me or some man, had any limiting effect on what I would do as a powered person in the world. I was challenged to go further than I'd ever gone before. And to that extent, it was an incredible experience.[3]

For Reagon and others, participation in the civil rights movement in general and in SNCC in particular, created new identities, both personal and political. Reagon and others continually expressed their newly found self-empowerment derived from movement participation. They were challenged to transcend not only personal boundaries but also political and social ones. Nothing was sacred, neither their identities nor society's boundaries. Reagon explains:

I think men . . . grew up—and we were growing up. This is what you need to understand. We were growing up as adults. Men who grew up in the Student Non-Violent Coordinating Committee were pushed as hard as we were in their own way to go beyond any models we had for behavior. All of us were, day by day, doing things that our parents thought would get us killed. So we'd been socialized to go as far as you can go, but don't go do X, Y, Z if you're Black. And SNCC was saying, "We're breaking this thing up. We're breaking it down. We're challenging this structure." So SNCC needed people who were willing to go further than they'd ever been trained to go. So we were all boundary breakers. And what I've experienced that doing, for me, was freeing me as a person in the world so that I never thought that anybody could tell me where I could go or not go. I thought that somebody else could kill me, but short of that, there wasn't any way they could stop me.[4]

While some movement theorists view social movements as ordinary organizations, this suggests that, for men and women alike, the movement provided a particular cultural context that transformed the identities of the participants beyond the confines of societal norms. It is clear that a strict adherence to gender norms was precluded by the context of the movement, even within the hierarchy of the church.[5] Bernice Johnson Reagon provides an example:

> You have to understand that I grew up in a church, and the women sat on one side in the Amen Corner and the men sat on the other side in the Amen Corner. The pulpit was in the center, and the only time the women went up was on Women's Day. Now, the civil rights movement was one time I saw women going up into the pulpit because they were leaders of the civil rights movement. . . . I say the leadership structure changed. . . . The woman was the most powerful person in the local community, like Fannie Lou Hamer, who was not a minister. She was always in the pulpit. I always during the mass meetings, saw women in the pulpit with the ministers. . . . And it had to do with your willingness to put your life on the line and your courage and your character. But we were all products of a culture that had roles for various people. My mother always belonged to a women's group. That is not a sexist phenomenon within the Black community. That is the way the organizations operated, to a large extent.[6]

Therefore, the movement cultivated a culture in which many societal norms were questioned. Within the context of a culture that was breaking down barriers, women and men often viewed women as capable leaders. Faye Bellamy, who late in SNCC's history became a member of the Executive Committee, recalls:

> One of the things about many of the people in SNCC was that they were very open to the fact that people were capable. So they didn't assume that you were not capable. They would assume that if you showed them that, but they would assume first that you are capable and, therefore, you can do certain things.[7]

As Judy Richardson notes, however, even though women were considered capable, few were elected to the Executive Committee. Yet Richardson emphasizes that this fact was irrelevant to the women activists who admired the men and women leaders and viewed themselves as strong and capable.[8] Fay Bellamy continues:

> I think of admiration of the persons because none of those people [Forman, Moses, or Carmichael] tried to take over or be the leader or annihilate or assassinate, by words or deeds, the other person. So that's why I say I don't think it was intentional that that occurred [these three men becoming leaders]. . . .
> For the most part, the males seemed to be the "leaders," and I think some of that is a throwback [to] the very sexism we grew up with in our universe and in our

personal environment. And certain things men tended to do more readily at that time. . . . But the males I've named—some of them, and there were more than just those three—had a little more say, sometimes based upon, I guess, the work they did or that they were male, or that they took that initiative, and sometimes that's what it takes.[9]

Moreover, Bellamy felt that men's power in SNCC was not intentionally claimed, but rather a by-product of their natural charisma. As discussed, charisma was not simply a natural state, but rather was socially constructed by traditional beliefs in educated men and/or male ministers as formal leaders. Therefore, while the movement culture served to transform gender norms, it did not entirely do so.[10] At the same time, she and other women activists felt their participation in SNCC was liberating. Faye Bellamy adds:

I never got the impression that most people were following a leader. We felt that we were all leaders, and that's what kept some of the balance there . . . like Ruby Doris [Smith Robinson], or myself, or Judy Richardson or Mildred Forman. I don't remember any of us thinking that we were less than. . . . [11]

One respondent indicated that what was most important was not what men thought of them but what they thought of themselves. She explained that since SNCC was a voluntary organization, no one told others what projects they could work on or that they had to participate in certain activities. Everyone in SNCC, by virtue of being a part of SNCC, was putting his or her life on the line. This act alone was a source of empowerment.[12]

This sentiment was expressed by other SNCC women as well. Though there were restrictions on the titled positions women could hold, they were still able to lead in particular areas and contribute in significant ways. Certain women were considered leaders, Bellamy recalls, because

they were workers, they were responsible people, they were not afraid to get involved in a showdown, struggle about a discussion to make a point or to have their point heard. There were . . . women, some of whom participated in movement activities, some of whom were project directors against the will of some of the men. . . . [Some men] were really afraid that these women would be harassed or brutalized in some kind of way because the project could be a very dangerous endeavor. The leader might be assassinated. . . . [While some men were afraid for the safety of the women,] there were some people . . . who just thought it was not a woman's place to play that kind of role. And there were some men who didn't want to work with women.[13]

Yet any misgivings that some men held about women's capabilities were not enough to stop women's leadership. Bernice Johnson Reagon recalls:

There wasn't [anything to stop women.] For instance, if you wanted to go into the field and somebody didn't want you to go into the field because you were a woman, that was their opinion. But it never stopped you from doing it. So when I talk about men's and women's relationships in the Student Non-Violent Coordinating Committee, I am not describing an organization where men were progressive when it came to women, and they were for women being equal, I'm not saying that. I am saying that we were in a movement, and the structure of that organization was such that you were the only person who could limit what you did. And you had to find the courage to challenge anything that didn't feel right to you, and you could do it in the organization.[14]

Women's status was gained through acts of courage, and gender divisions, while quite real, were irrelevant to their day-to-day struggle to survive as a people. The rarified atmosphere of ever-present danger precluded strict adherence to commonplace gendered expectations. Movement participants were constantly confronted with aggressive White southerners willing to stop their efforts by any means necessary. Dorie Ladner, a SNCC field secretary, recalls the dangerous circumstances in Mississippi:

My job was to go and try to organize my state, Mississippi. And each person had a similar goal that they wanted, and living under that type of intense pressure and danger—fear—that we lived under, I would say that a lot of times the guys might have wanted to protect us, but all of us were in [it] together. There was no hiding from anything. I can remember many a day that we were all out on the streets in the Mississippi delta. . . . We had been in Indianola the whole day, the guys and the girls. You must also understand that there in Mississippi, those of us who were working with Bob Moses, there were probably about five or six of us . . . there were only three girls and maybe four or five guys in the whole state. So we were running up and down the highways on these lonely, dark roads by ourselves. So when you talk about a particular role, we were all fighting a battle, like a war. It was war—not like war—it was war.[15]

Both Reagon and Ladner define their social locations in the movement primarily in terms of their racial identities, over and above gender. Race, in these dangerous circumstances and times, superseded other identities such as gender and class. "It was war," and the lines were drawn along color. Indeed, the dangers were real.

Therefore, in determining the nature of gender relations in the civil rights movement, what is of great significance is the way these relationships and the explanations for them have been shaped by racism. As Elizabeth Higginbotham notes,

in societies where racial demarcation is endemic to their socio-cultural fabric and heritage—to their laws and economy, to their institutionalized structures and discourses, and to their epistemologies and everyday customs—gender identity is inextricably linked to and even determined by racial identity. We are talking about the racialization of gender and class.[16]

In 1955, Emmett Till, a fourteen-year-old Black boy from the North, had been murdered in Mississippi for allegedly whistling at a White woman. When the body was found, his testicles had been cut off. So for Black women, the fact that men held offices or were the formal leaders was not perceived as the critical issue.

Black Women in Support of Male Leadership

Several of those interviewed suggested that Black men and women felt that it was the Black man's time to lead an organization to free all Black people. As Victoria Gray, who worked with several movement organizations, forcefully states,

> I know that I functioned fairly effectively. I did not feel that I was a threat or feel threatened by the male. . . . In our community we wanted that man wherever there was opportunity for him to be in authority. We wanted him to be there. We wanted him to be there. We wanted him to be there. We wanted whenever, wherever it was possible to put that man in some kind of position of authority or leadership. We wanted him there. That was just the way it was. This was our husband, this was our son, this was our brother, this was our lover. We wanted him there whenever there was an opportunity for this to happen and we would support him in whatever way that we could or that he would allow us. Our men have had a horrible existence in society, always. Horrible existence. Oftentimes that . . . had a lot to do with it. . . .
>
> The fact of the matter is that for those young men . . . [in] some local areas there were those strong men who were self-employed and more mature who took those roles. . . . Any time there is an opportunity for the Black man in the community to be in that leadership role, the community wants him there. I think there are a lot of reasons for that. Because there are just so few places where historically the Black male could have any authority, if you will. So that is not an accident, I assure you. Where that was possible, the community supported that.[17]

As stated by Mrs. Gray, it was the Black man's time to gain power, to lead in a society that prevented the Black people's representation. Mrs. Gray also suggests that conditions were much more dangerous and difficult for Black men than for Black women. Many women discussed the reasons why they or others supported and promoted Black male leadership and accepted less than formal leadership positions. One of the central explanations has centered on the belief that, throughout history, reprisals have been worse for Black men. The argument is generally made that men were lynched more often than were women. Yet throughout history women also suffered reprisals and were beaten, raped, and, though not as frequently as men, lynched.[18] As Jacquelyn Dowd Hall notes,

> the association between lynching and rape emerges most clearly in their parallel use in racial subordination. As Diane K. Lewis has pointed out, in a patriarchal society, black men, as men, constituted a potential challenge to the established order. Laws were formulated primarily to exclude black men from adult male prerogatives in the public sphere, and lynching meshed with these legal mechanisms of exclusion. . . . Lynchings served primarily to dramatize hierarchies among men.

In contrast, the violence directed at black women illustrates the double jeopardy of race and sex. . . . Black women were sometimes executed by lynch mobs, but more routinely they served as targets of sexual assault. . . . Rape sent a message to black men, but more centrally, it expressed male sexual attitudes in a culture both racist and patriarchal.[19]

Both Black men and Black women were subjected to violence, but the violence manifested itself in gendered ways. It is undoubtedly true that in a White patriarchial society, Black men, because they are men, pose the greatest threat to the social order and, therefore, face more life-threatening situations. What is at issue here is the extent to which this perception justified the exclusion of women from formal leadership positions. However, given the time—1954–1965—African-American men's bid for power was the most feasible and reasonable path to equality. The notion that Black men should be viewed as the equal of White men assumes inclusion into an already gendered and classed structure. If a civil rights movement were to be taken seriously by the White establishment, it would undoubtedly have to be led by men. Black men, then, were seeking access to the White man's power, and this power is associated with maleness. Moreover, tied to this perception is the view that without power, a man cannot truly be a man.[20] On the other hand, at that time and arguably now, women's identities and status were not generally determined by their access to societal power. This, of course, is significant and fraught with implications, not the least of which is the dependency of African-American women on the progress of Black men.[21] As is true for most women, their upward mobility and financial security were, and debatably are, largely determined by their fathers and husbands. Moreover, the rise of Black men to power is intricately interwoven with the position of Black women and their children in society, a dependency not only determined by gender but also by race and class. Such a view, however, does not sufficiently capture the reality of Black gendered relations except within the context of their respective relations to White society. Prathia Hall Wynn, currently a minister and former leader in SNCC, grapples with this complexity:

There is a sense in which I think Black women were—I'm going to use the word *complicitous* and probably bracket it for a moment—in the predominance of male leadership. I think, as I have reflected on that . . . that is reflective of the ways in which Black men and women have cooperated since slavery. When Angela Davis talks about equity in suffering, I think that that has been a factor that has influenced us at many points along the way. I am now, in my own research, looking at the religious women, the church women, and of course there is no place where women are more subordinated than the church. But some of that, I think, is also related to what I am about to say about SNCC, and that is that, because of the ways in which Black men have been demeaned, because there were no places in which Black men could give leadership with dignity except those places which were controlled by the Black community, and that would be the Black church and the Black movement organization . . . so in that sense, I think that there has been an attitude of support for Black male leadership by very, very strong, assertive Black women. And so on one hand, for instance, when the press was on hand, who did they interview? They interviewed men. Now part of that, then, had to do with the sexism in the culture, in that that's who the press people considered to be important to interview. . . . Women often went along with that, feeling that it was important to our community that Black males be seen as competent, standing up and giving strong leadership. I don't think, at the same time, that women felt that taking that posture was depriving them or taking anything away from them. I think that . . . [at] that time there was an attitude of partnership.[22]

Similarly, Faye Bellamy describes her experience of the complexity of gender relations when she was nominated as chair of SNCC:

I remember when I was nominated for chair, and Stokely was being nominated and H. Rap Brown was nominated. And I remember being so surprised that a number of the women said they didn't think it was time for women to be head of the organizational system. Now . . . some of the reasons were that they didn't feel that the community systems, the other nations, would be able to understand a woman being head of an organization such as SNCC at that time.[23]

These women ascribe sexism to the dominant culture, seeing themselves as empowered, strong, and assertive. The women's narratives locate them in relation to the dominant culture, to Black men, and to Black people as subjugated others. In this context, one's Blackness supersedes one's gendered location. The significance of gender identity is relational and interaction specific.[24] It is articulated that Black women's identities were clearly anchored to their race and that gender was secondary to their racial identity. In relationship to White society, Black women's identity was wedded to Blackness and the oppression of all Black people. When situated individually, as self to man, gender becomes significant. (But this significance is necessarily contextualized and constrained by the identities of gender in the other locations.) Yet as stated at the outset, this was not an issue for Black men and Black women in the movement. The goal was to free Black people, and any other agenda was viewed as divisive.[25]

Only with hindsight have some of the women reflected on the gendered nature of their positions in the movement. Septima Clark's view exemplifies this point:

But in those days, I didn't criticize Dr. King. . . . I adored him. I supported him in every way I could because I greatly respected his courage, his service to others, and his nonviolence. The way I think about him now comes from my experience in the women's movement. But in those days, of course, in the Black church, men were always in charge. It was just the way things were.[26]

Dorothy Cotton, a leader in the SCLC, offered similar explanations of women's views on sexism. That women deferred to men was not at issue; the goal was the freedom of Black people and this could be achieved only through a cooperative effort. She explains that "men were programmed to be chauvinists but we allowed it, too. Women deferred to the husbands. We deferred to the male."[27] In SCLC, the natural positions for women were supportive and secondary, though as Dorothy Cotton notes, women were not conscious of their positions as secondary.

While women may see their actions as "complicious" with what is now viewed as sexism, the fact that women did not feel oppressed by their gender at the time is significant. They have, quite rightly, conceived of themselves as leaders, as strong and assertive participants in the movement. They have recognized their successful contributions to the movement. Yet it is clear from most accounts of the civil rights movement that scholars have not often viewed women's participation as leadership. Rather, they have usually been perceived as local organizers or followers. In the historical record, the partnership between Black men and Black women, with men participating as formal leaders and women as bridge leaders, has not been accorded the recognition it deserves.

Indeed, most of the women interviewed either considered themselves leaders and/or felt other women were leaders. Their perceptions of themselves as empowered leaders are not consonant with theoretical and historical accounts of leadership in civil rights movement organizations. This incongruence is not, however, irreconcilable. The fact that women were not formal leaders should not obscure the ways that women led. An examination of the women's own perceptions of their leadership and participation, then, serves to broaden our understanding of gender as an organizing construct within social movements.

The following section illustrates that the activism of African-American women was neither new nor an anomaly; that they, alongside African-American men, provided many of the tactics and strategies that would later be associated with the heightened period of civil rights activism.

A Glimpse into Black Women's Historic Activism

Black men and Black women have shared a long and painful history of resistance to oppression, beginning as soon as blacks were forcibly removed from their homelands and brought to the shores of North America. Activism and resistance was and is a way of life, and women were and are central to the success of any movement for freedom. While the years 1954 to 1965 represent heightened civil rights movement activity, they by no means mark the sudden onslaught of activism. The movement was and is continuous. The development of nonviolent ideologies and strategies, as well as the culture of resistance which manifested itself during the heightened period of the "civil rights movement," developed in historical context. Many of those who were active in the 1930s and 1940s played crucial roles in the formation and sustenance of movement activity well into the 1960s.

While clearly the scope of this book cannot include an entire history of the activism of African-American women, it is nevertheless important to situate the context of women's activism in the civil rights movement as a part of a continuous struggle for freedom. An emphasis on the historic partnership between Black men and Black women provides a window to clearer understanding of the gendered nature of the civil rights movement.

Moreover, this history briefly illustrates the connections between pre–civil rights movement activists such as Mary McCleod Bethune, Pauli Murray, Bayard

Rustin, and A. Philip Randolph, and their influence on heightened movement activities.[28] The following section should serve as a sample of the ways in which, historically, women's activism in concert with that of men's contributed to the rise of heightened activity during the 1950s and 1960s. Prior to the 1950s, African-American women clearly acted as leaders, were often formal leaders, and addressed issues of gender and race simultaneously. When forced to choose, as they so often were, Black women's identities, just as those who followed, were strongly anchored to their Blackness.

Cooperation between Black men and Black women has been crucial to the success of their strides toward freedom. During slavery, Black women rebelled right along with men against the atrocities inflicted against their people.

> In 1721, the crew on board the *Robert* was stunned when they were attacked by a woman and two men intent on gaining their freedom. Before they were subdued by the captain and other crew members, the slaves, including the woman, had killed several sailors and wounded many others.... The woman had served as a lookout and alerted the leader as to the number of sailors on deck. She had also stolen all of the weapons used in the mutiny.[29]

> In another incident, in 1785, the Captain of a Bristol slaver was attacked by a group of women who tried to throw him overboard. When he was rescued by his crew the women threw themselves down the hatchway.[30]

This resistance continued throughout the slave period and into the civil rights movement of the 1950s and 1960s. Much of the ideological underpinning, as well as many of the tactics and strategies employed during the heightened period of the movement, were born in earlier years of activism. Women were involved in every aspect of resistance, working alongside men for freedom.

Mary McLeod Bethune and the National Association of Colored Women

In the earlier years, women's activism and leadership were often asserted through participation in Black women's clubs. In 1924, Mary McCleod Bethune took the helm of one of the first such organizations, the National Association of Colored Women (NACW). This organization possessed a long and distinguished history of activism, with Black women activists Ida Wells-Barnett and Mary Church Terrell, well-known educator and writer Anna Cooper, Black Baptist women's movement leader Nannie Burroughs, and founder of the National Association of Colored Women Josephine St. Pierre Ruffin as its former leaders. These women, along with many others who spearheaded club movements in their cities and states, were instrumental in the development of the National Association for the Advancement of Colored People (NAACP). Many of them had been part of its precursors, the National Afro-American League/Council and the Niagara Movement. The Niagara Movement split off from the Afro-American League and was led by W. E. B. DuBois, who advocated direct action in opposition to what he and others perceived as accommodation to Jim Crowism by the league.

In the early years, the women of the NACW worked tirelessly to garner support and to increase membership. These women often gave speeches rallying the Black community to pledge their support for the NAACP. Wells and Terrell, in particular, used their national and international recognition, and their connections to the Temperance Movement and the YWCA, to persuade both Black and White women to support the NAACP.[31]

Bethune's activism continued in the footsteps of her predecessors, and her connection to men who would later become a part of Dr. Martin Luther King's inner circle helped sow the seeds for heightened movement activity in the 1950s and 60s. She has been described as a very charismatic woman who was able to garner support and enthusiasm for her projects:

> Whenever Mary McLeod Bethune spoke, the most vibrant qualities in her personality became evident. She would stand silent for a moment, head tilted slightly upward, as though waiting for a message from above. Eyes half closed, she would intone the first words, and her audience saw the missionary, the spiritual messenger, heard the deep, rich resonance of a voice that was almost a bass. Using short sentences and clear-cut thoughts, moving slowly at first, building up a gradual crescendo until she reached a high-speed excitement that carried everyone with her on a wave of emotion, gradually slowing at the close of her speech, leaving her listeners with a deep sense of benediction, Mrs. Bethune stretched out her expressive hands and closed them quickly as though to turn off the sounds of her own voice.[32]

Bethune's activism emerged prior to her involvement in NACW. In 1915, she established the Daytona Normal and Industrial Institute for Girls. Building on that earlier work, Bethune led the NACW as it developed other schools for girls. Recognizing that many newly formed organizations such as the NAACP, which received White support, were doing a better job with civil rights and community welfare, she then turned the focus of the NACW to economic issues. With the deepening of the Depression, Black women were becoming the sole support of their families as Black men lost their jobs. At the same time, Black women's wages were falling. Generally barred from all but domestic labor and desperate for work, Black women were forced to underbid one another for a day's wage, producing a favorable labor market for White middle-class families. Envisioning a nationwide umbrella organization dedicated to the development of economic and political strategies, Bethune established the National Council for Negro Women. This coordinated effort brought many local professional women's groups into communication, particularly on the problems of unemployment and low wages.

Mary McLeod Bethune, the Roosevelt Administration, and A. Philip Randolph

Bethune's activism, which included attendance at a White House Conference on Child Welfare and participation in a National Council of Women conference, led her to meet First Lady Eleanor Roosevelt and the president's mother, Sara Roosevelt. Bethune greatly influenced Mrs. Roosevelt's views on racism and was later appointed to the administrative post of director of the Negro Division of the National Youth Administration. Although she worked tirelessly for separate but equal facilities, her efforts were often in vain. With unemployment at a record high, President Roosevelt's commitment to civil rights waned.[33]

Black women's activism continued throughout World War II, especially in the struggles for union representation. When allowed to join, Black women were actively involved in unions. "Black women led the organization of workers in laundries and in cleaning and dying establishments."[34] They were instrumental in successful tobacco strikes, an industry which the AFL had difficulty organizing until Black women were given their own union. "Emerging as a leader was Mamma Harris, a tobacco stemmer, who became known as 'Missus CIO in Richmond.' In the following year, she led a strike of . . . workers . . . some seven hundred of them."

This leadership continued through the peak of the war, as the federal government exhorted women to take up jobs in factories deprived of male workers and in the burgeoning defense industries. But during this time, when all hands were supposedly crucial to the war effort, Black men and Black women were, to a large extent, excluded. While Black organizations formed to fight this discrimination, the Roosevelt administration remained unresponsive.

The idea to shake up the administration with a march on Washington came from an unnamed Black woman. At a strategy meeting in Chicago, she said,

> "Mr. Chairman, we ought to throw fifty thousand Negroes around the White House —bring them from all over the country, in jalopies, in trains, and any way they can get there until we get some action from the White House". . . . A. Philip Randolph [activist and founder of the Alabama branch of the Brotherhood of Sleeping Car Porters, and later a part of King's inner circle] was said to have seconded the proposal, adding: "I agree with the sister. I will be happy to throw [in] my organization's resources and offer myself as a leader of such a movement."[35]

Their success resulted in the passage of a law forbidding discrimination based on race, color, creed, or national origin in the nation's defense industries.[36]

A. Philip Randolph was no stranger to Mary McLeod Bethune. He had attended Cookman Institute, making him one of "Mrs. Bethune's boys." Earlier, Bethune had rescued the ailing boys' school by merging it with her successful Daytona Normal and Industrial Institute for Girls. Bethune and Randolph often worked in tandem on special projects while lobbying the Roosevelt administration for the development of a commission and several task forces for civil rights.

One of their joint projects was the attempt to extricate a poor Gretna, Virginia, sharecropper from the grip of legal injustice. Odell Waller had been working for a poor White tenant farmer, Oscar Davis, who routinely exploited Black farmers. In 1940, Waller planted several wheat crops that his cousin and mother tended while he went to work in Maryland. Annie Waller also began to keep house for Davis's then ill wife. After several weeks of work, Mrs. Waller still had not been paid. She, in turn, refused to help Mr. Davis tend his tobacco crop. In retaliation, Davis evicted Mrs. Waller, keeping her share of the wheat crop. Odell, hearing of this injustice, promptly returned to Gretna to challenge Davis. Davis, who always carried his shotgun, became belligerent and threatened Odell. Odell, in fear for his life, shot and killed Davis. He was subsequently convicted by a jury comprising mostly White farmers and received the death penalty. His case became known to the Workers Defense League (WDL), a fledgling organization with few resources based in New York.[37]

The WDL, founded by A. Philip Randolph and others, had on its staff a young activist, executive secretary Pauli Murray. She was given the task of raising funds for Waller's defense. Lacking the $300 needed to file an appeal, Waller would be executed within two weeks. Murray brought Waller's plight to the attention of the NAACP in Richmond and to the Virginia Black Baptist Minister's Conference. Subsequently, Murray and Waller's mother traveled from coast to coast giving speeches at local NAACP and WDL chapters, as well as to the Brotherhood of Sleeping Car Porters. Eventually, they were able to raise enough money to cover all of Waller's legal expenses. Yet on October 13, 1941, the Court of Appeals of the Commonwealth of Virginia upheld Waller's conviction and refused to overturn the sentence of death by electrocution. Waller's lawyers successfully received several stays of execution, but the conviction, and sentence were continuously upheld.

Waller had fewer than thirty-six hours left to live when Virginia Governor Darden refused to commute the death sentence. In a desperate attempt to intervene, A. Philip Randolph, Pauli Murray, Mary McLeod Bethune, and representatives of the NAACP and the YWCA converged on the White House and demanded to see the president. He refused. Pauli Murray recalls:

> The day was one of unrelieved failure and humiliation. Mr. Randolph, whose threat a year earlier to lead 100,000 Negroes in a march on Washington had moved President Roosevelt to issue an executive order creating the nation's first Fair Employment Practice Committee, soon found that Negro discontent had low priority with an administration preoccupied with waging a global war. The delegation was shunted from office to office, and it became clear that the Odell Waller case was a hot coal no high official would touch.
>
> Vice-President Henry Wallace was walking toward his office building when he saw us approaching. He quickened his steps and tried to evade us, and Mrs. Bethune, who knew him well, was compelled to run after him in order to be heard. He brushed her off with a curt response, "I can do nothing, it is out of my jurisdiction." When we went to the office of an influential senator, his political secretary displayed contempt for the delegation by picking up Mrs. Bethune's cane (she suffered from arthritis) and twirling it like a drum major's baton as he talked to us. . . . No one at the White House would see us, and our last resort was Mrs. Roosevelt, whom Mr. Randolph had been trying to reach all day.[38]

That night, the delegation waited at the NAACP headquarters for a reply from Mrs. Roosevelt. When the call finally came, she expressed her deep regret that the president would not intervene. The delegation was heartbroken. The following morning, July 2, 1942, Odell Waller was put to death.

Deeply discouraged, the leaders continued their struggle throughout the 1940s, broadening their attention to include the plight of disenfranchised peoples throughout the world. With further developments in World War II, many Black intellectuals were comparing the Nazi position on "racial purity" with racist notions in the United States. They understood that U.S. outrage over Hitler's abominable actions and corresponding concern over the plight of the Jews (such as it was—lip-service, mostly) was an inherent contradiction, since the government did nothing about the oppression of Black Americans.

The Rise of Nonviolent Resistance

In the early 1940s, leaders such as Gandhi and Nehru were imprisoned for their civil rights activities. As activist Pauli Murray noted, "Ideas about the use of nonviolent resistance to racial injustice, modeled on Gandhi's movement in India, were in the air. A. Philip Randolph announced publicly in late December 1942 that the March on Washington Movement was considering a campaign of civil disobedience and noncooperation."[39] Although most of the established Negro groups criticized Randolph, the young people, many of whom attended Howard University, were supportive. Others, such as Bayard Rustin, who would later become a part of King's inner circle, and James Farmer, of the Fellowship of Reconciliation and the Congress of Racial Equality, were already implementing the Gandhian techniques.

In January 1943, a formative incident occurred in which three Black Howard University coeds were refused service at a lunch counter in Washington. They demanded to see the manager, and when they were told he was not in, they refused to give up their seats. A policeman was called, and he ordered the waitress to serve them, whereupon they ordered hot chocolate drinks. When the bill came, they found they had been substantially overcharged. Leaving what they owed on the counter, the three proceeded to exit the restaurant and were subsequently arrested. Charges were dropped, and they were remanded to the university officials. This incident triggered campus-wide discussions and groups formed to develop organized protests based on Gandhi's work.

One young woman, Ruth Powell, was in the forefront of these nonviolent protests and leader of the Direct Action Committee on campus. Powell had been raised in an upper-middle-class family in Massachusetts and had experienced little of the Jim Crowism so entrenched in the South. One day, as a newly arrived student at Howard University, Powell stopped at a restaurant to get lunch and experienced for the first time the humiliation of the segregated South. After the refusal of the restaurant staff to serve her, Powell fled in tears. Spurred by that outrage, she staged repeated one-woman sit-ins at local restaurants. Powell, upon entering an establishment which refused her service, would occupy a seat for several hours while fixing her gaze upon one waiter or waitress. Pauli Murray recalls, "Once a soda fountain clerk became so provoked . . . that he came around to Ruth's side of the counter, unscrewed and removed the stools on either side of her, and placed a card on the counter reading COUNTER CLOSED AT THIS END."[40]

As Powell's actions demonstrate, nonviolent protest had been operating long before its incorporation into the civil rights movement. Pauli Murray, commenting on the 1942 March on Washington (which fell short of the anticipated thousands of protesters and actually took place in New York), notes:

> A few activists in 1942 had pointed the way to the massive nonviolent protest demonstrations led by Dr. Martin Luther King, Jr., in the 1950s and 1960s. And our solemn protest did not end on a totally somber note. After the ceremony in Union Square, a truckload of marchers . . . rode back to Harlem along the parade route. This time we sang freedom songs and shouted a lively chant: "Hey, Joe, whaddye know; Ole Jim Crow has got to go![41]

During 1942 and into the summer of 1943, largely in response to the inherent contradiction between the government's concern over racism in Europe and the corresponding lack of concern about racism at home, spontaneous riots broke out in Los Angeles, Beaumont (Texas), Detroit, and Harlem. Many Black men had enlisted in the armed services or were drafted. They were dying for their country, and yet they were treated as less than citizens upon their return. Despite the worst rioting in decades, President Roosevelt continued to turn a blind eye to the plight of Black people. Pauli Murray, exasperated by these events, wrote a collection of poems entitled "Dark Testament and Other Poems." Some were published in *Crisis*, the NAACP's newsletter.

> Hope is a crushed stalk
> Between clenched fingers . . .
> Hope is a song in a weary throat.[42]

In another poem ironically entitled "Mr. Roosevelt Regrets," Murray asks:

> What'd you get, black boy,
> When they knocked you down in the gutter . . .
> What'd you get when you cried out to the Top Man?[43]

Both spontaneous and more organized forms of nonviolent protest developed during the late 1940s. Protest cultures became prevalent as soldiers returned home to unemployment and oppression while Black women, and women in general, were pushed out of the workforce to make room for the White men returning home from war. The irony of fighting a war against the racist Nazis and then returning home to a country that tolerated and perpetuated racial discrimination created intolerable discontent among Black people. The Reverend Jesse Jackson, speaking at the 1996 Democratic National Convention, powerfully told of how his father and other Black soldiers, returning from War World II on trains, were forced to sit behind Nazi War criminals because they were White. These experiences of racism stood as glaring contradictions to American ideals. Many Whites as well could not ignore this ingrained hypocrisy. These post–World War II experiences served to escalate and buttress the already growing protest culture of the early 1940s.

In 1942, in Chicago, an interracial organization developed call the Congress of Racial Equality. It arose from a Christian-pacifist group, the Fellowship of Reconciliation (FOR), whose doctrine and principles were based on the Gandhian concept of "*Satyagraha*, or nonviolent direct action, to the resolution of racial and industrial conflict."[44] Just three weeks after the sit-ins by the Howard University coeds, CORE staged a similar protest at restaurants in Chicago. James Farmer, a divinity graduate of Howard University, and Bayard Rustin held the formal leadership of CORE. Farmer, like Pauli Murray and others, had been a student of Dr. Howard Thurman, a Howard University professor, Methodist pacifist, and FOR vice-chairman.

Around the same time, and into the early fifties, Mary Church Terrell, an activist, and first president of the National Association of Colored Women, shifted her tactics. Previously, while an advocate for women's and Black civil rights, she had used more traditional modes of protest such as letter writing, petitions, and speeches. But led by the Truman administration, the national political climate began to change, augmented by three major Supreme Court rulings that undermined segregation:

In *Sweatt v. Painter*, the court held that equality involved more than physical facilities. In *G.W. McLaurin v. Oklahoma*, the court stated that a Black student, once admitted, cannot be segregated. In *Elmer W. Henderson v. United States*, the court rendered segregation illegal in railroad dining cars.[45]

This political shift created an atmosphere of hope in which the eighty-seven-year-old Terrell began new direct-action campaigns that included picketing, sit-ins, and boycotts.

Terrell's targets were segregated diners and those which refused outright to serve Blacks. In 1949, she formed the racially integrated Coordinating Committee for the Enforcement of the D.C. Anti-Discrimination Laws (CCEAD). Groups of CCEAD activists requested service at stores and restaurants all over Washington and Baltimore. If they were refused, the group would try to reason with the owner and, that failing, they would then picket. Such picketing resulted in resounding victories with such giants as Kresge Stores and the Hecht Company desegregating their lunch counters. Leaflets were passed out in an effort to gain support from Whites. One stated: "I have visited the capitals of many countries, but only in the capital of my own country have I been subjected to this indignity."[46] In 1954, Mary Church Terrell's achievements were celebrated at a White House reception in her honor. She died several months later, at the age of ninety.

Conclusion

What is abundantly clear is that African-American women activists did not feel oppressed by their gender. Rather, they experienced feelings of empowerment and were inspired to transcend societal constraints imposed by racist institutions and cultural norms. These women's gender identities were "inextricably linked to and even determined by racial identity."[47] That women activists supported men as formal leaders, even though it meant their own exclusion, does not suggest a false consciousness in which they contributed to their own oppression. Rather, given the years 1954–1965, this support was developed within the context of a racist,

White patriarchal society. Because of the dangerous circumstances in which move-ment activists worked, Black women found many of the barriers to their leadership participation weakened. Moreover, despite their exclusion from formal leadership positions, Black women found ways to lead and did not feel constrained or limited.

African-American men and women share a long history of mutual support in their struggle for freedom. Although this history is beyond the scope of this book, the chapter provides a glimpse of the decades of activism that preceded the height-ened movement activity of the 1950s and 1960s. Historically, African-American women participated in civil rights struggles through their work in the women's club movement, the NAACP, and many other activist groups prior to the 1950s. Their efforts, alongside those men who would later become formal leaders of their own movement organizations or a part of Dr. King's inner circle, illustrate the many strategies and tactics, including the use of nonviolence, sit-ins, pickets, dem-onstrations, and boycotts, which were to lead to the success of the civil rights movement.

THREE

Women and the Escalation of the Civil Rights Movement

Early Resistance to Segregated Transportation

Challenges to interstate, state, and local Jim Crow transportation laws had occurred since the 1800s, with Black women and men refusing to relinquish their seats or to cooperate with segregated transportation facilities. One of the earliest cases of this resistance occurred when seventy-year-old Sojourner Truth was assaulted and injured by a conductor. Truth, an ex-slave and forceful antislave and women's rights advocate, often staged sit-ins on public transportation.[1] Many conductors either refused to stop for Black riders or would force them to run for the car.[2] Truth sued the rail line and won. In response to her triumph Truth replied:

> It created a great sensation, and before the trial was ended, the inside of the cars looked like salt and pepper. . . . Now they who so lately cursed me for wanting to ride, would stop for black as well as white, and could even condescend to say "walk in ladies."[3]

In 1872, Josephine DeCuir,

an apparently wealthy Louisiana plantation owner, moved to sue a steamship line. After being sold a ticket, DeCuir was refused a cabin and required to take her meals after white passengers had dined. A District Court had responded to her $75,000 suit by awarding her $1,000. Eventually the United States Supreme Court overturned the decision and DeCuir ended up without even a consolidation award.[4]

Ida B. Wells, a civil rights and women's rights activist, also confronted the illegalities of such practices. While traveling from Memphis to Woodstock, Tennessee, Wells took a seat in the first-class train car. When the conductor came by, he advised her to move to the smoking car, which was the only car in which Blacks could ride. When she refused to move, the conductor attempted to drag her from the car. She bit the back of his hand and secured her feet under the seat in front of her. The conductor went for help; three men then pried her loose, dragged her to the door of the train, and at the next stop threw her out. "Bruised, the sleeves of her linen duster torn, she tumbled down the steps to the platform while her white fellow passengers stood and applauded."[5] Wells sued the railroad and won. The Tennessee Supreme Court overturned the decision on appeal. If upheld, it would have challenged the 1883 nullification of the Civil Rights Bill passed during Reconstruction. Wells was the first Black to challenge this bill. In her diary, Wells wrote about this painful event:

I felt so disappointed because I had hoped such great things from my suit for my people generally. I have firmly believed all along that the law was on our side and would, when we appealed to it, give us justice. I feel shorn of that belief and utterly discouraged, and just now, if it were possible, would gather my race in my arms and fly away with them.[6]

News of the failure of many of these women to gain justice in the court system traveled quickly throughout women's clubs and became one of the central issues discussed at the 1896 meeting to create the National Association of Colored Women. "A representative of the Cambridge, Massachusetts Golden Rule Club complained of the 'recent disgraceful decision of the United States Supreme Court in regard to the Jim Crow Car System.' "[7] While the women realistically understood that they could never get the courts to uphold justice, they did agree to use direct action to effectuate change. They "enthusiastically endorsed" a proposal to boycott the railroads:

We hereby condemn . . . the excursions and picnics of our race which patronize the railroads . . . where the separate car law is in operation, and pledge ourselves to do everything in our power through the press and pulpit to educate . . . on this point. The recent decision of the U.S. Supreme Court convinces us that we must depend upon ourselves in this matter. So long as we continue to spend thousands of dollars every year on needless excursions, we enrich the railroads at our expense. Cut off this source of revenue because of the "Jim Crow Cars" into which the wives, mothers, sisters and daughters of the race are forced to ride and the railroads will fight the separate car law through self interest.[8]

This tradition of noncompliance with segregation laws in public transportation continued into the 1940s, when Pauli Murray and her friend Adelene McBean traveled by Greyhound bus from New York to Durham, North Carolina, changing buses in Richmond, Virginia. McBean had never fully experienced southern Jim Crowism. While riding south in the back of the bus, her seat, which was over the wheel, dislodged. The women notified the driver, who would not allow them to switch seats. McBean began to feel a sharp pain in her side and once again requested to move her seat. The driver proceeded to threaten them both. When they stopped in Petersburg, some twenty miles later, McBean and Murray moved up but remained behind the White passengers. As new passengers boarded the bus, the driver yelled for them to move back. McBean refused and suggested that she would be willing to leave the bus if the driver agreed to refund her money. At this, the driver became belligerent and left the bus, returning with the police.

When they arrived, Murray was frightened, but McBean looked the officers squarely in the eyes and told them that she was not afraid. The policeman then asked the bus driver to fix the broken seat, whereupon McBean and Murray moved back. The driver, however, proceeded to pass out cards to the White passengers requesting that they fill out their names and addresses, so he could call upon them as witnesses if there was an accident. None of the Black passengers received cards. When Murray protested this treatment, the policeman was resummoned, and both Murray and McBean were arrested. Such incidents were numerous throughout the decade of the 40s and continued in the South into the 50s.[9]

Many of the women who began the Montgomery bus boycott credited their anger at such humiliating treatment as powerful motivation. Having to fight for justice had been a daily reality for too many years. Finally, in the mid-1950s, the possibility of real change seemed feasible. In the past, the U.S. Supreme Court had failed to uphold the rights of Black Americans; recent rulings suggested a more favorable outcome. Women and men all over the nation were celebrating the strides made by other women and men. These changes, coupled with the long history of womanist resistance to inequality on public transportation, set the stage for events that moved civil rights activism out of abeyance and into its heyday.

The Women's Political Council of Montgomery

In 1946, for personal and political reasons, scholar and Alabama State College professor Mary Fair Burks founded the Women's Political Council of Montgomery, Alabama. That same year, Mrs. Burks had been in a traffic accident that involved a White woman. A White onlooker had summoned the police, claiming that Mary Fair Burks had cursed the White woman. Prior to the civil rights movement, accusations of this nature were taken as sufficient evidence for incarceration. It came as no surprise, therefore, when Mrs. Burks was arrested and taken to police headquarters. She was interrogated and released only after the White woman exonerated her.

This humiliating experience prompted Mary Fair Burks to begin an organization that would work within the community to educate individuals about their constitutional rights and encourage them to register to vote. This group was primarily composed of professional women. Men, Mrs. Burks claimed, were intentionally excluded because they "would take it over and women wouldn't be able to do what they could do."[10] So from the very beginning the Women's Political Council was a political organization designed to combat the institutionalized racism of Montgomery, Alabama, and it was an organization that provided leadership opportunities for women.

Jo Ann Gibson Robinson, a young professor at Alabama State College, joined the WPC in 1949 and became its president one year later. Under her direction, the WPC developed chapters statewide and began to discuss ways in which some of the laws might be changed. In an interview, WPC member Mrs. Johnnie Carr recalls: "People like Jo Ann Robinson, Mary Fair Burks, and Mrs. A. W. West worked very hard as leaders to get us organized. We had been working for years together."[11]

The women of the WPC had long been concerned about segregated public services such as the bus lines and parks. Like many other women, Jo Ann Robinson suffered degrading treatment on the segregated buses. And like Mrs. Burks, her participation in the WPC sprang from personal as well as political experience. As she recalls:

> I suffered the most humiliating experience of my life when that bus driver had ordered me off the fifth row seat from the front and threatened to strike me when I did not move fast enough. . . . I had not forgotten that ordeal. I had not told it to anybody, not even my closest friends, because I was ashamed for anybody to know. Yet I could not rid my mind, my thoughts, my memory of it![12]

Throughout 1954 and 1955, the women of the WPC met six times with the mayor and city bus officials in an effort to negotiate better bus service, though they did not request an end to segregation. In March 1954, the women threatened a citywide boycott of the buses if their demands were not met.[13]

On December 1, 1955, Mrs. Rosa Parks refused to relinquish her seat to a White man. The previous spring, there had been a similar incident with the arrest of Claudette Colvin, who refused to give up her seat on the bus. Her case was tried at the state level, and she was found guilty. The effort to press the case at the federal level was abandoned because E. D. Nixon, a highly respected formal local leader and former president of the local NAACP chapter, and others believed that her character was unsuitable for a desegregation case. They felt that such a case would, most assuredly, receive press attention, and she was not only an immature teenager but pregnant as well. Another opportunity arose in October 1955, when Mary Louise Smith also refused to give up her seat on a bus. She too was arrested and found guilty under the segregation law, but again E. D. Nixon did not find her character suitable. She came from extremely impoverished surroundings, and her father was known for his bouts with alcoholism.[14]

The women of the WPC disagreed with these decisions and felt that the emphasis should be on challenges at the local, rather than federal, level. At the very least, they surmised, pursuing these cases should entail challenging local segregation laws through confrontation with city officials. The suitability of these women's characters, they insisted, should not preclude local leadership from pressing for change within the local government.[15] Clearly, women were pressing male leaders to act against the system of segregation long before the Montgomery Improvement Association and the Southern Christian Leadership Conference came into existence. They had continuously challenged the system on their own initiative.

Recent accounts of the civil rights movement indicate that Mrs. Rosa Parks was not, as popular accounts would have it, simply tired from long hours of work when she refused to relinquish her seat on the bus.[16] Her tiredness was more a product of years of humiliation by, and frustration over, segregation in the South. Mrs. Parks recalled:

> I was thinking that the only way to let them know I felt I was being mistreated was to do just what I did—resist the order [to stand]. . . . I simply decided that I would not get up so a white person could sit, that I would refuse to do so.[17]

Twelve years before, Parks had also refused to relinquish her seat and had been thrown off of the bus. Ironically, this 1955 incident involved the same bus driver, only this time he called the police. Her decision to resist this system was based on years of civil rights activism. Mrs. Parks had been an active member of the NAACP for fifteen years and at the time of her arrest was secretary of the local chapter. She had participated in a committee with Reverend Martin Luther King Jr., Jo Ann Robinson, and Alabama State Professor J. E. Pierce that discussed grievances with city officials during the time of Claudette Colvin's arrest. Mrs. Parks had also created local youth chapters of the NAACP. Her activism clearly illustrates that she was a community bridge leader prior to her arrest. Moreover, she was well acquainted with Ella Baker, a seasoned activist and director of the New York chapters of the NAACP, who later became the first director of the Southern Christian Leadership Conference. Every time Baker was in town, she and Parks got together to discuss the NAACP's Leadership Conference.

Baker had been traveling extensively throughout the South, holding leadership training courses, and had done so in Montgomery just prior to the boycott.[18] Additionally, Parks had attended Highlander Folk School in Monteagle, Tennessee, during the summer of 1955. At this unique interracial facility, she attended workshops for activists. Many of these civil rights workshops were led by Septima Clark, a longtime NAACP activist whose Citizenship Education Program would later become the foundation of the Southern Christian Leadership Conference's Voter Registration Program. Parks's decision to refuse to relinquish her seat on that bus came from a long and persistent ideological and action-oriented resistance to segregation, a continuum of movement activity. And she was well acquainted with other contemporary activist women whose bridge leadership was central and critical to the successful outcome of the movement. In *Ready From Within* by Septima Clark, Mrs. Parks, in an interview with the editor, Cynthia Stokes Brown, recalled her feelings about Septima Clark and Highlander Folk School:

> I am always respectful and very much in awe of the presence of Septima Clark because her life story makes the effort that I have made very minute. I only hope that

there is a possible chance that some of her great courage and dignity and wisdom have rubbed off on me. When I first met her in 1955 at Highlander, when I saw how well she could organize and hold things together in this very informal setting of interracial living, I had to admire this great woman. She just moved through the different workshops and groups as though it was just what she was made to do, in spite of the fact that she had to face so much opposition in her home state and lost her job and all of that. She seemed to be just a beautiful person, and it didn't seem to shake her.

While on the other hand, I was just the opposite. I was tense, and I was nervous, and I was upset most of the time. I can't describe my attitude too well, not in this polite company. However, I was willing to face whatever came, not because I felt that I was going to be benefited or helped personally, because I felt that I had been destroyed too long ago. But I had the hope that the young people would be benefited by equal education, should the Supreme Court decision of 1954 be carried out as it should have been. . . .

[Highlander founder] Myles Horton just washed away and melted a lot of my hostility and prejudice and feeling of bitterness toward white people, because he had such a wonderful sense of humor. I often thought about many of the things he said and how he could strip the white segregationists of their hardcore attitudes and how he could confuse them, and I found myself laughing when I hadn't been able to laugh in a long time.[19]

Cynthia Stokes Brown quite rightly concludes:

As Mrs. Parks talked, the story of the civil rights movement began to fall into place for me. Mrs. Parks had been able to do what she did because of Myles Horton and Septima Clark and E. D. Nixon. Events had not happened in a random way; they were hooked together through the relationships that people had established and with each other. There had been no single leader.[20]

Three months after her return from Highlander, Mrs. Parks refused to relinquish her seat to a White man. This single act was to set in motion the heightened period of civil rights activism. Mrs. Carr, secretary of the Montgomery NAACP and leader in the Women's Political Council, recalls the sequence of events that led to the boycott:

When Mrs. Parks was arrested, a lady was on the bus and saw the arrest. She went to a person that knew Mrs. Parks, told her that they had arrested Mrs. Parks; this lady in turn went to Mr. Nixon. Now, they didn't go to the Political Council. They went to Mr. Nixon. He in turn called . . . the lawyer, Clifford Durr. Clifford Durr, Mrs. Durr, and Nixon went down to the jail and got Mrs. Parks out of jail. . . . Mrs. Parks knew Mrs. Durr and Mr. Durr, and of course she'd been sewing for Mrs. Durr. . . . When she went home, then Mr. Nixon sat down and talked to her. He said, "Mrs. Parks . . . what do you think about us making a test case out of this?" So it wasn't the Political Council that did it. But when this idea was brought out . . . then everybody fell in line to try to make it work.[21]

When Jo Ann Robinson and the women of the WPC heard of Mrs. Parks's arrest, they decided to call a bus strike. The women of the WPC had, for several years, discussed the possibility of a bus boycott, and how they would achieve it. They developed tactics like distributing flyers as a means of mass communication, and mechanisms for gaining cooperation from the Black community. Mrs. Thelma Glass, an active member of the WPC recalls:

> We had all the plans and we were just waiting for the right time. We had discussed
> . . . well, every angle of it had been planned. We talked about transportation and we
> talked about communication, and all the things that would happen when we finally
> decided to do this. . . . At one of the meetings, we had asked Mr. Nixon . . . to hear
> our plans and to talk with us. It was planned years in advance before it actually came
> to fruition.[22]

They realized that, although they worked closely with others within their respective neighborhoods, they possessed neither the necessary legitimacy nor the institutional power within the Black community to maintain support for a boycott. Some within the community did not even know of the existence of the WPC. Any successful boycott, they decided, would need a "legitimate," well-respected leader within the Black community. When asked if women leaders such as Jo Ann Gibson Robinson were viewed in a similar light as E. D. Nixon and Rufus Lewis, another respected community leader, the secretary of the WPC, Mrs. Thelma Glass replied:

> No, by some people. Now, by me she was. But just by people in general, it looks
> like, I don't know, a male-dominated world. And it was still in existence and I guess
> it still is. And so somehow the male comes up and gets the attention. Others seem
> to just respect male leadership more. I think the men have always had the edge. . . .
> Traditionally it has just been a male role.[23]

Mrs. Carr, currently the first and only woman president of the MIA, also addresses the question:

> Do you know how long we've been fighting for women to stop being housewives and
> the maid and the cook so that we could pick our places in the job market? And do
> you know how long we've been fighting for that? Women were in [the past] . . . were
> considered secretaries, [anything] but a president. And this is just how society was
> and you can't get away from that.[24]

Mary Fair Burks stated that the members of the Women's Political Council were mostly professional women who did not have extensive community support. Mobilization, she believed, could be achieved only through the formal leadership of the ministers. Of special significance is the fact that, though excluded from formal leadership, women understood their own power to move the community to action. It is this understanding that characterizes the relationship between the formal and bridge leadership. This symbiotic or mutual-exchange relationship has important implications for understanding the ways in which mobilization occurred in the civil rights movement.

Jo Ann Robinson's understanding of these relationships did not prevent her from initiating the boycott. Acting as a community bridge leader between the desires of the community and those of the formal leaders, she, along with two students, drafted and mimeographed leaflets to be distributed throughout the community.[25] Jo Ann Gibson Robinson remembers:

> On Friday morning, December 2, 1955, a goodly number of Montgomery's black clergymen happened to be meeting at the Hilliard Chapel A.M.E. Zion Church on Highland Avenue. When the Women's Political Council Officers learned that the ministers were assembled in that meeting, we felt that God was on our side. It was easy for my two students and me to leave a handful of our circulars at the church, and those disciples of God could not truthfully have told where those notices came from if their lives had depended on it. Many of the ministers received their notices of the boycott at the same time, in the same place.[26]

Women had a full understanding of the limitations on their status and power. The women of the WPC were not without the knowledge or tactical skills needed for mobilization, yet they knew that as women they could never gain community sanction to act as primary formal leaders. Although gender was not the sole exclusionary category for achieving such a leadership position, it did override any amount of innate talent a woman might possess.

Over the next several days, the WPC contacted many local women, requesting that they distribute the flyers within their neighborhoods. One such woman was Mrs. Johnnie Carr, a respected leader of her community and one who stood up for the rights of others. Though it was E. D. Nixon who first notified her of Mrs. Parks's arrest, it was Mrs. A. W. West, a leader in the WPC, who first contacted her about the boycott.

> It was from Mrs. A. W. West who called and asked if I would take an area to distribute the leaflets. I told her I was going out of town to Birmingham for a meeting but that I would see to it that there would be people in the community that got those leaflets out. So I got about five people in my neighborhood to do that.[27]

So women within and between their communities had a communication network for dispensing information and soliciting cooperation. The women, as formal leaders of the WPC acting as community bridge leaders, used these existing structures to great advantage; their efforts were not organized from the pulpit. By the time the meeting of community leaders took place that Friday evening at Dexter Avenue Baptist Church, most of the members of the various congregations—mainly women—were already aware and in support of the boycott.[28]

The women of the WPC had achieved their goal. Through neighborhood linkages, they had gained community support and pressured the ministers and local leaders to support the boycott. Mary Fair Burks believes that both the support of the ministers and the support of the local women were essential to the success of the boycott. Although women, through their community networks, could gain the initial support for a boycott, she believes it could not have sustained itself without "legitimate" leadership—that is, the ministers. And she also notes that the boycott would not have happened at all without the initial thrust by Jo Ann Robinson: "Jo Ann worked as hard as any minister [for the boycott]. She worked as hard as Ralph Abernathy."[29]

Mary Fair Burks suggests that it was women who were most affected by the conditions on the buses. Most cars owned by Blacks were owned by men, and ministers were not among the population that daily experienced the degrading conditions on the buses. In 1955, most families owned only one car, if any, and it was the man who drove it to work. Consequently, as Mrs. Burks states, "it was the woman who saw more of [the degrading conditions on the buses]."[30] Given that women were most affected by the conditions on the buses, it is they who were most receptive to the initial suggestion of a bus boycott. Their acute feelings of humiliation, degradation, and anger propelled them to support the boycott despite the risk of arrest.

The actual organizing of the boycott took place on the evening of Friday, December 2, 1955. Though both men and women were present at this meeting of community leaders, and though without the initiative of the WPC attendance may have been considerably less than the 100 present, men controlled the meeting. Mrs. Erna Dungee, WPC secretary and later financial secretary of the Montgomery Improvement Association, describes the boycott meetings as male dominated:

> Women listened to men. They passed the ideas to men to a great extent. Mary Fair Burks and Jo Ann Robinson were very vocal and articulate, especially in committee meetings. But when it came to the big meetings, they let the men have the ideas and carry the ball. They were kind of like the power behind the throne.[31]

Mary Fair Burks and Jo Ann Robinson informed the ministers of the details of the boycott and the methods worked out for getting people to work on Monday morning. They wanted to be sure the ministers would pass on the correct information to their congregations on Sunday morning.[32] Mrs. Dungee continues:

> We really were the ones who carried out the actions. Driving the cars, though men eventually took over that. But we organized the parking lot pick-ups and many things like that. Finally, Mr. Rufus Lewis and Reverend B. J. Simms took over that transportation committee.[33]

So vocal leadership by women was suitable behavior as long as it did not emerge from "behind the scenes" into the public arena. While at the outset women's leadership was relatively visible, as formalization of activities and organization structures developed men were given titled positions and the power to delegate duties, while women's visibility and power declined. Women's duties were redirected to more "appropriate" spheres, such as the preparation of meals and the distribution of flyers.

After the success of the first day of the boycott, there was a mass meeting at

Holt Baptist Church. Here, too, the WPC was responsible for the distribution of the flyers taken door to door by local people. The leadership still had not picked an individual to lead the boycott, but that evening Dr. Martin Luther King Jr. was chosen despite the long-standing leadership status of E. D. Nixon, who was the former President of the NAACP.

In his account of the Montgomery bus boycott, Martin Luther King Jr. gives the women of the WPC the credit for initiating the bus boycott, and suggests that it was E. D. Nixon "who readily concurred. . . . He agreed to spearhead the idea."[34] Though Jo Ann Robinson had a great deal of respect for E. D. Nixon, she states that

> the leaders were not political leaders. They were businessmen. Sometimes they were given little tokens that kept them satisfied. Mr. Nixon was one of them but Mr. Nixon was very limited educational wise. And that affected him as a potential leader. And he was sort of an agitator. But then when the whites recognized it he sort of cooled it down. People respected Mr. Nixon for his bravery. But he wasn't always able to follow up. See, he could expose trouble but then he couldn't take it from there. He just couldn't go any further. He was willing, I've never seen anyone more willing, but I think his leadership stopped where he couldn't go any further.[35]

Mrs. Johnnie Carr concurs: "Now, Mr. Nixon was a hardworking man, a fine leader and everything, but he doesn't have that thing that could weld people together in a movement like ours."[36] Mr. E. D. Nixon, no matter how well respected as a local leader, was not suitable as a primary formal leader. He, too, for lack of an education as well as his nonminister status, was excluded. Yet as a part of the inner circle of Montgomery's formal leadership, he served in a crucial capacity as a secondary formal leader, located between the women of the WPC and the ministers. In this position, Nixon was to serve as a mediator between the desires of the bridge leaders and the decisions of the primary formal leaders.

The Formation of the Montgomery Improvement Association

Though there had been considerable factionalism among community groups that had prevented unified challenges to segregation, it was the women of the WPC who had taken the initiative and mobilized other women to push for a bus boycott. Now, after the success of the first day of the boycott, it was time for formal leaders, who were mostly men clergy, to decide whether or not to continue the protest. On the evening of the first day of the boycott, the formal leaders assembled to discuss what should happen next. Many of the ministers did not want to continue the boycott, or, if they were to support it, they wanted to do so anonymously.

> E. D. Nixon rose in anger. "How do you think you can run a bus boycott in secret? . . . Let me tell you gentlemen one thing. You ministers have lived off these wash-women for the last hundred years and ain't never done nothing for them. . . . We've worn aprons all our lives. It's time to take the aprons off. . . . If we're gonna be men, nows the time to be mens".[37]

Nixon pointed out that the women had risked arrest, and now it was the time for men to step forth in support. He then threatened to tell all the parishioners of the various congregations that their preachers were cowards. E. D. Nixon as a secondary formal leader was able to gain the support of the ministers, acting as a mediator between the desires of the bridge leaders and the community they represented and the primary formal leaders. With this, the ministers agreed to support a boycott and to form the Montgomery Improvement Association.

Indeed, Nixon had long been a trusted man in the community, president of the Progressive Democratic Association and a forerunner of civil rights activism. Just as women bridge leaders did, Nixon earned his community recognition through acts of resistance and courage. Nixon also shared ties with A. Philip Randolph. Both men had organized the Black Brotherhood of Sleeping Car Porters Union in Montgomery. What distinguishes his position from that of the women was his male status. Although excluded from primary formal leadership, Nixon did earn a position in the inner circle as a secondary formal leader of the Montgomery Improvement Association. He was nominated for president, elected its first treasurer, and also served on the negotiating and finance committees.[38]

Women bridge leaders did not enjoy such privileges. Their leadership, however, was no less important to the development of the Montgomery bus boycott and the Montgomery Improvement Association than was the male- and minister-dominated leadership. Women initiated, planned, and strategized, providing momentum for the boycott. They understood the normative constraints that prevented them from becoming formal leaders of the boycott, and so thrust their energies into activities that would force its inception.

As an organization, the Montgomery Improvement Association's gender patterns strongly followed those of the church. Officers generally were men. Only one woman served in such a capacity at its inception, Mrs. Erna Dungee (later Allen), secretary of the Mount Zion Church, appointed financial secretary. Though Mrs. Dungee was an officer, she was also part of the paid staff, which included Mrs. Maude Ballou, Dr. King's personal secretary; Mrs. Hazel Gregory, office manager; and Mrs. Martha Johnson, secretary-clerk. As the sole woman officer, Mrs. Dungee's bookkeeping activities were overseen by E. D. Nixon and later by Reverend Ralph Abernathy.[39]

On the MIA Executive Board, Jo Ann Robinson and Mrs. A. W. West were chosen to represent the Women's Political Council. On committees, men generally outnumbered women. For example, Rosa Parks was the only woman to serve on the Committee to Write the MIA constitution, and Mrs. A. W. West was one of nine, eight of whom were men, on the Committee to Establish a Bank and Savings Association. Mrs. Erna Dungee, Mrs. Alda Caldwell, and Mrs. R. T. Adair were on the Finance Committee with four men. Women did chair certain committees, such as the Welfare Committee and the Membership Committee, however. Both areas were the responsibilities of women in the church and illustrate the extent to which bridging community members to the movement was women's work. Women who were on the Welfare Committee were responsible for the well-being of those who might suffer economic reprisals for participation in the boycott—that is, loss of jobs or eviction.[40] These two areas of the MIA were, however, critical to the boycott's success and to the life of the MIA.

It was not that women were prevented from participating in important ways but that gender assumptions limited their participation options. This was not, however, a point of contention between Black men and women. Mrs. Carr, a community bridge leader, recalls:

> I never did find time to find fault with how people were selected for doing what they did because I had been asked to serve in so many different capacities. . . . I was se-lected to go to various places to speak for the organization . . . state meetings . . . like the NAACP . . . or Baptist women.[41]

Though Mrs. Carr asserts that she was not an exception, and she dislikes the pursuit of those who feel they did not get adequate credit for their participation in the movement, she later agreed that while women could chair a committee or hold office as a secretary, they would not be elected president.

> Well, it was not a stated thing but just an understood thing. . . . Now, of course, when you spoke out against things like that, a lot of times you were even criticized by other women that felt like . . . this is not what we ought to be doing. I think we just accepted the servant [role] and done what we could because we felt like togeth-erness was the point.[42]

The central concern, as many women indicated, was "togetherness," a view centered on the solidarity and progress of the community rather than on individual glory. While women were excluded from formal leadership positions, they were relied upon to be leaders in local activities. It was not that women could not be viewed as possessing leadership qualities; such capabilities were viewed positively for both sexes within the community. Rather, it was that, in women, these qualities were suitably displayed through local activities and committee duties. The work of the welfare committee served to sustain the efforts of the boycott participants against the many economic reprisals exacted by employers. Likewise, it served to provide linkages between those in the organization and those citizens who it pur-ported to represent.

Women often acted on their own initiative to provide support for the boycott. Early on, it became clear to women such as Georgia Gilmore, who also had been arrested on a bus,[43] and Inez Ricks that financial support was critical to the op-eration of the carpool. These indigenous bridge leaders immediately organized neighborhood bake sales. They created local fund-raising clubs, Mrs. Gilmore's No-Name Club on the east side of town and Mrs. Ricks's Friendly Club on the west side, which competed to raise the most funds for the boycott. Each club provided about $100 per week.[44] Though considerably more money was needed and outside support would later become central to success, the initiative and organizing skills of these women sustained the MIA in its infancy. Mrs. Gregory, the MIA office manager, elaborates:

There was the Club from Nowhere. Georgia Gilmore [started that on] the east side of town. And the Friendly Club was on the west side of town and that was [started by] a lady named Inez Ricks. . . . In the beginning the first two years, it was so many people going to the mass meetings until they had to have a mass meeting on . . . the east side of town and the west side of town. . . . So these ladies and men, they would be there, and . . . they would raise money. They raised all the money. They would come and sell a lot [a seat or pew] of church to one another and to families because people would be getting off of work to come and get a seat. And I feel like those people, a lot of them, that no one ever mentions them, no one ever talks about them. And those are the people that I feel were really the people that made it work. Because if you hadn't had those people, then you would not have been able [to succeed]. . . . And I will say this, there were many ministers who would not have gone as far had it not been for their members. They wouldn't have let them show up in their pulpit on Sunday if they had not participated.[45]

Later, northern organizations such as In Friendship, which was based in New York, raised money for the boycott. In Friendship was formed by Ella Baker, A. Philip Randolph, Bayard Rustin, and Stanley Levinson. Rustin was a long-time Black activist and Levinson was a Jewish New York attorney sympathetic to the movement. In Friendship raised money to support activism throughout the South. And their numerous discussions with Dr. King would eventually lead to the development of the Southern Christian Leadership Conference.

In the meantime, at the mass meetings which were minister led, the words of Dr. Martin Luther King Jr. were eagerly awaited. His words echoed throughout the hall, serving as an inspiration to all. While women's activities were also acknowledged at these meetings, they were generally given only three-minute slots to provide updates on the progress of their endeavors on the Membership and Welfare Committees. Or anecdotes of their acts of courage might be recounted to encourage the audience to forge ahead. This gender discrepancy was also demonstrated in the MIA newsletter, edited by Jo Ann Robinson but subject to approval by Dr. King. It contained little information on the activities of women, focusing instead on the activities of the primary formal leaders—the ministers—or the secondary leaders.[46]

Though men became the formal leaders of the Montgomery bus boycott, it is clear that without the support of the women bridge leaders and the community, their efforts would have proved fruitless. Mrs. A. W. West, though quite elderly, made four trips every morning between seven and eleven A.M. to transport individuals to work. Virginia Durr, a local White activist, recalls: "And that's why Mrs. West was called a queen, because she was the type of lady in our community who did not have to do it. Because she could have stayed at home and said that she was, you know, elderly."[47]

While men made organization-wide structural, tactical, and financial decisions, women made similar kinds of decisions within the bridge tier of their leadership. As previously mentioned, indigenous bridge leaders Mrs. Georgia Gilmore and Mrs. Inez Ricks provided economic support, initiating fund-raising activities and organizing competitive community bake sales. Mrs. Carr describes the contributions of

Mrs. Odessa Williams: "[She] was a very forceful leader in the voter registration drive and she worked with the young people and did a beautiful job."[48]

Mrs. Gregory elaborates:

Odessa Williams was very, very active from the beginning and follow[ed] Dr. King [down to help with] the integrating of the University of Mississippi. She was in that March. She . . . participat[ed] in everything, and every phase of the civil rights movement.[49]

The chair of the Welfare Committee and a community bridge leader, Mrs. Johnnie Carr took responsibility for the well-being of those who were punished for boycott actions, lessening their fear of participating. Mrs. Carr remembers:

They would cut you off of Welfare or they would put you outdoors and all those things they were doing to people. Those type of things had to have somebody . . . investigate and see the needs of the person and report back to the organization.[50]

Women also took responsibility for providing lunches and dinners for the mass MIA meetings and for marches. Mrs. Carr continues: "In this we really had to work because we had to get people to give food and we had to get people to prepare food."[51] Though these activities do not possess the glamour of formal leadership, they were no less critical to the success of the boycott. Such efforts required a capacity to lead, to be creative, and to be committed. Still others participated in whatever ways they could. Virginia Durr recalls,

One day, I shall never forget, I stopped to pick up a lady. She was elderly. . . . I stopped and asked her where she was going. And she told me. And I said, "Well, I'll take you." And she said, "Well, I appreciate it very much . . . but if nobody picked me up, I was going to walk . . . because I am determined if my walking is going to help my people to get justice, I will walk." And her entire journey would have taken her approximately twelve miles of walking. . . . And I carried her to her destination. But before I picked her up, she had made about seven miles of her journey walking to see about a job and was on her way back home.[52]

Such an act is illustrative of the ways in which community members exhibited personal leadership. Although we will never know the name of this woman, she provided others with the inspiration and courage to follow her example, and not yield in the pursuit of freedom. Mrs. Thelma Glass, a leader of the WPC, provides her perspective of the movement in these early days:

When you finally look at it, I think it was a grassroots movement that had basically the women behind it in service and support. I would say they gave the greatest service and sacrifice for it in the movement. And leadership when invited. . . . And I kind of think that since it was one thing that affected all of the people, I think that they sacrificed and pooled what money they could give with what types of services they could give to keep the movement going and helping with all these hundreds of people who were in Montgomery because they have to be fed and all the other things. So they did that kind of thing and gave leadership where they could. The women attended mass meetings. It's just like every church. I'm not saying men aren't religious, but just population comparison you have more women than you do men. . . .

And then those in terms of leadership, for example with communication, you had to have a newsletter and all of that. Women were right there in that type of leadership. I would have to say that they gave administrative support too, but not to the extent—I guess. Did you look at the membership of the MIA? You didn't have but two women? That's what I meant when I was talking about grassroots support. It was a hundred percent among the women.[53]

Mrs. Glass is suggesting that women led whenever and wherever they could, but that they were not often asked to lead in any formal context. Her recollection that only two women served in the leadership on the board of the MIA is correct, as is her view of the women's leadership as instrumental for the success of the Montgomery bus boycott. Moreover, she discusses the disproportionate representation of women in movement activities. Some movement observers and participants have attributed this skew to the relatively greater risk to Black men.[54] When Rosa Parks was asked why men did not risk arrest, as she had, she replied, "I wouldn't want to minimize the action or the will of the Negro male [or] to take his place. But in the white South it would usually be fatal or so near fatal, in most cases, if they take a stand."[55]

Early in the movement, men were the primary targets of extreme violence because of their formal leadership positions, though later a similar degree of violence was extended to include women. On January 30, 1956, the home of Martin Luther King Jr. was bombed. E. D. Nixon's home was bombed the following month. Undoubtedly, had women been formal leaders, they too would have been victims of such extreme attacks. Johnnie Carr adds: "It was and still is because Black men still have a rough time now. They have a much rougher time than women have. That's a fact."[56]

Women, though, were not exempt from retaliation. While the reprisals against the women of the MIA were less extreme, they were no less life threatening. As E. D. Nixon noted above, women had risked arrest by initiating the bus boycott. Mrs. Dungee, the MIA financial secretary, Jo Ann Gibson Robinson, and many other boycotters were the target of violent reprisals. A large rock was thrown through the front window of Jo Ann Robinson's home; she and two friends narrowly escaped the spray of shattered glass. Later, acid was poured over her car and destroyed much of its exterior.[57] In addition to the loss of her job, Rosa Parks describes the level of harassment she received during the boycott: "Well, I did suffer quite a bit of harassment during the boycott, not physically, but there was, you know, the constant ringing of my telephone and threatening calls."[58]

In February 1956, the entire MIA was arrested and brought before the grand jury on charges of conspiracy. In addition to the arrests of Dr. King and other male leaders, women such as Mrs. Rosa Parks, Mrs. A. W. West, Mrs. Gregory, and Jo Ann Robinson were arrested. City officials felt that the arrests would deter the majority of Black citizens from participating in the boycott. The effect was quite the opposite, as is described by Reverend Simms. On the morning of the arrests,

> blacks had come from every section of town. Black women with bandannas on, wearing men's hats with their dresses rolled up. From the alleys they came. That is what frightened white people. Not the tie and collar crowd. I walked into there (to be indicted) and the cops were trembling. . . .
>
> I got in line behind the late Mrs. A. W. West. . . . One of the police hollered "allright, you women get back." Three great big old women with their dresses rolled up over work pants told him and I will never forget their language, "We ain't going nowhere. You done arrested us preachers and we ain't moving." He put his hand on his gun and his club. They said, "I don't care what you got. If you hit one of us you'll not leave here alive." That was the thing we had to work against, keeping those blacks from killing these whites.[59]

It seems fitting here to point out that mobilization often rested on emotional appeals, spontaneous or planned. Not all mobilization work was organized in advance, with careful tactics and strategies. The unnamed women who led this group responded spontaneously and emotionally to a situation in which formal leaders, and in this case even bridge leaders, were unable to respond. Such actions provided energy critical to mobilizing the people's continued commitment to acts of resistance. Without such support by these women, the efforts of the MIA would have been severely weakened.

Of all those arrested, only Dr. King was indicted and found guilty. Though the state court upheld the constitutionality of segregated buses, that decision was later overturned at the federal level. The Black population of Montgomery had won its first battle against the system of segregation.

Reprisals for boycott activities did not stop when the boycott ended, however. In 1960, both Mary Fair Burks and Jo Ann Robinson suffered investigation of their civil rights activities by a state-appointed committee. And since Alabama State College was funded by the source of that investigation, pressure was placed upon Dr. Trenholm, president of Alabama State, to insist that Jo Ann Robinson and Mary Fair Burks resign from their jobs. Professor Burks expressed shock when first confronted by this request. Montgomery was her home, now she would be forced to leave it.[60] Similarly, Jo Ann Robinson left Alabama and began teaching at Grambling State College in Louisiana. While the departure of these two heroines created a void in community leadership, the abiding change they spearheaded in Montgomery altered the entire course of history for Black people in the United States.

Conclusion

It is clear that without the initiative of the women of the Women's Political Council, the support of parishioners, primarily women, and the mediation efforts of E. D. Nixon, as well as the cooperation of ministers, the Montgomery bus boycott would never have taken place. Yet the initial efforts of the women to put the boycott in motion, and their subsequent efforts to mobilize and sustain it, were no less crucial to the success of the movement than were the efforts of formal male leaders. In point of fact, their work created a stable and solidified base for the boycott. During the Montgomery Improvement Association's infancy, women utilized their community connections to organize financial support and maintain the welfare of movement participants. This was the cornerstone of continued mass-movement activities.

It is equally clear that, (1) women participated in these activities for personal as well as political reasons; (2) they understood the normative legitimacy of a minister's authority and therefore assumed bridge leadership positions; and (3) they possessed a clear sense of their goals while employing astute tactics and strategies focused on achieving those ends.

Furthermore, women were not simply led into the movement by men or ministers, but provided the impetus for the development of movement organizations. As community bridge leaders, women of the Women's Political Council initiated resistance activity prior to the inception of the larger scale, formalized protest organization, the Montgomery Improvement Association. These women, because of their leadership positions within the local community, were the essential mobilizers in the initial protest effort.

That women were denied access to formal leadership positions should not obscure the fact that their self-motivated approach to participation escalated movement activism and required not only commitment but also leadership ability. Women relied heavily on their preexisting networks and organizations to provide a base for the movement. Bridge leadership, while invisible to the media and many scholars, provided a critical link between the MIA and the community. These women served to bridge potential "legitimate" leaders to an already mobilized constituency, illustrating that formal leaders are not always the initial mobilizers of movements.

Finally, and most important, is the fact that although these community networks provided the tool for mobilization, equally important was the extent to which spontaneity and emotion stimulated grassroots support for the boycott. As pointed out, these women could empathize with the humiliation suffered on the buses. It was their emotional responses to inequality that provided the impetus for their initiation of and participation in the boycott. Given the context of their lives, their anger and humiliation served as the basis for their strategic and planned activities.

The assumption that emotional responses are irrational or irrelevant has served to obscure the symbiotic relationship between emotionalism as a tool of mobilization and planned action as a process of coordination. There were many instances of spontaneous and emotionally energizing acts by movement participants that were the impetus for the initiation of planned activity. For example, this was illustrated above in the descriptions given by Mary Fair Burks and Jo Ann Gibson Robinson of their feelings of humiliation on city buses which initially led to the development of the Women's Political Council and later became the impetus for the Montgomery bus boycott. Additionally, E. D. Nixon's emotional appeal served to sway the ministers to support the boycott. And Reverend Simms's moving description of women's emotionally charged vocal challenges during the arrest of the MIA leadership served to sustain the momentum of resistance. These events should not be discounted or ignored because they are the by-product of emotions. Nor are they any more irrational than planned strategies and tactics. In fact, given the reprisals meted out to leaders of the boycott, one could argue that continuing such actions was quite irrational: both activities could easily result in death. The central point is that the boycott was a success not only because of resources such as indigenous funding or careful strategies and tactical planning but also because of emotional responses and spontaneous activism. Bridge leaders effectively mobilized many movement participants by appealing to emotions and seizing upon the high energy arising from the spontaneous.

❧ FOUR ❧

Sustaining the Momentum
of the Movement

Miss Ella Baker and the Origins of the Southern Christian
Leadership Conference

The Montgomery bus boycott lasted a year and was sustained by local as well as outside resources. On November 13, 1956, the state court of Alabama issued an order declaring car pools illegal. This devastating news proved short-lived, however. On the same day, the U.S. Supreme Court ruled that Montgomery's segregated transportation laws violated the Constitution of the United States, thrilling the boycotters. They had achieved a monumental victory. Yet that triumph did not propel Black leaders to organize boycotts in other cities throughout the South.

After the success of the Montgomery bus boycott, the members of In Friendship—Miss Ella Baker,[1] A. Philip Randolph, Bayard Rustin, and Stanley Levinson—began to discuss the lack of protest momentum in the South and the possibility of developing a southern-based organization that would challenge the oppressive order. With the passage of the Civil Rights Act of 1957, designed to protect the constitutional rights of Black voters, voter registration became a priority. It was the first civil rights act to be passed since 1875, and gave the federal government the right to sue a state on behalf of anyone denied his or her legal right to vote. It also established the Civil Rights Commission, which studied the conditions of Black people in the United States.[2] Nevertheless, persuading Black people to register remained difficult given the severity of physical and economic reprisals exacted upon those who dared to challenge the repressive system.

Ruby Hurley, southern regional director of the NAACP and professional bridge leader, explains the dangers of organizing in the 1950s:

> Much is said about what happened in the 1960s, but to me the fifties were much worse than the sixties. When I was out there by myself, for instance, there were no TV cameras with me to give me any protection. There were no reporters traveling with me to give me protection, because when the eye of the press or the eye of the camera was on the situation, it was different. It was different. A lot of people know about the marching of the sixties and the dogs of the sixties because television was there, and the cameras were churning while the dogs were snapping and while "Bull" Connor was behaving but we had to deal with "Bull" Connor long before the sixties. "Bull" Connor was [police commissioner] when the houses were burned on Dynamite Hill in Birmingham, when I first moved over there. The Negroes had moved into a section that had been white before. . . . I watched the smoke going up from one of those houses that burned to the ground. We know that that was arson, and the police department and the fire department had to have known what was going on, and they let it happen in Birmingham. I've seen all that. . . . 3

When Hurley arrived in Alabama, lynchings and murders of Blacks were commonplace. Part of Hurley's job was to investigate racially motivated murders. One of her cases involved the investigation of the murder of Reverend Lee, who on the eve of Mother's Day 1955, had been gunned down in cold blood for his efforts to register Blacks to vote. Hurley recalled:

> When I went in to investigate that case and saw the place where he had been killed, it was just cold-blooded murder. And then when I saw his body in the casket—I will not be able to forget how the whole lower half of his face had been shot away. A man killed because he, as a minister, said that God's children had rights as God's children and as American citizens.4

In 1955, Hurley was also sent to investigate the murder of Emmett Till, a fourteen-year-old boy who was visiting Mississippi from the North. She recalls:

> The boy was a fourteen-year-old who had infantile paralysis as a child and could not speak clearly. He whistled when he tried to enunciate words, rather than speak clearly. And this was the charge that was made against him, that he had whistled at [a white man's] wife in the store when he went in to get something for his cousins. Now I talked with his cousins, and they told me what they thought had happened, and the boys were too young to make up or to fabricate.
>
> There's no question in my mind that the [two white men] . . . decided that they were going to "get a nigger". . . . They took the child out and beat him, and then they tied him up with a chain from a cotton gin and dumped his body in the Tallahatchie River. But [they were] acquitted, and there were witnesses to the fact that they had the boy in the pickup truck with them and [that] they went on to the

plantation of a brother of [one of the men], and when they left, the boy was not seen, but the tarpaulin was pulled down over the back of the pickup truck. The witnesses who saw this and heard the screaming from the barn where the beatings were taking place, a youngster of sixteen or seventeen and a woman from across the road, sent word they wanted to talk to me and tell me some information.[5]

Hurley, disguised in "cotton-pickin" clothes, traveled to the plantation to obtain the eye-witness accounts of the events that led to the murder of Emmett Till. She recalled her journey for truth:

I really got a feeling of what the Underground Railroad during the days of slavery was all about-how word would be passed by just the look in an eye, never the exact phraseology being used, never the clear language, always in some form that you have to sorta try to figure out what the people meant. And it was only after going through . . . four different families, going to four different places, did I finally get to the people who had sent word that they wanted to talk to me. You never went directly to a place. You had to go through . . . you were cleared all the way. Protection was there for me all the way and I didn't know it until many years later. There were men around with shotguns standing in various spots to be sure that I got where I was going and got back. . . . [6]

Hurley received numerous threats for her activities. Bombs were thrown at her house. Others would drive by her home shouting "We gon' get you." And she was awakened numerous times in the middle of the night with threats. Yet Hurley continued to press for justice. She attended the trial of the two men accused of murdering Emmett Till and described the atmosphere in the courtroom:

It was just like a circus. The defendants were sitting up there eating ice-cream cones and playing with their children in court just like they were out on a picnic. Everybody was searched going into the courtroom to make sure that none of the Negroes carried any weapons. White folks were not searched. It was something that I won't forget. . . . All because Negroes wanted freedom in Mississippi.[7]

Yet it was Blacks who were more in danger than Whites. Hurley continued her activities and was eventually joined by Medgar Evers, an activist who was later murdered. Hurley recalls the precautions she and Evers tried to take:

Many times when Medgar and I would be driving together, Medgar would tell about carrying his gun. I said, "Medgar, its not gon' do any good to carry a gun." He used to sit on it under his pillow. Said, "Medgar . . . if they're gon' get us, they're gon' get us. Because the way they behave, they're cowards. They're not gonna come and tell you, 'I'm gonna shoot you.' And sure enough, that's the way he died: A sniper got him. . . . Medgar didn't get it until 1963, but that was a buildup from the time he came on the staff in December of 1954.[8]

Yet despite any precautions that one might take, the violence continued. In 1956, right after the bombings of Dr. King's house on January 30 and E. D. Nixon's yard on February 1, Hurley along with NAACP attorneys oversaw the desegregation of the University of Alabama. Following the 1954 Supreme Court decision that struck down the constitutionality of separate but equal school facilities for Black and White youngsters, the NAACP filed a suit to force the admission of the first Black student, Autherine Lucy, to the campus. Because of the crowds that had gathered in protest, Lucy had to be escorted by car to each of her classes. While jumping out of the car and running for the building, Lucy was struck on the shoulder by an object. The crowd followed her shouting, "Let's kill her, let's kill her." She ran into the library and could hear their jeers "Hey, hey, ho, where in the world did Autherine go? . . . Where in the hell did that nigger go?"[9] The next day rioting continued and Lucy was expelled by the university trustees for, they stated, her own safety.

The court upheld the decision of the trustees. Hurley and the NAACP were outraged and wanted to pursue Lucy's admission, but the ordeal had proved too stressful for Lucy and she refused to continue.[10] The backlash against desegregation continued with a legal ruling barring the NAACP from activity in Alabama. It was not until eight years later that the NAACP could legally operate in that state. During 1956 and 1957, the NAACP was tied up with legal cases,[11] and its southern leadership could see no reason to engage in direct action. Moreover, they viewed the passage of the 1957 Civil Rights Act, though unenforceable, as a victory even if no federal protection existed for those who chose to exercise their constitutional right to vote.

Realizing that the momentum of protest was waning, Rustin and Levinson met with Dr. King in New Orleans several times in 1957. Miss Ella Baker also attended two of these meetings. On one occasion she questioned King about the lack of momentum following the bus boycott and "he said it was a natural let down." Her assessment was somewhat different. She recalled asking Dr. King why the MIA, with its successes and lessons learned, wasn't proceeding to organize other areas of the South. King, she claimed, became irritated. She states:

> At that stage neither of the two young men, who were Ralph Abernathy and Martin, had had too much organizational experience and I don't think anybody will claim that the Montgomery Improvement Association provided a great deal of organizational know-how to people who hadn't had any. So the services that were rendered were in the direction, you know, of consulting.[12]

Baker believed that the momentum of the movement should continue, especially in light of the government's seemingly favorable shift toward Black voter registration. She felt that King and Abernathy, because they had little activist experience, did not understand how to lead or to harness the enthusiasm following the boycott. King would later describe his own lack of experience during the bus negotiations, which took place shortly after he arrived in Montgomery.

I was asked to serve on this committee. We met one afternoon in March 1955 in the office of Mr. J. E. Bagley, manager of the Montgomery City Lines. Dave Birmingham, the Police Commissioner at the time, represented the city commission. This was the first time that I had been in the presence of a city official and a representative of the city's large businesses. . . . We left the meeting hopeful; but nothing happened. The same old patterns of humiliation continued.[13]

Scholars have often attributed King's rise in the Southern Christian Leadership Conference to organizational skills and leadership know-how acquired as a matter of course through education and his position as a charismatic minister.[14] As previously discussed, his legitimacy as a leader rested on the culturally prescribed traditional authority of an educated male minister, yet this does not automatically imply possession of the kinds of organizational and leadership proficiency best suited to a civil rights movement. Unlike Dr. King and Ralph Abernathy, Miss Ella Baker possessed a great deal of civil rights leadership and organizational experience. She was clearly a professional bridge leader. In 1938, she joined the NAACP and by 1943 she became its national director of branches.[15] She was the first woman to serve as president of a chapter.[16] From 1955 to 1957, at the request of the mayor of New York City, Baker served as a member of the Commission on School Integration. By 1957, as a freelance consultant to civil rights groups, Miss Baker worked with In Friendship, initially to aid southern Blacks displaced by economic reprisals resulting from the 1954 *Brown vs. The Board of Education* decision. Later, the organization raised considerable funds to support the Montgomery bus boycott.

Despite King and Abernathy's lack of experience, the northern group decided that these young ministers were the most suitable leaders for a new southern organization. Both had proved they could not be coerced by the southern White establishment, and both had been courageous enough to risk their lives during the Montgomery bus boycott.[17] Though King may not have possessed civil rights experience or organizational know-how, he did possess certain qualities essential for southern leadership. He was educated, a man, and a minister capable of charismatic appeal.

On January 10, 1957, in Atlanta, Georgia, King assembled the South's Black leaders, mostly male ministers, and the Southern Christian Leadership Conference was born. The leaders conceived of the SCLC as an umbrella organization that would link other groups together in their mutual battle against the institutionalized racism of the South. Dr. King and Ralph Abernathy were, however, unable to attend the meeting. They had received word that Abernathy's home, as well as that of White minister and MIA member Reverend Robert S. Graetz, had been bombed the night before. This left Ella Baker, Bayard Rustin, Mrs. King, and Reverend Fred Shuttlesworth, head of the Alabama Christian Movement for Human Rights, in charge of the meeting. That night Dr. King was elected its first president.

While during the boycott the factions in the community had managed to work together, the momentum began to die and divisions reemerged. Civil rights movement scholar David Garrow notes that

Mrs. Durr felt that "there is a good deal of bitter feeling" in the black community, and believed that the pre-boycott factionalism was reemerging. "It is the old class split coming to the fore again," the division between mass and elite that had existed before both Nixon and [Rufus] Lewis had united behind King.[18]

Rufus Lewis was a prominent businessman and ex-football coach for Alabama State. He was Nixon's chief rival and headed the Citizen's Steering Committee in Montgomery, a group which also addressed civil rights issues. King found it difficult to overcome the local dissension, as well as the NAACP's leaders' fears that the SCLC would tread on their turf.[19] As the year progressed, King found himself unable to achieve many of his goals, and in October 1957, in his annual report to his Dexter Avenue Baptist Church Congregation, he stated that "almost every week— having to make so many speeches, attend so many meetings, meet so many people, write so many articles, counsel with so many groups—I face the frustration of feeling that in the midst of so many things to do I am not doing anything well."[20] In the meantime, as the rift between the various factions widened, E. D. Nixon resigned from the MIA. King's frustration and inability to capitalize on the momentum of the boycott continued throughout the year.

The Movement Gains Momentum

Movement activities, however, did not come to a standstill in other parts of the South. The NAACP continued to forge ahead with legal challenges to segregated schools. While the NAACP was succeeding in the courts, as in the Lucy case, implementing desegregation was proving a daunting task. In addition to the violence they met at the University of Alabama, Black parents and children in Clay and Sturgis, Kentucky, were met by mobs, forcing the governor to call out the National Guard. Afterward, the attorney general expelled the students, who subsequently, through the NAACP, filed a suit that resulted in only marginal integration in the high schools and none in the elementary schools.[21]

Undaunted, the NAACP then turned its attention to Little Rock, Arkansas, whose school board developed a plan of compliance. In 1957, Little Rock's Central High School was to become integrated. The school board immediately began to hear complaints and threats of noncompliance by parents. In reaction, the board backed down and began to consider a six-year plan of integration. In 1957, there were seventy-five Black applicants to the school. The board only accepted nine: Minniejean Brown, Elizabeth Eckford, Ernest Green, Thelma Mothershed, Melba Patillo, Gloria Ray, Terrance Roberts, Jefferson Thomas, and Carlotta Walls. Mass hysteria began in Little Rock with White parents refusing to send their children to school with Blacks. The KKK and other White supremacist groups organized meetings to plan ways to prevent integration. A group called the Mothers' League of Little Rock Central High School was formed and one of its members, Mrs. Clyde A. Thomason, filed a suit seeking a temporary injunction to halt the integration. The governor of Arkansas appeared as a witness and the judge granted an injunction against integration.

The next day, NAACP attorney Wiley Branton and special NAACP attorney

Thurgood Marshall went before a federal judge, who overturned the injunction. Integration was to proceed. Several days later, the Little Rock Nine, as the children were called, were to enter Little Rock Central High School. On September 2, 1957, the evening prior to their entry, Governor Faubus announced that he would not allow integration in Little Rock and vowed that "blood will run in the streets" if the Black students attempt to enter. He ordered the National Guard to surround the school.[22]

Daisy Bates, an active member of the NAACP and owner of a local and highly political Black newspaper, became involved in the controversy. Bates, an associate of Miss Ella Baker and a longtime activist, had been jailed for publishing stories accusing the Arkansas judicial system of improprieties.[23] She had served as co-chairman of the NAACP's State Conferences Committee for Fair Employment Practices and was president of the Arkansas State Conference of NAACP branches.[24] Bates was a dynamic woman with an ax to grind. In her infancy, Bates's mother was allegedly raped and murdered by three White men. Discovering this at the age of seven, Bates also learned that her father, overwhelmed by the pain, had left her in the care of his closest friends, people whom she had previously believed were her parents. Around the same time, she suffered humiliating experiences in her daily interactions with Whites. From that time on, Bates vowed to get revenge. Her anger was so great that from his deathbed, her father counseled her:

> You're filled with hatred. Hate can destroy you, Daisy. Don't hate white people just because they're white. If you hate, make it count for something. Hate the humiliation we are living under in the South. Hate the discrimination that eats away at the soul of every black man and woman. Hate the insults hurled at us by white scum—and then try to do something about it, or your hate won't spell a thing.[25]

Daisy Bates heeded her father's advice. Propelled by the desire to stop the humiliation and discrimination of Black people, she went into action. In their article about Daisy Bates, Carolyn Calloway-Thomas and Thurmon Garner, although theorizing her actions in organizational terms, describe her leadership in the Little Rock crisis:

> She created a form of organization based on centalization of information and command. For example, as early as the first day that the "Little Rock nine" (as the students who integrated Central High were called) were scheduled to enter school, realizing that Blossom [the school superintendent] had given the students little assurance that they would be protected from violence, Bates tackled the problem, concentrating on what should be done as well as when and how. . . .
>
> Bates demonstrated her organizational prowess in other ways as well. She orchestrated the movement of the children and their parents including when they were to arrive at her home, the route they would take to school, and even the door through which they would enter.[26]

The morning following the governor's announcement, White students passing through the line of National Guardsmen entered Central High. In the meantime, the school board met and suggested that the Little Rock Nine wait to attend school the following day. They did not want the parents to accompany the children, since adults would be harder to protect if violence broke out.

All that day, Bates stayed in touch with the parents, listening as they expressed their fears.

> Typical of the parents was Mrs. Birdie Eckford. "Mrs. Bates," she asked, "what do you think we should do? I am frightened. Not for myself but for the children. When I was a little girl, my mother and I saw a lynch mob dragging the body of a Negro man through the streets of Little Rock. We were told to get off the streets. We ran. And by cutting through side streets and alleys, we managed to make it to the home of a friend. But we were close enough to hear the screams of the mob, close enough to smell the sickening odor of burning flesh. And, Mrs. Bates, they took the pews from Bethel Church to make the fire. They burned the body of this Negro man right at the edge of the Negro business section. Mrs. Bates do you think this will happen again?"[27]

Mrs. Bates would comfort them and continued to encourage them to allow their children to fight segregation. That evening, a White newspaper reporter and friend of the Bates's came by their home to warn them of the increasing tension. He told Bates that there were at least five hundred people at the school and many people were coming from out of town to join their ranks. He stated that people he'd known all of his life had gone mad, and he feared that sending the students alone was an act of murder. After he left, Bates considered the options. While the presence of parents might inflame the situation, the presence of ministers might defuse it. "Her plan required two ministers 'in front of the children' and 'two behind' until they approached the beginning of the long line of guardsmen."[28] She passed her idea on to Reverend L. C. Crenshaw, president of the Little Rock branch of the NAACP. He thought her idea a sound one, so she phoned a White minister, Reverend Ogden, who was president of the Interracial Ministerial Alliance. He, in turn, called several other White ministers, but was able to garner support only from a few. Calloway-Thomas and Garner continue:

> To ensure that her plan to protect the children worked, Bates notified the police, gave them persuasive reasons as to why their services were needed, and explained her particular plan carefully. Because the school was occupied by the National Guard, Bates learned that it was impossible for them to escort the students to the front door. Bates was undaunted, however, and contacted the parents about the change in plan.[29]

Bates recalled, "At three o'clock [in the morning], I completed my last call, explaining to the parents where the children were to assemble and the plan about the ministers. Suddenly I remembered Elizabeth Eckford. Her family had no telephone."[30] Unable to contact her, Bates decided to try and reach her in the morning.

The following morning, Bates drove to the spot where the students were to meet and prayed that the ministers would be there as well. When she arrived, she found two White ministers and two Black ones. The local police were also there, as Bates requested. On the radio she heard that a Black girl was being mobbed. Bates described her reaction, " 'Oh, my God!' I cried. 'It must be Elizabeth! I forgot to notify her where to meet us!' "[31] Elizabeth was in grave danger. In recalling her experience, Elizabeth said

> I walked across the street conscious of the crowd that stood there, but they moved away from me. [Then] the crowd began to follow me, calling me names. I still wasn't afraid, just a little bit nervous. Then my knees started to shake all of a sudden. . . . Even so, I wasn't too scared because . . . I kept thinking that the [guards] would protect me . . . the guards let some white students go through [into the school]. . . . I walked up to the guard who had let [them] in. He didn't move. When I tried to squeeze past him, he raised his bayonet and then the other guards moved in and raised their bayonets. . . . Somebody started yelling, "Lynch her! Lynch her!"[32]

Elizabeth frantically walked to a bus stop and sat on the bench. The crowd followed shouting, "Get a rope and drag her over to this tree." A White man sat down next to her and put his arm around her. It was Dr. Benjamin Fine, who had won the Pulitzer Prize for the *New York Times*. He was on the scene, as the education editor of the paper, reporting to the *Times*. As he comforted Elizabeth, the crowd jeered and called out "nigger lover." Suddenly a White woman appeared and yelled for them to leave the girl alone. The woman, Mrs. Grace Lorch, the wife of a professor at Philander Smith College, tried to enter a store and call for a cab, but the owner blocked her path. As she tried in vain to find a telephone, a bus pulled up and the woman escorted Elizabeth onto the bus, sat next to her, and dropped her off at her mother's place of employment. Fine, who remained at the bus stop, was taunted and called "a dirty New York Jew." A woman spat in his face. To his dismay, the National Guard did not try to assist but, rather, threatened to arrest him for inciting a riot.

Some time later, the other students accompanied by the ministers and Daisy Bates proceeded to the front door of Central High. The guardsmen blocked the entrance and refused them entry. The group retreated and headed for the superintendent's office, but he would not see them. Feeling frustrated, but determined to force the opening of the school to Black students, the group proceeded to the U.S. attorney's office. Since it was the ruling of the federal court that had called for the immediate integration of Central High, they reasoned it was Attorney Osco Cobb's duty to enforce it. Cobb was surprised to see them and decided that they should go to the FBI Office to report the incidents. "Yet," as Daisy Bates later recalled, "no action was taken against anyone by the Office of the United States Attorney, Osco Cobb, or the Department of Justice."[33]

In the days that followed, Thurgood Marshall and Wiley Branton, attorneys for the NAACP, sought an injunction from the federal court to prevent Faubus's use of the National Guard to prevent integration. They won, and Faubus made an announcement that he was complying with the court, but that he hoped Blacks would not come to Central High.

On September 23, 1957, the Little Rock Nine met, just before heading for the school, at the home of Daisy Bates. Bates devised a plan to drive the children to a side entrance. When they arrived, as they had hoped, the crowd was in front of the school. Someone noticed the children and shouted, "They're in! The niggers are in!" The crowd rushed toward them. Since the children were safely inside, Bates and the ministers jumped in their cars and sped off.

Just prior to the arrival of the students, the local Black press had arrived. Screaming, "Here they come!" the crowd rushed toward them. "The women screamed, 'Get the niggers! Get them!' " The mob attacked and proceeded to beat and kick members of the Black press. The arrival of the students had saved the journalists by diverting the crowd's attention to the side of Central High. Daisy Bates recounts the incident:

> The frenzied mob rushed the police barricades. One man was heard to say, "So they sneaked them in behind our back. That's all we need. Let's go get our shotguns!" Hysterical women helped to break the barricades and then urged the men to go in and "get the niggers out!" Some of the women screamed for their children to "come out! Don't stay in there with those niggers!" About fifty students rushed out, crying, "They're in! They're in!"[34]

Later that morning police chief Gene Smith realized that his force could not hold back the enraged mob, so he arranged for the children to escape through a back entrance. The mob then turned its rage on reporters, beating the mainly White *Life Magazine* staff mercilessly. The city was in utter chaos with Blacks being attacked, pulled from their cars and beaten. That evening police protected the homes of the Little Rock Nine, as well as the home of Daisy Bates.

Bates's husband, L. C. Brice Miller, a reporter for the United Press International, local dentist Dr. Freeman, and several other members of the media stayed up all night, some of them with their shotguns in their laps. Shortly after 10:30 P.M., police sirens could be heard approaching the Bates house. When a policeman entered, he shouted for them to turn off the lights, explaining,

> We just stopped a motorcade of about one hundred cars, two blocks from here. When we followed [a] car that passed, we ran into the mob head on. We radioed for help and a whole group of city and Federal agents showed up. We found dynamite, guns, pistols, clubs, everything, in the cars. Some of the mob got away on foot, leaving their cars. We don't know what will happen tonight, so no one leave the house.[35]

Everyone remained awake. At 2:30 A.M., Daisy Bates answered the telephone. A man threatened to "get her" if she persisted in bringing the children to Central High. The following morning none of the Little Rock Nine attended the school while they awaited news from the White House. In the afternoon, word came that President Eisenhower had declared the State National Guard under the direction of the federal government. They were now directed by the secretary of defense. In addition to these ten thousand troops, one thousand paratroopers were sent to Little Rock. The following morning, the Little Rock Nine again met at the home of Daisy Bates. Shortly after 8:30, the 101st Airborne accompanied the children to Central High in army jeeps with a helicopter circling overhead. Soldiers armed with rifles and bayonets pushed back the angry crowd. Each student was assigned to a soldier and other soldiers were posted throughout the school.

Several days later, Daisy Bates experienced an escalation of harassment and threats. "The *New York Times* ('Little Rock,' 1957, p. 18) observed, '[Bates] had borne the brunt of the integration dispute here. She had been vilified, abused, threatened and intimidated.' "[36] Daily, carloads of White thugs rode past her home throwing fire crackers and rocks and shooting into the windows. Crosses were burned on her front lawn and she received continuous threatening letters and telephone calls. One day, a White woman visited her and told her that she had less than a day to publicly call for the Black students to return to the all-Black high school. If Bates did not comply, she was warned, she would lose everything. The following morning at 9:00 A.M., Daisy Bates received a telephone call asking her about her decision. Bates gave a firm no. Within a few weeks every advertiser had pulled its ad from Bates's paper. Long-time clients such as Southwestern Bell Telephone Company, Arkansas-Louisiana Gas Company, and many local merchants cancelled their contracts. Still Daisy Bates persisted.

The following year the governor, in seeking to keep the Black students from returning to Little Rock Central High and overriding the federal court's judgment in favor of immediate integration, closed the schools. Tensions escalated as did the violence. On several occasions, bombs were tossed onto the front porch of the Bates's home. Moreover, many of the parents of the Little Rock Nine lost their jobs. Five of the nine families moved away. By the summer of 1959, the laws by which Governor Faubus closed the schools had been ruled unconstitutional. Faubus was threatening to create new laws that would make all the schools private. In the meantime, tensions continued to mount. Distressed by the turn of events but unwilling to retreat, Bates sent a telegram to the U.S. attorney general.

Last Night, July 7, 1959, at 10:08, a bomb hurled from an automobile exploded in our front yard. The bomb fell short of its target and only the lawn was damaged from the explosion which rocked dwellings for several blocks. As adviser to the litigants in the Little Rock School case, my home has been under constant attack since August 1957 by lawless elements of this state, and many threats have been made upon my life and the lives of my immediate family. Incendiary bombs have been thrown at our home from automobiles. Three KKK crosses have been burned in our lawn. Fire has been set to the house on two occasions. All the glass in the front of the house has been broken out and steel screens had to be made to cover the front windows to protect our home. To this date, no one has been apprehended by the law enforcement officers of this city or state. We have appealed to the city and county for protection, yet these attacks on us and our home continue. We have been compelled to employ private guards. Now as a last resort, we are appealing to you to give us protection in Little Rock, United States of America.[37]

Two days later, Assistant Attorney General W. Wilson White replied.

The Attorney General and I have read the distressing account of your telegram of July 8, 1959, of the harassment which you have suffered since the institution of the Little Rock School desegregation case, culminating in the explosion of a bomb on July 7. After careful consideration, however, we are forced to conclude that there is no basis for federal jurisdiction. Any investigation and prosecution of persons responsible for the incidents which you described in your telegram would be within the exclusive jurisdiction of state and local authorities. Inability or failure on the part of such authorities to take effective action does not authorize the federal government to intervene. This department can take action only when there has been a violation of federal law. The information which you furnish in your telegram fails to disclose any such violation.[38]

The harassment and violence continued and Daisy Bates was compelled to make a plea to President Eisenhower, who also turned a blind eye to the situation in Little Rock.

Dear Mr. President, despite repeated bombings, attacks by gunfire and rocks, and other assaults on our home—attacks provoked by the fact that we have stood steadfast for this community's compliance with the federal law—both local and federal authorities have declined to provide the minimum physical protection that we have requested, now state police have begun to arrest and harass the upstanding citizens who have provided us with volunteer protection, leaving us defenseless before those who constantly threaten our lives. I appeal to you, Mr. President, to provide the basic protection that will give us the freedom from fear to which citizens of our free American Society are entitled.[39]

Several days later, she received a telegram from Deputy Assistant to the President, Gerald D. Morgan.

Your telegram of August thirteenth to the President is acknowledged, although the matter seems to be one within the exclusive jurisdiction of local authorities. The President has referred your telegram to the Department of Justice from which I am sure it will receive prompt appropriate consideration.[40]

No action was taken by either state or federal officials to protect the Bateses or those who assisted them. In the meantime, organizations and individuals sent money to help support the Bateses, but after eighteen years of hard work, the *State Press* was shut down in the latter part of 1959. Even so, Bates never regretted her decision.

By 1962, just seventy-five Black students had been admitted to Little Rock's White junior and senior high schools. Still, a major battle was won that signaled to other cities and states that, despite violence, harassment, and intimidation, Black people would continue to struggle for freedom. Mrs. Bates, along with her husband, continued the fight, and she eventually served on the board of the SCLC.

Conclusion

Bates, even as president of the NAACP State Conference of Branches, operated much as a formal local community bridge leader, sustaining the efforts of the students and their families. She linked the support of ministers to their cause, and despite the threats of reprisals persisted to desegregate Little Rock High School. Bates, as were many bridge leaders, was an activist before the inception of the Little Rock crisis. In this capacity, she was ready to respond to the structural and far-reaching rulings of the courts. Mrs. Bates's activism in this local event captured widespread media attention[41] and gave rise to the continuation of nationwide activism. Bates, atypical of bridge leaders, did have direct contact with the national government. Yet even in her correspondence to the president, she did not identify herself in a position of authority with the NAACP. Rather, she described herself as an "advisor" to the students. Clearly she was much more than that, yet in her book *The Long Shadow of Little Rock*, she was sure to give credit to Roy Wilkins, then national executive secretary of the NAACP, for his role in the Little Rock crisis. She wrote:

> The story of the "Battle of Little Rock" is a story of people. But it is also a story of organizations and groups that at every turn were in the forefront of the struggle, giving leadership where it was needed and whenever it became necessary.
>
> The organization that was the prime target of all segregationists—from Governor Faubus down—was the National Association for the Advancement of Colored People. The record this organization wrote in the "Battle of Little Rock" will stand as a monument in man's eternal yearning for human rights and decency. And in this effort, Roy Wilkins will long be remembered.
>
> As Executive Secretary of the NAACP, it fell to Mr. Wilkins to make many decisions that have since made history. Few are aware as I am of the energy and wisdom, the fortitude and patience this man brought to the leadership of the NAACP during its hour of need.[42]

The Little Rock case in particular illustrates the complexity of movement mobilization. The activism in Little Rock stemmed from the efforts of national-level formal leadership in the NAACP. The NAACP attorneys operated much as secondary formal leaders, carrying out the wishes of the formal leadership, but also interacting with local community leadership.

Despite the disagreements between Wilkins and King and their two organizations, as primary formal leaders they joined forces to castigate the Eisenhower administration for not being more forceful and supportive during the crisis. On October 16, 1957, SCLC voted to send a telegram to Eisenhower requesting that he assemble his already-approved Civil Rights Commission. At a rally that evening, King told the crowd that the telegram sent "will be effective according to the political activity of the masses of Negroes at the local level."[43] Though fighting over turf, the formal leaders of the NAACP and the SCLC were able to form an alliance to challenge the White House.

In late May of 1958, the SCLC again voted to send another message to the

White House, expressing their strong disapproval of Eisenhower's lack of support for enforcing the *Brown* decision and asking that President Eisenhower meet with Black leaders. Presidential Assistant Rocco C. Siciliano called King and requested a meeting with him to ascertain what Black leaders wanted to discuss with Eisenhower. At the meeting, King suggested that not only he but also A. Philip Randolph and Roy Wilkins should meet with the president. The final meeting was to consist of Dr. King, Roy Wilkins, A. Philip Randolph, and Lester B. Granger of the National Urban League. Prior to their scheduled meeting with the president,

> King and the other three men traded thoughts about what to say to Eisenhower. They agreed that a written statement should be presented to the president, and several quick drafts were circulated. They met at 8:00 P.M. . . . [and] hammered out a statement that made nine points. The principal ones called upon Eisenhower to declare that the law, i.e. *Brown*, would be enforced, to call a White House conference to promote peaceful desegregation, to support the enactment of stronger federal civil rights laws, to order the Justice Department to become more active concerning voting discrimination, and to recommend an extension of the temporarily established Civil Rights Commission. The four men agreed that Randolph would make an opening statement for them, with King, Wilkins, and Granger each then speaking about three of the nine specifics.[44]

It is clear that the formal leadership consisted of men in primary formal and secondary formal movement organizations who had greater access to national government officials. They were able to rise above their internal disagreements to work as a unified force within the movement sector. Bates, although a formal leader in Arkansas, clearly did not have this access and never had direct contact with the president. While Daisy Bates represents many of the women who were already formal local leaders and activists prior to the rise of heightened movement activity, it is equally clear that these women were rarely included in national-level negotiations.

The secondary tier of formal leaders, primarily the NAACP attorneys, served to carry out the wishes of the NAACP's primary formal leaders. As you will recall, the Lucy case ended in defeat. According to Jack Greenberg, one of the attorneys on the Little Rock case, Thurgood Marshall, who was special counsel to the NAACP, was deeply disturbed by the outcome and

> raised the question of whether we should not be "reexamin[ing] strategy" with a view to revising it and considering "what we should do . . . *to prevent another Lucy case* [emphasis in original] so that we can arrive at the point that when the court stated a plaintiff goes in she will be permitted to enter." But Roy Wilkins responded that while there was indeed great resistance in the Black Belt, we had a moral obligation to proceed there. The meeting arrived at a "consensus": "Since we have the Supreme law of the land on our side we are obligated morally and legally."[45]

The attorneys did proceed with the Little Rock case, working between the courts, the primary formal leaders, and Daisy Bates.

Still, the Little Rock crisis illustrates the strength of community bridge leaders who were able to sustain activism in the face of grave dangers. It is a story of the courage not only of a bridge leader but also of those ordinary citizens who risked their lives for freedom and justice.

Interestingly, the attorneys for the NAACP were unable to proceed in many of the areas most resistant to change. Jack Greenberg recalls:

While we did file in areas of high resistance, courts rarely ordered extensive desegregation in the face of physical resistance. In most of the worst places we did nothing because there were few, if any, plaintiffs prepared to face the very real risks involved. Carsie Hall, our lawyer in Mississippi, reported, "There is not one town ready for a school segregation case." Thurgood informed the board, "We must realize that as far as school cases are concerned, there will have to be a delay in Mississippi." Perhaps we might file a voting rights case, he suggested, against the Mississippi procedure of asking prospective voters questions like "How many bubbles in a bar of soap?" Another factor in favor of pursuing voting rights cases, according to Thurgood, was that if we won the cases and "nothing happens to the plaintiffs, it will show the people in Mississippi that they can go to court and nothing will happen to them. It will then give them the impetus to proceed on other cases."[46]

These extreme dangers facing participants served to quell the tide of support by ordinary citizens. Yet if the movement were to succeed, it required just such risk taking by those who would come to lead or join the movement. It was precisely the recognition of this obstacle that led Miss Ella Baker and Mrs. Septima Clark to become central leaders in the recruitment process.

Sowing the Seeds of
Mass Mobilization

The Roots of Micromobilization

Daisy Bates's efforts as a community bridge leader were not unique. Black women all over the nation were leaders in the struggle for civil rights. During the 1950s, sit-ins occurred in such cities as Baltimore, St. Louis, Tallahassee, Rock Hill, Miami, and Oklahoma City. Most of these direct-action groups were affiliated with either CORE or the NAACP. Their tactics included picketing and sit-ins. In Oklahoma City, a successful effort to desegregate amusement parks, restaurants, swimming pools, and theaters was launched by Clara Luper, a community bridge leader, high school teacher, and formal local leader of the NAACP Youth Council. Luper admired Dr. King and the successes in Montgomery, and she believed that such tactics would work in Oklahoma City. In August 1958, Luper led her young charges to the food counter of a local segregated drugstore. Little did they know that their fight would last six years.

Yet beyond the efforts of the NAACP and the targeted protests, there was a need to mobilize a larger constituency of supporters. As Thurgood Marshall and others noted, many were afraid to join the movement. And as long as this fear persisted, areas of resistance to equality would remain intact. Rustin and Levinson continued to me•t with Dr. King through 1958. The momentum of the movement continued to slacken and worsened with the near fatal stabbing of King by a crazed woman. This put King out of commission from mid-September to the end of October.[1]

Earlier in the year, King opened an Atlanta office. Rustin and Levinson, recognizing the lack of organization within the SCLC, decided that Ella Baker, with her professional leadership experience, was the individual needed to develop a strong protest base. They had a difficult time convincing King that anyone who was not a minister could provide the SCLC with the help and guidance it so desperately needed. King finally agreed that Baker could become its "acting" director while he and his fellow ministers searched for someone more "suitable."

Upon arriving in Atlanta, Baker discovered the extent of disarray at the SCLC.

There was no office. There wasn't anything. I got a room at the Hotel there on Auburn Avenue. I stayed there a week. I worked out of my vest pocket and whatever access I could have to a telephone at Ebenezer Baptist Church. Frequently, I had to make use of pay coin telephones. So that went on for maybe a week. I know I didn't have any contact with Dr. King.[2]

Her job was to work on the SCLC's first project, the Crusade for Citizenship, and to organize simultaneous meetings in twenty-one cities. The meetings, which were held one month after she arrived, were designed to encourage Blacks to register to vote and to educate them about their civil rights. All too often, these meetings proved ineffectual when the ministers failed to sustain registration efforts in their own communities or provide support to those who wished to register.[3]

Miss Baker also set up an office in Shreveport, working tirelessly without staff on The Crusade for Citizenship. Although Miss Baker performed many duties that might be construed as secretarial in nature—answering correspondence, typing letters, and mimeographing flyers—she clearly operated as more than a secretary. Miss Baker had little contact with King. Her organization of the SCLC and development of clear tactics and strategies designed to increase the number of registered voters were self-initiated. King's lack of interaction with Baker signaled the degree to which her position as acting director was not taken seriously. He treated her largely as a secretary.

Miss Baker, not one to succumb to frustration, continued to assert her abilities as a leader. On at least one occasion, she met with the legal assistant to the director of investigations for the Civil Rights Commission. They discussed King's request to testify at a hearing on voting in the South. Baker, acting on her own, informed King by letter of her actions. She indicated what was discussed, and provided suggestions as to the content and format of King's presentation.[4] Miss Baker's unwillingness to defer to the authority of ministers would eventually lead to her departure from the SCLC. In the interim, however, she asserted her ideas and her leadership, maintaining her focus on the development of the SCLC. Though locked out of any permanent formal leadership position, Baker began working to bridge several segments of the Black population to the movement and to nurture the expanding energy of resistance sparked by the boycott.

Meanwhile, Dr. King continued to be frustrated by the lack of support from many of the MIA leaders. " 'There was nothing he could get going,' one member recalled. 'When he began to talk about school desegregation—and he's talking to black teachers primarily . . . nobody was willing to go out on the limb on that.' "[5]

King began to focus his speeches as attacks on Eisenhower and Governor Faubus, stating of the latter, " 'His irresponsible actions brought the issue to the forefront of the conscience of the nation' as nothing else had, 'and allowed people to see the futility of attempting to close the public school.' "[6] His attacks on Eisenhower were even more condemnatory:

> I fear that future historians will have to record that when America came to its most progressive moment of creative fulfillment in the area of human relations, it was temporarily held back by a chief executive who refused to make a strong positive statement morally condemning segregation.[7]

That same year Miss Ella Baker, as acting executive director of the SCLC, began to consider the Citizenship Education Program at the Highlander Folk School in Monteagle, Tennessee. The program at this unique school became a powerful tool for the development of movement mobilization. Baker believed that it was largely for the lack of a well-developed organizing scheme that the SCLC's voter registration drive had failed. To pursue this interest, Miss Baker traveled to Highlander, one of the few multiracial schools in the South. Highlander was well known for its Citizenship Education Program, directed by Septima Clark. Mrs. Clark had participated in civil rights activities for some time. She understood the importance of door-to-door contact as a tool of mobilization. She states:

> In 1918–1919, I went door-to-door for the NAACP, getting signatures to petition the South Carolina Legislature that Negro teachers be placed in the public schools of Charleston. We got the teachers in, in 1920. Then in 1956 I refused to disown the NAACP, and lost my job as a public school teacher in South Carolina as a result of my membership and inter-racial activities. Finally, in 1959, while directing the educational program at the Highlander Folk School, I was arrested for allegedly possessing whiskey (which was found by the courts to be untrue, and the case dismissed). This attack was made on me, I feel to scare me, the only Negro resident, so I would leave. I stayed.[8]

Many of the women who were active in the Montgomery bus boycott had also attended Highlander. As discussed in chapter 3, Rosa Parks returned from Highlander only three months before her arrest. Mrs. A. W. West, of the Women's Political Council, and Mrs. Erna Dungee, the only woman officer of the Montgomery Improvement Association, had also attended Highlander's Citizenship Education Program. Miss Baker went to Highlander with the intention of incorporating such a program into the fabric of the SCLC's Crusade for Citizenship program. It would not be instituted until late in 1959. In the meantime, the SCLC continued to fail in its voter registration project.

The seeds of a model for rural mobilization were planted by Septima Clark, a professional bridge leader, at the Highlander Folk School. Morris has described Highlander as an important movement halfway house that served to create associations among movement participants. While many important associations were formed among already active participants, Highlander had failed as an institution to link with the rural Black masses. Fear of reprisals prevented Highlander from attracting nonmovement participants. Mrs. Clark's Citizenship Education Program, however, had achieved tremendous success in the area of voter registration. Mrs. Clark, along with Esau Jenkins, a former student and an indigenous bridge leader, were able to develop a connection with the masses within the rural community. Although many scholars credit either Myles Horton or Esau Jenkins with the development of the Citizenship Education Program, it was Mrs. Clark who developed much of the program.[9]

An often overlooked aspect of the recruitment process is that institutional and formal organizational networks often failed to elicit the support of those in rural and small-town communities. It was the activities of bridge leaders and their efforts to connect through interpersonal ties that facilitated recruitment of the rural masses. The SCLC had been continually frustrated by the lack of response on the part of the African-American community in the rural South. In a report to the Marshall Field Foundation, the Citizenship Education Program reported that

> motivation is one of the big problems in arousing the Negro community to vote in the South. Many efforts have been made through preaching, mass media and public relations gimmicks from time to time, but it is our feeling that no one has ever taken the time to explain to the masses of people in our society how politics determines the course of their lives and specifically how their vote contributes to this process.[10]

In 1959, at Miss Baker's prodding, Dr. King and Myles Horton, the founder, agreed to establish a facility in which Mrs. Clark and a staff could train local people to become activists.

But there was an enormous gap between the desire to train local activists and convincing them to come to the workshops. Clark understood the complexities of gaining local trust. She explains:

> Now the people on Johns Island knew me, so I went down first and introduced them to Bernice. But Bernice had already been working with Esau Jenkins, who was one of them. They had worked together on voter registration drives for the NAACP. When you can work through "one of them," as they say, you can get the real feeling from them that you're somebody that they can trust. Esau could be trusted on the island, and because he could be trusted, he could introduce us to numbers of others who would trust us. People on the island didn't want to trust black people coming from the city. They just thought that you were so high-falutin that you were going to try to make fun of them.[11]

Septima Clark's understanding of what it would take to mobilize the masses often conflicted with Myles Horton's view of how to go about gaining their support. She elaborates:

Myles thought we could just go into communties and get people registered to vote. But I knew that these people had had no schooling, because according to U.S. statistics we had 12 million illiterates in the South. If they were illiterate, with the laws that we had, they would not be able to read enough to register in most southern states.

Myles thought I could go right into the community and get a large group of people, talk to them, then bring them up to the registration booth and get them registered. You can do that now, because the laws have changed, but then black people had to read.

So Myles and I had to just shout it out. That's what we did—shouted at each other. . . . Finally, we hit on the plan that was right, but we weren't doing too good at first. Myles would ask me about methods, and I would say, "Don't ask me about methods. Let me tell you how I'm going to do this thing." Myles would go back home and think about what I had said; then he would come back the next day and get things typed up the way I suggested. This is what we did.

Myles thought I had new-fangled ideas. But my new-fangled ideas worked out. I didn't know they were going to work out though. I just thought that you couldn't get people to register and vote until you teach them to read and write. That's what I thought, and I was so right.[12]

Connecting Prefigurative Politics to Strategic Politics

McAdam, Piven, and Cloward argue that central to the development of a civil rights movement was a cognitive change in consciousness.[13] Most Black people in the rural community were well aware of racial inequality. What they did not have was the basic information necessary to transform their prefigurative politics, based on personal experience, to an understanding of their constitutional rights and the strategic politics of the movement. Therefore, the primary task of the Citizenship Education Program was to provide the rural potential constituents with the information necessary to persuade them to join the movement. One of Septima Clark's successes as a professional bridge leader was her ability to connect the politics of the movement to the needs of the people. She did so through frame extension, by making the needs of the people one of the SCLC's priorities. She found that by listening to the problems of the potential rural constituents, the latter then became willing to listen to the teachers' transformative message.[14] She explains:

But I changed, too, as I traveled through the eleven deep south states. Working through those states, I found I could say nothing to those people, and no teacher as a rule could speak with them. We had to let them talk to us and say to us whatever they wanted to say. When we got through listening to them, we would let them know that we felt that they were right according to the kind of thing that they had in their mind, but according to living in this world there were other things that they needed to know. We wanted to know if they were willing then to listen to us, and they decided that they wanted to listen to us.[15]

Mrs. Clark solicited the help of her cousin Bernice Robinson, a quintessential teacher. Although lacking a teaching credential, she understood deeply that the key to good teaching is the ability to engage student interests. Mrs. Clark recalls:

> Bernice and her students would tell stories about the things they had to deal with every day—about growing vegetables, plowing the land, digging up potatoes. Then they would write down these stories and read them back. Any word they stumbled over, Bernice would use in the spelling lesson.[16]

The core of Septima Clark's program was teaching members of the community to read and write. She felt that literacy was the only way to enlighten the rural masses about their citizenship rights, and the best way to do this was to become actively involved in the pupils' lives. For example, Robinson would teach individuals to fill out money orders, sew, and crochet.

So Clark and her staff began the transformation process by teaching literacy and by connecting people's personal concerns to the strategic politics of the movement. Bridging in both directions at once, they simultaneously extended the SCLC's awareness of and involvement in local problems while implementing the goals of the Citizenship Education Program among rural folk: self-pride, cultural pride, literacy, and a sense of one's citizenship rights. Mrs. Clark often became involved in the plight of these poor communities, and the SCLC provided food and clothing to those in need. Registration was the goal, but one could not achieve this without intimate involvement within the community. Mrs. Clark explains:

> The first night . . . we would always ask people to tell the needs of the people in their community. The first night they gave us their input, and the next morning we started teaching from what they wanted to do. But what they wanted varied. We had to change. Down in the Southern part of Georgia, some woman wanted to know how to make out her own check. . . . The next morning we started off with asking them: Do you have an employment office in your town? Where is it located? What hours is it open? Have you been there to get work? The answer to those questions we wrote down on dry cleaners bags, so they could read them. We didn't have any blackboards. That afternoon we would ask them about the government in their home town. They knew very little about it. . . . We had to give them a plan of how these people were elected, of how people who had registered to vote could put these people in office, and of how they were the ones who were over you.[17]

This transformation process also involved frame amplification, most clearly illustrated by attempts to reshape the religiosity in rural communities to include activist philosophy and action. In 1963, the Citizenship Education Program reported that

> we are attempting to hold conferences for ministers on "The Bible and the Ballot" in cities across the South in an attempt to help overcome some of the ill effects of a pious, personalistic religion which has no prophetic concern for the community.

Our experience has been that this gives ministers some theological basis for participating in voter registration.[18]

This amplification of religious doctrine was also presented to the rural constituency. Septima Clark and her staff were able to (1) bridge those who were already
predisposed to join the movement by providing them more information; (2) extend
the interests of the SCLC to include the daily concerns of the rural population as
a means to increase rural support; (3) amplify already existing religious tenets to
emphasize compatibility with movement ideology; and (4) transform prefigurative
and personalistic frames to include the strategic politics of the movement. In these
ways, they were able to reach out to the potential participants from the rank and
file as well as to the unsupportive ministers.

Mrs. Clark's techniques would prove to be pivotal in the SCLC's efforts to
increase voter registration throughout the rural South. After the first class of three
men and eleven women successfully completed the program, the graduates opened
other schools. Enrollment in both the teacher training workshops and local citizenship schools increased rapidly. A study conducted by Robert Green, education
director of the SCLC, indicated that 56 percent of those attending the workshops
were women, mean age 31, one-third of whom had children. Most were without
a high school diploma. According to the study, these women "were—(a) highly
motivated to come; (b) were concerned with bringing about social change at their
local level; and (c) were willing to risk social and economic ostracism from citizens
in both white and Negro communities upon their return."[19] It is also important
to note that the risks to teachers and students alike went beyond ostracism and
shaped the citizenship school experience. Annelle Ponder, who joined the Citizenship Education Program later, describes her experience in a local community:
"Because the people were so afraid, it was impossible to find a place where we
could hold training sessions in the evenings, we were limited to daytime hours for
our work."[20]

By the spring of 1961, Highlander had trained eighty-two teachers to work in
Alabama, Georgia, South Carolina, and Tennessee. Clark was traveling all over
the South, visiting the schools and recruiting new teachers.[21] In one year, according to a report compiled by Mrs. Clark, Black voter registration was increased by
thirteen thousand in Alabama, sixteen thousand in Arkansas, sixty-eight thousand
in Florida, sixty thousand in Georgia, thirty-one thousand in Louisiana, twenty-
eight thousand in Mississippi, eighty-three thousand in North Carolina, one hundred and thirty thousand in South Carolina, seventeen thousand in Tennessee,
seventy-four thousand in Texas, and sixteen thousand in Virginia. Approximately
three hundred were trained as community leaders and returned to their communities to develop local citizenship programs.[22]

In these ways, bridge leaders established and expanded a sense of group identity,
collective consciousness, and solidarity between rural and small-town communities
and the wider movement; they did so by bridging the gaps between the formal
movement organization's message and the day-to-day realities of potential constituents.

Bridges between the organization and the rural communities were further expanded through the new Dorchester Cooperative Community Center, located in Dorchester, Georgia. Septima Clark recalls:

> Three of us from SCLC drove all over the South recruiting people to go to the Dorchester Center. Andy Young was the administrator, Dorothy Cotton was the director or the educational consultant, and I was the supervisor of teacher training. The three of us worked together as a team, and we drove all over the South bringing busloads of folk—sometimes seventy people—who would live together for five days at the Dorchester Center. . . . Once a month for five days, we'd work with the people we had recruited, some of whom were just off the farms. Like Fannie Lou Hamer, who stood up and said, "I live on Mr. Marlowe's plantation." She talked about how Pap, her husband, had to take her to the next county because they were going to beat up Pap and her if she didn't stop that voter registration talk. She taught us the old songs in the meetings to keep their spirits up. We sang a lot in the workshops at Dorchester, just like at Highlander. . . . Those who came had to feel that we could get away with it or that we didn't mind if we had to die.[23]

This bridging aspect of movement mobilization was critical to movement success. Through Septima Clark's program, the SCLC was able to reach out to thousands of potential participants at the grassroots level. Indigenous bridge leaders—women such as Fannie Lou Hamer, who later became a central leader in the movement—received training at the Dorchester Center. Septima Clark's program became the foundation of the movement.

Bridge Leaders, Gender, and the Southern Christian Leadership Conference

While the SCLC's membership recruitment and registration of voters increased, Ella Baker remained dissatisfied with gender bias in the organization. Men, ministers in particular, consistently maintained their domination of the upper ranks of the SCLC hierarchy. At the executive staff level, there were only two areas in which women actively participated: the Citizenship Education Program and the Fund-Raising Department. In a 1959 newsletter, Miss Baker was pleased to announce the election of the first female staff officer. Baker's article states:

> This is in keeping with the expressed need to involve more women in the movement, and we believe that Mrs. Whickam will bring new strength to our efforts. The National Beauty Culturist's League, Inc., of which she is president, has strong local and state units throughout the South, and voter-registration is a major emphasis to its program.[24]

Mrs. Katie E. Whickam had been elected assistant secretary. As for the board of directors, until 1965 their membership included one woman at most and often no women at all. At the time Mrs. Whickam was elected to the staff, one woman also served on the board, Mrs. Daisy Bates. Neither of these women, however, retained her position for more than a year or two.[25] In 1964, Mrs. Marian B. Logan of New York City served as the only woman member of the board. By 1965, there were three women board members: Mrs. Erna Dungee, Mrs. Logan, and Mrs. Victoria Gray. Thirty-nine males constituted the rest of the board roster during that time.[26]

Even when they were privy to board and executive staff meetings, women found their contributions to organizational or structural decision making and to discussions of strategies for the future stifled. Most notably, Ella Baker was consistently frustrated by the dominance of the Baptist ministers and their lack of confidence in her skills. In commenting on why she decided to leave the SCLC, she replies:

> In the first place, I had known, number one, that there would never be any role for me in a leadership capacity with SCLC. Why? First, I'm a woman. Also, I'm not a minister. And Second, I am a person that feels that I have to maintain some degree of personal integrity and be my own barometer of what is important and what is not, which meant that even if there had been any inclination on the part of the leadership—which I'm sure it never would be—of me being in an important leadership role there, I knew that my penchant for speaking honestly about what I considered directions would not be well tolerated.
>
> Also, . . . the combination of being a woman, and an older woman, presented some problems. Number one, I was old enough to be the mother of the leadership. The combination of the basic attitude of men, and especially ministers, as to what the role of women in their church setups is—that of taking orders, not providing leadership—and the ego that is involved—the ego problems involved in having to feel that here is someone who had the capacity for a certain amount of leadership and, certainly, had more information about a lot of things than they possessed at that time—this would never had lent itself to my being a leader in the movement there.[27]

This feeling of not being allowed to rise in the ranks of the the SCLC leadership was echoed by Septima Clark. Though she credits Andrew Young with acknowledging the Citizenship Education Program "as the base on which the whole civil rights movement was built," she considered the SCLC to be a man's domain. She recalls:

> I was on the Executive Staff of SCLC, but the men on it didn't listen to me too well. They liked to send me into many places because I could always make a path in to get people to listen to what I have to say. But those men didn't have any faith in women, none whatsoever. They just thought that women were sex symbols and had no contribution to make. That's why Rev. Abernathy would say continuously, "Why is Mrs. Clark on this staff?"[28]

While we have seen that men did recognize women's ability to bridge the organization to the masses, Mrs. Clark's and Miss Baker's comments reflect the degree to which women's contributions were controlled by conventional belief in the leadership supremacy of male ministers. Mrs. Clark also understood other women to be unwilling to speak out at all. Recalling the times Mrs. King and Mrs. Abernathy would attend meetings, she relates:

> Mrs. King and Mrs. Abernathy would come and they were just like chandeliers, shining lights sitting up saying nothing. They never had anything to say at the conventions. They were introduced by someone but that's all.[29]

At most of the SCLC conventions the only women to regularly participate were Septima Clark, Dorothy Cotton, and Diane Nash. Nash was the youth group coordinator. Mrs. Clark and Mrs. Cotton were usually afforded a few minutes to report on the progress of the Citizenship Education Program, while Diane Nash ran a youth group workshop. At both board meetings and executive staff meetings, women's comments were scarce and usually treated without serious consideration, especially if they were policy suggestions.[30]

Dr. King's intended preface to Septima Clark's autobiography, *Echo in My Soul*, indicates his view of women's positions in the struggle for civil rights. He wrote.

> *Echo In My Soul* epitomizes the continuous struggle of the Southern Negro woman to realize her role as a mother while fulfilling her forced position as community teacher, intuitive fighter for human rights and leader of her unlettered and disillusioned people.[31]

The young Baptist minister believed that women, while capable of leadership, did not and should not exercise this ability by choice. A woman's natural, not forced, position was as a support to her husband and a mother to her children.

And at the First Southwide Institute on Non-Violent Resistance to Segregation held during July 1959, which few Black southern male leaders attended, Reverend Palmer notes that "he [Dr. King] made excuses for others who were not there, and how great it was for women to be concerned in the struggle."[32]

Dr. King's ambivalence toward women extended into his dealings with other women staff. Carole F. Hoover was the daughter of a minister in Chattanooga, Tennessee. She began working for the SCLC in 1962, and served as an aide to Wyatt T. Walker, the executive assistant to the SCLC. In 1964 Mr. Walker was relocated, leaving Miss Hoover uncertain of her status. Repeated attempts to discuss her situation with Dr. King failed, and in a letter to him she wrote:

> I regret that I have to communicate by this means with you, however, it seems that it is impossible for me to be afforded an opportunity to talk with you. . . . I need to know specifically what my responsibility will be and also my job classification. . . . My second concern stems from the fact that I am so obviously excluded from meetings where programming, policy and future plans for the organizations are dealt with. Consequently, I am poorly informed which is bad, because I am constantly before groups for promotions, fund raising and other things where it is mandatory to be equipped with information on our present program. At present, I do not know what cities we will be in this summer for direct action. I feel that if I am to remain on the staff at least I should be informed.[33]

Carole Hoover was not part of the executive staff, though her position clearly required such participation. (By 1965 she was included in these meetings.)[34]

While women were routinely excluded from official positions of status, men acting as secondary leaders within the organization were generally elevated to oversee the tasks women did perform. One of the more positive examples is Andrew Young, one of Dr. King's trusted confidants. Though given oversight of the Citizenship Education Program, he chose not to exercise his authority over Septima Clark and Dorothy Cotton. While the three of them traveled throughout the South, they worked in a cooperative fashion to implement the program in local communities.[35] In a memorandum to Mrs. Clark, Mrs. Cotton, and Dr. King, Young wrote:

> For some time now I have been meaning to try to put into words the understanding that I have of our program and how it relates to the total work of SCLC. This is an attempt at such a statement. This in no way intends to be final or authoritative, it is only my thinking. I hope that others will add their thinking to it.[36]

This passage suggests that Young did not feel comfortable asserting power over a program he had not developed or usurping the decision-making ability of those who had. This understanding was critical to the success of the program, which enjoyed relative autonomy in relation to the formal leaders.

The exclusion of women from official positions of power extended itself into the field staff. It was not until 1965 that the SCLC acquired one woman field staff director, Shirley Mesher of Dallas County, Alabama. Most women were either part of the secretarial staff or, if in the field, remained assistants.[37] At the local level, affiliates of the SCLC were generally minister led, though there were some exceptions. One such exception was Mrs. Carolyn Daniels of Dawson, Georgia, a thirty-six-year-old Citizenship School teacher, whose home was fired with thirty rounds from an automatic rifle. She was struck in the foot, and while at the hospital, her home was bombed.[38] Other exceptions included Mrs. Sarah Small, president of the Williamston unit of the SCLC, and Mrs. Outerbridge, another North Carolina leader, both of whom were hit, cursed, and thrown against police cars while leading a march to integrate the local public library.[39]

Even in the SCLC publications, women's efforts were scarcely mentioned, particularly in press releases. Newsletters were more inclusive, though recognition was limited to the achievements of Mrs. Cotton, Mrs. Clark, and Miss Hoover, and often took the form of a "paternalistic pat on the head," as Dorothy Cotton recalls.[40]

Conclusion

It is clear that the momentum of the boycott had begun to slacken by 1958. Miss Ella Baker's keen understanding of the need to build support from the bottom up was central to the mobilization of a mass effort. Baker, as a professional bridge leader, recognized that local leadership was the key to gaining the trust and support of the rural masses, particularly in areas most resistant to change. Yet it is equally clear that despite Baker's efforts, she was disregarded as a formal leader.

In spite of women's limited official power within the SCLC, their contributions as bridge leaders were critical. Though women did not generally hold positions as officers, they did bring to the organization all the skills in their possession, leadership included, exercising those abilities wherever they found themselves. And as leaders women can be credited with building the SCLC's mass base of support. Miss Ella Baker provided the organizational foundation for the SCLC. Mrs. Septima Clark, also a professional bridge leader, imparted her knowledge and skills regarding citizenship education and literacy to hundreds of others, who in turn spread the word throughout their communities, dramatically increasing voter registration throughout the South. Miss Carole F. Hoover's initiative in fund-raising provided the SCLC with an economic base to sustain its protest efforts. Although these women worked diligently, the public and the media rarely saw their efforts; the spotlight stayed focused on the formal Black male leadership and has remained there.

❦ S I X ❦

Bridging Students to
the Movement

BY THE EARLY 1960S, student-organized protests were spreading to southern cities such as Nashville, Tennessee, and Greensboro, North Carolina. The direct-action events in Greensboro precipitated by four students—Ezell Blair Jr., Franklin McCain, Joseph McNeil, and David Richmond, all of North Carolina Agricultural and Technical College—received widespread media attention and created a rash of similar sit-ins at lunch counters throughout the South. With the momentum of these events in mind and frustrated by the dominance of ministers within the SCLC, Miss Ella Baker turned her energies to the development of a national student movement organization. She believed that student activists across the South would benefit from contact with one another, and she discussed her idea with the SCLC. Baker comments about the need to coordinate the sit-ins:

> It hadn't gone on so long before I suggested that we call a conference of the sit-inners. . . . It was very obvious to the Southern Christian Leadership Conference that there was little or no communication between those who sat in, say, in Charlotte, North Carolina, and those who sat in at some other place in Virginia or Alabama. They were motivated by what the North Carolina four had started, but they were not in contact with each other. . . . You couldn't build a sustaining force just based on spontaneity.[1]

Miss Baker began the process of bridging the students to one another and to the movement as a whole. She sent announcements to college campuses regarding a conference that was to take place on April 15–17, 1960, at Shaw University in Raleigh, North Carolina. Baker and Dr. King did not agree on the selection of the keynote speaker. Miss Baker had selected Reverend James Lawson, known for his rapport with the Nashville students and his commitment to nonviolence, while Dr. King wanted a speaker from the SCLC, who would encourage the students to form an organization that would be an arm of the SCLC. Miss Baker recalls:

> The Southern Christian Leadership Conference felt that they could influence how things went [with the students]. They were interested in having the students become an arm of SCLC. They were most confident that this would be their baby, because I [was the one who] called the meeting. . . . Well, I disagreed. I wasn't one to say yes, because it came from the Reverend King. So when it was proposed, that [SCLC] could influence . . . what [the students] wanted done, I was outraged. I walked out.[2]

Though Reverend Lawson was the keynote speaker, the issue of student sovereignty was hotly debated. The compromise eventually reached accepted that the student organization would not become an arm of the SCLC, but added that Dr. King would join Miss Baker and Reverend Lawson as one of its advisors. The meeting in Raleigh was a great success, with attendance exceeding expectations. Instead of the one hundred youth expected to attend, there were approximately three hundred. Black and White students attended the conference representing many colleges and student groups from both the North and the South. The students decided to establish a committee with representatives from each organization or college.[3] Three times as many men as women were chosen delegates. However, it was the women who provided the groundwork necessary for the establishment of the Student Non-Violent Coordinating Committee (SNCC).

SNCC set up office in an unused portion of the SCLC headquarters in Atlanta. Jane Stembridge, a White student at the Union Theological Seminary in New York, volunteered to work in the office for a small stipend. The goal of SNCC was to dispense information and act as a clearinghouse for protest activity. The group published a newsletter that kept student activists abreast of interstate protest work.

Marion Barry, an active participant in nonviolent demonstrations in Nashville at Fisk University, was elected chair of the coordinating committee.[4] Diane Nash, who was president of the Nashville student movement, served as a member of this coordinating committee composed of student representatives. Also in attendance were several adult leaders from various organizations including CORE, SCLC, YWCA, ACLU, the National Student Association (NSA), and the NAACP.[5] Generally, there were more men in attendance and they dominated discussions, though several women were quite vocal.[6] The most vocal women were either those who came to SNCC with status from participation in local activist groups or those who, through their activism in SNCC, proved themselves to be courageous. That most women remained less vocal in meetings than men should not obscure the fact that their activities were essential to the development of a solid base from which SNCC was to operate.

In addition to creating SNCC's structure, Ella Baker contributed her clear philosophy regarding leadership, goals, and tactics. Many of Baker's ideas were formed during the Harlem Renaissance. In the twenties and thirties, Harlem flourished with writers, poets, and other intellectuals discussing the plight of Black people in America. Some wondered whether black people would have a better life in a communist or socialist state. Baker took part in many of these discussions. She comments: "Wherever there was a discussion, I'd go. It didn't matter if it was all men, and maybe I was the only woman . . . it didn't matter. . . . New York was the hotbed of radical thinking."[7]

At the outset of the Depression, Baker went to work for a Harlem newspaper and met George Schuyler, a prominent Black newspaper writer. She and Schuyler were not willing to sit back and watch as Black people struggled to feed and clothe themselves. They developed a cooperative in Harlem so that people could obtain necessities below cost. The ideal of mutual assistance and communal support was central to Baker's notions of activism. She did not believe that leaders should define a movement, and she often stated that "strong movements don't need strong leaders." Instead, her focus was on development of community leadership and grassroots mobilization.[8] Baker's views became central to the operation of SNCC.

Early in SNCC's development, conflicts arose between student groups. The Fisk University and Howard University students were more articulate than the other southern university students and tended to dominate discussions. Students from Fisk had already experienced direct confrontations with the police and had the benefit of Reverend Lawson's nonviolent teachings. The groups were not simply divided by experience and articulation, however, but also by philosophical orientation. The Nashville group believed in nonviolent direct action while another contingency supported political action—that is, voter registration. Tensions arose over who would be the chairman; it was suggested that SNCC divide, but Miss Ella Baker intervened to prevent such an action. She recalled:

> It was one of the few times, I suppose, that I had anything to say in terms of that type of discussion. I usually tried to present whatever participation I had in terms of questions and try to get people to reach certain decisions by questioning some of the things themselves. But in this instance I made a little plea against splitting, pointing out the history of organizations among black people and the multiplicity of organizations and the lack of effectiveness as a result of this, to the extent that they decide[d] against it. . . . [9]

Because of her extensive experience, Miss Ella Baker gained immediate respect from the students. She encouraged them to think for themselves and did not attempt to dominate. With Ella Baker's guidance, it was decided that rotating the chairmanship would ease some of the tensions between groups and would prevent a single "strongman" from usurping power. Unlike the centralization of power within the other movement organizations, SNCC was a decentralized organization. There were rotating chairs and an executive committee. The official positions within SNCC, much like those in other movement organizations, were dominated by men, but women in SNCC were more visible and held more power than those in other organizations. These differences are attributable to Miss Ella Baker, whose emphasis on group-centered leadership required that decisions be made through group consensus. Such a consensus automatically included women's input. As Carol Mueller, in her description of Ella Baker's philosophy, states:

> the emphasis on participation had many implications, but three have been primary: (1) an appeal for grassroots involvement of people throughout society in the decisions that control their lives; (2) the minimalization of hierarchy and the associated emphasis on expertise and professionalism as a basis for leadership; and (3) a call for direct action as an answer to fear, alienation, and intellectual detachment.[10]

This emphasis on group participation and the decentralization of power in the decision-making process created an environment in which everyone was expected to participate fully, even women. This tended to mitigate, though not eliminate, traditional beliefs that had encouraged deference to males or ministers as leaders because, even if one held the belief, one was expected to participate.

Yet there is still a disparity that needs clarification. Though the women in SNCC held considerable power, here too they were not part of the primary formal leadership. Although SNCC's decentralized structure prevented the development of oligarchy—rulership by the few—it did not ensure that power was any less gender determined than that of the centralized organizations. Though their philosophy was one of group-centered leadership, visibility was still heavily dictated by traditional beliefs about the legitimacy of male authority. Even SNCC, with its decentralized structure and relatively decentralized power relations, was dominated by male leaders. As Faye Bellamy states,

> I think there was a hierarchy. I think there was more than one, let me say that. I think that hierarchies oftentimes come from personalities and charisma of various individuals. So in SNCC there was a Foreman kind of hierarchy. There was a Stokely kind of hierarchy. [A] Bob Moses kind of hierarchy . . . [11]

According to Bellamy and other interviewees, three distinct groups emerged through which power was organized. While these power groups each formed around a male leader, taken as a whole women had greater access to organizational power here than in groups where power was centralized around one key figure. Even within SNCC, men were perceived as the representative leaders by both men and women. As Diane Nash states:

> Before the women's movement, men and women tended to see the males as naturally in leadership positions. . . . The thing that we didn't do is to take the out-front positions, and when the TV cameras were around I know I for one and I think many other women were content to let the men who were interested in dealing with the press be with the press.[12]

However, because of the townhouse, "consensus required" nature of decision making, and the relatively decentralized nature of leadership, a few women were able to become secondary formal bridge leaders, though many remained community bridge leaders. Yet the secondary formal bridge leadership tier was gendered. Men in this position, though working just as their female counterparts, could advance to the primary formal bridge leadership tier. However, despite the lack of primary formal leadership positions, women did enjoy greater power in this organization than in primary formal and secondary formal organizations.

Moreover, the organization possessed many powerful women leaders, and Diane Nash was one. Nash became a key figure in the development of SNCC and the movement in general. Committed to the philosophy and principles of nonviolence, she and fellow Fisk student Peggi Alexander outlined the purposes of SNCC in a paper entitled "Non-Violence Speaks to the Movement." This paper included recommendations on ways that SNCC should approach protest.[13]

Reverend Lawson, a member of King's inner circle, has been credited by numerous scholars with producing SNCC's statement of purpose; an early SNCC newsletter indicates that Lawson prepared the statement himself. No credit is given to either Diane Nash or Peggi Alexander. Certainly Lawson, who conducted nonviolence workshops with college students, influenced the philosophy of SNCC; nevertheless, Nash and Alexander's handwritten document clearly contributed a great deal to the organization's statement of purpose. Once again, this demonstrates the visibility differential between formal leaders and those who work as bridge leaders, behind the scenes. By her writing and through the several nonviolence workshops she led during the SNCC conferences Nash set the tone for the strategies and tactics employed by SNCC's membership.

Diane Nash, a much younger woman than Ella Baker, was a formal local community bridge leader whose capacity to lead placed her well on her way to becoming a professional bridge leader. The initial respect of her activist peers was gained because of her activities in the Nashville movement as the organizer and leader of several protests. She recalls:

> I ran into some real problems in terms of being the only woman at the stage where we were just setting SNCC up as an organization. It was really rough not being just one of the guys. They did tend to look at me that way. However, they had to tolerate me because I had such a strong local base in Nashville, and at that time I had gotten probably more publicity than any other student in the movement and had been on the cover of *Jet* magazine a couple of times and things like that. . . .
>
> Even though they disagreed a lot of times, they tolerated me because they didn't want me to say that these guys just really aren't okay. I had a real good image because I took truth and love seriously, the basic tenets of non-violence. And people who knew me and worked with me knew that and so my word would tend to be taken seriously. I was taken seriously by a lot of people. That's what's helped me. . . . [Otherwise] they'd have wiped me out.[14]

However, as had happened during the development of the MIA, most of the women rank and file found themselves listening to men. In the momentum-building years, one of the central factors contributing to a woman's acceptance as a leader was her record of previous actions, which needed to be of an extraordinary nature. However, as the organization grew and the number of projects increased, women's leadership options expanded.

Community Bridge Leaders as Temporary Formal Leaders

During its formation, SNCC was primarily a men's organization: no women served on the field staff. During an interview, one respondent pointed out that while most mothers would be reluctant to have their sons participate in SNCC, they would adamantly oppose their daughters doing so. This particular female volunteer was disowned for her active participation.[15] In correspondence sent to the SNCC office in 1962, a prospective female volunteer wrote:

> Many of us are interested in the possibility of going to the South but are hesitant because from the information we have received about SNCC we could find only male students' names in the accounts of students working there.[16]

In response, Julian Bond, a SNCC field secretary, replied:

> Although we do not presently have any girls on our field staff, we do have a very capable office manager who is very female. Diane Nash one of the leaders of the Nashville Student Movement, was a leader on SNCC's staff until her recent marriage. Glen Green, Joy Reagan, Bertha Gober, and other college girls have been members of the staff in the past as well. . . . In addition, let me say that if we were able to hire a girl to type some of our correspondence, I wouldn't have made as many mistakes as I have.[17]

However, many more women began to join SNCC and their positions began to change in February 1961, when students in Rock Hill, South Carolina, were arrested. Among them were several women whose reputations as loyal activists would elevate their power in SNCC. Hearing of the arrests, four SNCC workers—Diane Nash, Charles Sherrod, Ruby Doris Smith, and Charles Jones—traveled to Rock Hill to stage a sit-in as a show of solidarity. Before 1961, SNCC had initiated no formal group actions; in their capacity as a clearinghouse, they dispensed whatever information about protests they could come by through the "Student Voice," their newsletter. When the SNCC workers were arrested in Rock Hill, they decided to follow their comrades' example by choosing to serve their full thirty-day jail term. In this way use of the "jail-no-bail" tactic gained momentum. Other organizations began to use this approach for arrests of their members, conserving badly needed money for uses other than bail.[18]

During 1961, CORE began development of a project called the Freedom Rides, in which a busload of Black and White activists would ride from Washington, D.C., to New Orleans to test the desegregation of local bus and transportation facilities. The goal was to force the southern states to comply with the 1960 Supreme Court decision banning segregation on interstate trains and buses. Moreover, they were challenging the segregated facilities in the terminals, rest rooms, and lunch counters that served the passengers. The first ride took place on May

4, 1961 and proceeded through the South without much difficulty until it reached the Rock Hill, South Carolina, terminal. There two of the Black male riders were beaten by a mob of White men for attempting to use the rest rooms designated for White men only. They continued the rides, however, making it safely through stops in Winnsboro, South Carolina, and Augusta, Georgia. After a stop in Atlanta, they thought it best to divide up, with half of the Freedom Riders boarding a Greyhound bus and the other half a Trailways bus. When they reached Birmingham, Alabama, a mob tore into the riders, beating them severely. Many were near death. Ruby Doris Smith, a participant in the rides and later a central figure in SNCC, recalls the request for federal protection prior to the attacks.

> I remember Diane Nash called the Department of Justice from Nashville, and Lonnie King—you know he was head of the Atlanta student movement—also called the Department. Both of them asked the federal government to give protection to the Freedom Riders on the rest of their journey. And in both cases the Justice Department said no, they couldn't protect anyone, but if something happened, they would investigate. You know how they do. . . . [19]

Eugene "Bull" Connor, Birmingham's commissioner of public safety, was known for his intolerance of Black civil rights. (As discussed in chapter 4, Ruby Hurley had encountered him during her work in the 1950s.) Police were not sent to the mob scene for nearly a half hour. Though the CORE riders were unable to continue, Diane Nash phoned Reverend Shuttlesworth, a leader in Birmingham and part of King's inner circle, to insist that the rides continue. She told Shuttlesworth, "The students have decided that we can't let violence overcome. We are going to come into Birmingham to continue the Freedom Ride." Shuttlesworth responded, "Young lady do you know that the Freedom Riders were almost killed?" She replied, "Yes, that's exactly why the rides must not be stopped. If they stop us with violence, the movement is dead. We're coming; we just want to know if you can meet us."[20] Spontaneous decisions were often made by community bridge leaders during moments of crisis, when they were propelled into temporary formal leadership positions. Many felt that "the spontaneity was as important as being organized."[21]

Diane Nash organized a group of Nashville students to begin a ride to Birmingham. Emotions ran high as the students who volunteered contemplated the consequences of continuing the rides. Lucretia Collins, one of the volunteers, recounts her decision to join the rides:

> I could see how strongly someone would have to be dedicated because at this point we didn't know what was going to happen. We thought that some of us would be killed. We certainly thought that some of us, if not all of us, would be severely injured. At any moment I was expecting anything. I was expecting the worst and hoping for the best.[22]

Diane Nash explained the high emotions of the riders:

These people faced the probability of their own deaths before they ever left Nashville. . . . Several made out wills. A few more gave me sealed letters to be mailed if they were killed. Some told me frankly that they were afraid, but knew this was something that they must do because freedom was worth it.[23]

Although realistically afraid and contemplating their own deaths, the students overcame their fears and continued the rides. Eight student volunteers boarded the bus, were stopped on the outskirts of Birmingham, jailed for a night, and driven by the police chief, "Bull" Connor, to the Tennessee border. Nash and others returned to Nashville and assembled even more students to ride to Birmingham. Ruby Doris Smith joined the group in Birmingham, and they struggled to persuade a bus driver to take them on to Montgomery. This time, the Kennedy administration convinced Alabama's Governor Patterson to send police to escort the bus from the outskirts of Montgomery to its bus terminal. The police kept their word until the city limits were reached, then disappeared. When the bus pulled into the terminal, it was met by hundreds of angry Whites brandishing clubs and baseball bats. Several Freedom Riders were severely beaten.

That evening Ralph Abernathy's First Baptist Church hosted a gathering to honor the Freedom Riders, at which Dr. King, Ralph Abernathy, Diane Nash, and John Lewis (another SNCC leader) held a press conference. Though King rallied in support of the rides and supported their decision to continue, he did not join the riders as they continued to Jackson, Tennessee. SNCC activists were increasingly becoming disillusioned with Dr. King's decisions.

Off the record, SNCC member Julian Bond bluntly voiced the growing student perception of King: "He has been losing since he left Montgomery. He lost when he didn't go on the Freedom Ride when the students begged him to go on the Freedom Ride and he didn't go. I think he's been losing for a long time. And I think eventually that more Negroes and more white Americans will become disillusioned with him, and find that he after all is only another preacher who can talk well.' "[24]

Within the movement sector, SNCC operated much as a bridging organization. The primary goal of SNCC was to develop leadership within each community of entry. They did not want to act as leaders for the community. While the SCLC did some of this, as in the case of the Citizenship Education Program, its primary objective was to mobilize communities in an organized and nonviolent fashion with the ultimate goal of securing state legitimacy and support. Dr. King became the legitimate voice of the movement, and he was the central figure around which the movement revolved. Yet his decisions could not be made without careful consideration of the state's response. Consequently, SNCC and the SCLC were often at odds because of their distinctly opposing foci and philosophies of leadership. James Forman, in *The Making of Black Revolutionaries*, states: "I recalled . . . King's statement that he was not going to take a Freedom Ride because he was then on probation and his advisors had told him it would be unwise." He continues:

Even Diane Nash, who had strong convictions but tried not to speak evil of anyone, expressed a mixed opinion of Dr. King. "He's a good man but as a symbol of this movement, he leaves a lot to be desired. He has been affected by a lot of middle-class standards. If he wanted to, he could really do something about the South. He could go to Jackson and tell those people why they should participate in and support the Freedom Rides."[25]

As a community bridge leader, Nash was able to come to the fore when the formal leadership was either unable or unwilling to risk alienating their legitimacy with the state. Because she was without such responsibilities, Nash could acknowledge and build upon the emotions of the masses. At that time, the momentum of the movement depended on the continuation of the Freedom Rides. They had become a critical factor in mobilizing support from mainstream America, who watched the coverage of the horrible beatings on the evening news.

Angered by the police betrayal, the Kennedy administration sent in federal marshals to protect the riders on the last legs of the journey through Meridian and Jackson, Mississippi, to New Orleans. The following morning a bus left for Jackson, escorted by National Guardsmen. Upon arrival, the riders attempted to use the all-White facilities and were arrested. Frank Holloway describes the scene:

When we got there we met several men in ten-gallon hats, looking like something out of an old Western, with rifles in their hands, staring at us. . . . Soon they took us out to a room, boys on one side and girls on the other. One by one they took us into another room for questioning. . . . There were about eight guards with sticks in their hands in the second room and the Freedom Rider being questioned was surrounded by these men. Outside we could hear the questions and the thumps and whacks, and sometimes a quick groan or a cry. . . . They beat several riders who didn't say "Yes, sir. . . ." Reverend C. T. Vivian of Chattanooga was beaten pretty bad. When he came out he had blood streaming from his head. . . . We could hear somebody slap a girl Freedom Rider, and her quick little scream. . . . She was about five feet tall and wore glasses.[26]

Ruby Doris Smith and others were sentenced to prison for their activities. The first two weeks of her sentence were spent in a four-bunk cell with twenty-three others. Though crowded, the conditions were not as dismal as those in Parchmen, where she spent the next six weeks of her sentence. Here they were stripped, issued clothing, and placed in cells with hardened criminals. The cells were filthy and infested with bugs. In the Hinds County jail, they had been allowed to sing; here they had to remain quiet under the threats of the guards, who removed mattresses for such infractions. Many women refused to comply and spent several nights on steel springs, while cold air was deliberately blown into the cells.[27]

Just like their male comrades, women risked their lives for the movement. Some even risked the lives of their children. Diane Nash, who married SCLC Field Secretary James Bevel, was four months' pregnant when she was brought to trial in Jackson, Mississippi, for "contributing to the delinquency of minors." Her offense was teaching workshops on nonviolence to young Black children. Instead of pleading guilty and accepting a fine, she allowed the charges to go to trial. She was sentenced to two years' imprisonment, but served only ten days. Prior to Dr. King's arrest in Albany, he stated his intention to remain in jail without bond, but within hours of his arrest he allowed a bond to be posted for his release. Many members of SNCC were deeply disappointed with King's action, and Diane Nash Bevel addresses this issue in a memo describing her decision to serve a full two-year term rather than to accept bail. She wrote:

> I believe that the time has come, and is indeed long past, when each of us must make up his mind, when arrested on unjust charges, to serve his sentence and stop posting bonds. I believe that unless we do this our movement loses its power and will never succeed. We in the nonviolent movement have been talking about jail without bail for two years or more. It is time for us to mean what we say. . . . If we do not do so, we lose our opportunity to reach the community and society with a great moral appeal and thus bring about basic changes in people and in society. . . . I think we all realize what it would mean if we had hundreds and thousands of people across the South prepared to go to jail and stay. There can be no doubt that our battle would be won. . . . We have faltered and hesitated. . . . I can no longer cooperate with the evil and corrupt court system of this state. Since my child will be a black child born in Mississippi, whether I am in jail or not he will be born in prison. I believe that if I go to jail now it may help hasten the day when my child and all children will be free—not only on the day of their birth but for all their lives.[28]

Dr. King's decisions, while a disappointment to those in SNCC, were made based, in part, on consideration of his image in the eyes of the state. King and the SCLC needed to remain credible. This was, after all, a movement for inclusion, and recent civil rights legislation and court decisions indicated some support for the movement by those in power. It was critical that King not alienate his state supporters. His primary task was to maintain a balance between the needs of the movement and the judgment of the state.

An obvious strength of the community bridge leadership tier was their relative autonomy. The emotions and the spontaneity so critical to movement momentum and mobilization could be harnessed by community bridge leaders. Moreover, this freedom in leadership served constantly to remind formal leaders of the flesh-and-blood constituency they represented. Nash's decision to remain in jail undoubtedly influenced Dr. King's decision to remain in jail after his sentencing in Albany, Georgia.[29] This symbiosis between the formal and bridge leader tiers ensured that movement momentum would not be sacrificed to governmental reluctance.

Community Bridge Leaders as Secondary Formal Leaders

In addition to their spontaneous leadership during moments of crisis, community bridge leaders took on more formal leadership positions as the movement grew. By the summer of 1964, SNCC had begun its Freedom Summer program, which established thirty-one Freedom Schools across the state of Mississippi, swelling the number of volunteers to nearly one thousand.[30] This ambitious expansion required an increase in the number of field workers who could supervise the activities of these novices. With the greater need for seasoned supervisors, women began to gain titled positions with greater responsibility over the activities of others. Early in SNCC's development, most women were less vocal in meetings, but by 1964 women seemed to participate fully by setting the agenda, making proposals, and guiding the discussions, though men still chaired meetings and initiated discussions to a greater extent than did women. Although Ella Baker, Ruby Doris Smith Robinson, and Diane Nash Bevel were always considered a part of the leadership, and women such as Gwen Robinson, Prathia Hall Wynn, Muriel Tillinghast, Cynthia Washington, Lois Rogers, and Mary Lane as community bridge leaders were considered essential to SNCC operations, the sharp increase in demands upon leadership resources placed these respected and capable women in new positions of responsibility and power as secondary formal bridge leaders.[31]

With the exception of Ella Baker, Diane Nash Bevel, and Ruby Doris Smith Robinson, most of the newly arrived cadre of women leaders came to SNCC after its first few years of operation. From the beginning, a core of males remained central in various positions of power. Such men leaders as James Forman, John Lewis, Marion Barry, Bob Moses, Worth Long, Courtland Cox, Ivanhoe Donaldson, and later Stokely Carmichael were either chairs of SNCC or representatives on the Executive Committee. While this is an important factor, since "longevity was the standard by which people were chosen for leadership,"[32] it still remains that women did not acquire comparable titled positions, despite longevity. Instead, women tended to rotate in or out of the Executive Committee positions and to align themselves with primary formal leader Forman, Moses, or Carmichael.[33] Muriel Tillinghast, one of the most vocal and powerful secondary formal bridge leaders, felt that "there was a band of people right around [the core]." This band included many women community bridge leaders and the few secondary formal bridge leaders.

Though women were viewed as capable and many participated in ways that endangered their lives, titled positions remained gender based. In 1964, the Atlanta staff, which included Administration, the "Student Voice," Photography Department, Research Department, Northern Coordination, Southern Coordination, Communications, office managers, telephone operators, Financial Department, Freedom Singers, and the category listed in SNCC papers as "others" were generally headed by men. Similarly, the office managers and telephone operators were supervised by men.

Carol Merritt was the only woman in Administration; she directed the education program. The executive secretary, program director, administrative assistant, chairman, Freedom Summer coordinator were all men. There were no women on the staff of the "Student Voice." At the most, one or two women worked in each area within SNCC, with the exception of the telephone operators and the Financial Department, which were exclusively women.

Listed in that "others" category mentioned above was Ruby Doris Smith Robinson's position, in charge of personnel.[34] While she was responsible for hiring and firing volunteers, and for signing the checks dispersed to the various SNCC projects, giving her a great deal of power, she had no formal title.[35] There were also women campus travelers who solicited funds and volunteers. These included Jean Wheeler, Enoch Johnson, Joyce Brown, and Judy Richardson.[36]

A 1964 Atlanta office list of job descriptions and personnel clearly illustrates that job title and job descriptions adhered to gender-based divisions of labor. For example, the executive director, the office manager, and the staff coordinator were all men. The descriptions of their jobs included words that indicated authority over others, such as *supervises* and *directs*, while women's job descriptions, such as those of Forman's secretary and of the women coordinators, included the verbs *answers* and *handles*, connoting production rather than leadership. The receptor of women's authority was generally an object, namely correspondence.[37]

In a 1964 office staff meeting, Horace Julian Bond, the director of communications, indicated his dislike of working with women and was honored with the appointment of a male as his coworker. As the staff minutes state, "Julian doesn't like working with women. . . . Would like to have Mike Sayer as requested earlier." Given that this was before the women's movement, there was no attempt to confront this issue by either the men or women present at the meeting.[38] Later that year, in an Executive Committee meeting that included four women and fourteen men, the group discussed the possibility of training a SNCC member to become a fund-raiser. In the minutes of this meeting, Forman suggested:

> Let's discuss whether we should have someone from own ranks or hire someone for lots of money. This person should have "internal drive," should be someone who feels fundraising is very important, who is willing to learn and who can move into cities and move the people there, who will attend to details, who will travel, who won't dump the program because of a commitment to be in the South. Ivanhoe [Donaldson] could do this. . . .
>
> Some discussion on the person to fill this job. T. Brown asked if it had to be a male and suggested Prathia [Hall Wynn]. John Lewis suggested we refer the names to a committee but Forman thought it was too important a question to be referred to committee. Forman mentioned that male would be better since job involved living virtually out of a suitcase.[39]

Clearly, gender-based assumptions governed decisions regarding certain jobs. Yet women's leadership was never viewed as unimportant by either women or men. Rather than extinguishing their desire to lead, women shaped their participation in ways that sustained their feelings of empowerment and complemented the efforts of primary formal bridge leaders.

Women, Power, and Titled Positions

Within SNCC, women often avoided titled positions. Such positions were gendered even though the structure was decentralized—that is, titled positions meant office work. Since women could type and men generally could not, women would end up doing the typing. Within SNCC, the combination of an emphasis on grassroots leadership and the decentralization of decision making created an atmosphere where women could lead as long as the position was untitled or was given a unique title (though a few women, as discussed, did hold titled leadership positions). Yet titles in SNCC were relatively unimportant because the absence of a title or a relatively unimportant title did not mean one lacked power.

Many of my respondents stated that women did not want to be relegated to the office but preferred to work in the field. One respondent recalls, "If you had a title, you were in the office."[40] It is important to recognize that, for women, titled positions often translated to less power, while the titled positions for men often signified greater decision-making power. If a woman was titled, her duties would be restricted to clerical activities. On the other hand, when she participated without a title, her workload could more easily stretch beyond the duties contained in her job description. In other words, it was unsuitable for a woman to hold a titled position with an undue amount of power. Women could have the power without the title or the title without the power.

That titles failed to reflect women's authority in the movement is clearly illustrated by those given to Diane Nash, Miss Ella Baker, and Ruby Doris Smith Robinson. In Nash's case, her titled position of office manager completely disregarded her repeated leadership during moments of crisis. Miss Baker was an outside consultant, though clearly her influence dominated and created SNCC's structure and philosophy. Like Miss Baker, Ruby Doris Smith Robinson's position as personnel manager and bursar was uniquely buried, placed in the "others" category.

Women leaders wasted no energy challenging these inequalities, aware of the vastly greater goal all those in the movement pursued. Cognizant of the fact that titles restricted their leadership opportunities, women chose to either avoid them or ignore the restrictions imposed by their titles.

Women preferred to work in the field, though here, too, they did not often hold titles. Still, such positions allowed for more autonomy. They worked at canvassing in local communities and on a day-to-day basis were able to make decisions within the local community. Canvassing included finding out what was on people's minds—what kinds of things they would like to see done; getting individuals to register to vote; and recruiting individuals for local demonstrations.

Few women became project directors or secondary leaders, though more were appointed to the position at the beginning of the 1964 Freedom Summer. Between 1964 and 1965, of the fifty staff in Mississippi, there were twelve women. In Mississippi, southwest Georgia, and Alabama, there were twenty-nine project directors, seven of whom were women. These included Muriel Tillinghast in Greenville, Mississippi; Mary Lane in Greenwood, Mississippi; Willie Ester McGee in Itta Bena, Mississippi (she worked alongside Stokely Carmichael who was the district director); Mary Sue Gellatly in Shaw, Mississippi; Lois Rogers in Cleveland, Mississippi; Cynthia Washington in Bolivar County, Mississippi, and Gwen Robinson in Laurel, Mississippi. Women project directors did not generally supervise more than one field worker, while most men supervised three or more.[41] Additionally, some of the women received the position because no man was willing or able to take it on. Muriel Tillinghast, for example, received her position after Charlie Cobb, her friend, decided to move on. Tillinghast had had movement leadership experience as a member of NAG in Washington, D.C. prior to her involvement in SNCC. Later she would become project director in Jackson, Mississippi, in an equally spontaneous way. Tillinghast elaborates:

> Jesse Morris, in the Jackson office where COFO [Council of Federated Organizations] was headquartered, announced that he was giving up running the office. He was exhausted. He had been working, I guess, for the better part of a year. Anyhow, he said that if anyone wanted to take over, he'd be leaving on such and such a day by 12 o'clock. I drifted in on that day to see what the story was. Turns out that I was the only one who showed up, and Jesse handed me the keys and left. . . . By the time[I] got to Jackson, the major civil rights organizations had pulled their people and their money out. I guess the killings . . . really frightened a lot of people.[42]

In 1963, under extremely dangerous conditions, another powerful community bridge leader, Prathia Hall Wynn, though not on the official roster of project directors, became head of the project in Selma. Hall Wynn explains:

> Jim Forman and I (and I don't even know why I was asked to go, but Jim asked me) went to Selma. It was an extremely dangerous time. I remember the first mass meeting and how the church had been ringed by the sheriff on horseback and carrying these huge carbines and rifles and Al Lingo and the Alabama State troopers surrounding the church. . . . In the week . . . which followed . . . all of the men who had been involved in the project were in jail and at that moment I became the project director. . . . Need determined how people were utilized.[43]

Dangerous circumstances prevailed throughout the South, and it was impossible to plan and organize every decision and activity. Women moved in and out of positions frequently and served the movement in ways that were critical to its continued sustenance. The fact that women's participation options as titled staff members were limited neither suggests that women were not leaders nor that they were not looked to for leadership. Likewise, the women interviewed did not perceive their activities as limited. Women felt themselves to be an important and integral part of SNCC. They would not be simply relegated to office duties and felt that titled positions were restrictive since they were supposedly limited to office work.

Women Bridge Leaders and Their Heroines

Black women understood their centrality in the community and in the leadership. They did not feel sexually discriminated against; instead they felt empowered by their activities in the movement. Most of these young women were aware of the courageous leadership of older women such as Mrs. Daisy Bates, who had fought for school desegregation in Little Rock, Arkansas. For example, Prathia Hall Wynn was well aware of the critical leadership that had been supplied by Mrs. Boynton, an activist who knew Mary McLeod Bethune. Hall Wynn explained:

Now of course there had been a local Selma movement with Mrs. Boynton, who was clearly, it seemed to me, if not *the* leader—in my experience she was the leader of the local movement. There were men and ministers and others who were leaders, but it seemed to me that she was clearly respected as a peer among them. And she certainly was by the SNCC people.[44]

Women participants understood that women's leadership was no less important to the movement than men's. Miss Ella Baker, who was considerably older than the students in SNCC, provided a role model for both the young men and women. One woman respondent, who wished to remain anonymous recalls.

In terms of the organization's basic philosophy, strategy and tactics, both Diane [Nash Bevel] and Miss Baker were key in those processes. As far as I know, they didn't have any titles . . . but as far as a young woman coming into the organization, I saw people trying to arrange meetings with Miss Baker . . . saying I don't understand this, let's go talk to Miss Baker. And it was the same thing with Diane. Well . . . they didn't have to have titles.[45]

Young people of both sexes understood the courage demonstrated by women, such as Rosa Parks and later Fannie Lou Hamer. These youth were surrounded by strong, intelligent, and capable women who treated them with respect. These women leaders were often featured in *Jet*, a popular Black magazine, and routinely spoke in churches. Young Black people were aware of them and considered them heroines. Before coming to SNCC, Black women, as one respondent states, were aware that "women played pivotal roles in history . . . and could change the course of history."[46] Gloria Richardson, the leader of the Cambridge, Maryland, movement describes the relationship of Black women's history to her own involvement in the movement.

I think mine was more an extension of Eastern Shore history because I came from an area that's like fifteen minutes from Harriet Tubman's home in Sharptown. And grandchildren of the Tubman family had gone to school with my children. . . . So we had come up in that environment, so for us it was like an extension of that.[47]

Indeed, Black women have had a long and continuous history of rebellion and struggle. During slavery, women who did not want to leave their children would rebel in other ways. They would slow their work or verbally confront or strike the overseer. These defiant acts often led to brutal beatings.[48] Frederick Douglass describes such a rebel:

When the poor woman was untied, her back was covered with blood. She was whipped, terribly whipped, but she was not subdued and continued to denounce the overseer and to pour upon him every vile epithet of which she could think.[49]

Many women, however, did manage to escape. Best known among these and known to Gloria Richardson, was Harriet Tubman. Born into slavery, Tubman escaped alone in 1849. Upon reaching freedom in Philadelphia, she realized that

> I had crossed the line which I had so long been dreaming. I was free, but there was no one to welcome me to the land of freedom. I was a stranger in a strange land, and my home, after all, was down in the old cabin quarter, with the old folks, and my brothers and sisters. But to this solemn resolution I came; I was free, and they should be free also; I would make a home for them in the North, and the Lord helping me, I would bring them all here. . . . [50]

Returning numerous times to Maryland, Tubman succeeded in freeing approximately three hundred people, including her parents, rescued in 1857. None of her escapees were ever recaptured. Tubman was a fierce and wily leader who planned the tactics and strategies necessary for the survival of her charges.[51]

She is less well known for her leadership during the Civil War. Tubman helped John Brown plan his attack on Harper's Ferry, and would have accompanied him had she not been ill. Later she led three hundred Black soldiers in a famous June 2, 1863, raid on South Carolina's Combahee River. According to the *Commonwealth*, a Boston newspaper, dated July 10, 1863, Harriet Tubman inspired, originated, and conducted the raid. "Many and many times she has penetrated the enemy's line and discovered their situation and condition, and escaped without injury, but not without extreme hazard."[52]

Therefore, as the anonymous interviewee concludes, "the issue of women's participation had already been resolved" because the history of Black women's activism had preceded the activities of women in SNCC. Black women in SNCC were more concerned about living up to these role models than they were about gender equity in SNCC.[53]

Conclusion

It is clear that Miss Ella Baker's keen understanding of movement mobilization bridged students to the movement and provided an organizational base, an infrastructure, from which the movement could be bridged to the masses. SNCC, as a bridging organization, possessed a philosophy of leadership that facilitated the leadership of those who would ordinarily be excluded from formal leadership positions. Although women were not primary formal bridge leaders, because of the decentralized nature of power within SNCC and the need, after 1963, to expand the formal leadership tier, several women held titled positions as secondary formal bridge leaders. Women, it has been shown, are better able to obtain power where power relations are decentralized.

Several other arguments have been presented regarding women's participation. First, women's official positions did not always reflect their power. Leadership power, within the context of social movements, is not limited to the ability to make national decisions regarding tactics, strategies, and goals, but also includes the ability to influence formal leaders, represent the local and/or organization's constituency, harness the emotions of the constituency to sustain movement momentum, and inspire collective action in others. Women community bridge leaders, and those who later became secondary bridge leaders, acted in this manner even though their official positions were either untitled, titled in a unique way, or inadequately reflected their activities. The official mislabeling of women's actual work served as a means of giving legitimacy to women's positions of power without violating the norms surrounding legitimate authority figures. For example, Diane Nash was clearly more than an office manager, but she operated as a community bridge leader and never possessed a secondary bridge leadership title. Additionally, SNCC women often preferred untitled positions because titles meant that they were confined to positions that maintained gender norms. Untitled positions often brought the freedom to work semiautonomously and therefore exercise their leadership capabilities.

Moreover, I have shown that the community bridge leader's power increases during situations of organizational strain or crisis when normative views of authority break down and women receive greater external visibility—that is, that of the media and masses—as well as an increased visibility within the organization. Organizational strain may be defined as a situation in which the primary and/or secondary organization's primary formal and secondary leaders are either unable or unwilling to act to lead the masses. The situation that has become uncontrollable—for example, protest marches or Freedom Rides—may be one that was initiated through rational decision making and organizational planning but in practice fell apart. In such situations, community bridge leaders gain visibility.

Moreover, it has been illustrated that one's leadership position, as well as one's organization's position, within the movement sector can act as a powerful determinant in decision making. Specifically, primary formal leaders of primary organizations are often constrained by their relationship to the state. The foci of these leaders is in marked contrast to bridge organizations, whose allegiance is primarily with the constituency while relations with the state remain peripheral.

In this chapter, as well as in previous and subsequent chapters, several instances of protest in which rational planning was not always possible have been discussed. Although this in no way suggests that the civil rights movement was disorganized and unplanned, what it does suggest is that even when activities are planned, events emerge that either stifle the original plans or create disorder. In this sense, spontaneity and emotions are not divorced from planned action. It is during these crises, when the primary formal and secondary leaders are unavailable, that community bridge leaders emerge and act as formal leaders. Such an emergence is generally short-lived. Likewise, such leadership emerges when the organization expands and must draw upon these leaders as formal leaders, even if temporarily.

Finally, it is clear that young African-American women were influenced by the activism of their predecessors as well as older women in the movement. As older professional and community bridge leaders, these women inspired confidence in those who would risk their lives to change the oppressive system.

SEVEN

Race, Class, and Culture Matter

THE POWERFUL ROLE MODELS provided by older Black women were significant not only to young Black women but also to young White women. Women felt empowered by their participation in the movement. Although much has been written about gendered relationships in the Student Non-Violent Coordinating Committee, most of it has been about the relationships between White women and Black men,[1] a focus which is nonrepresentative of the majority of gendered relations between men and women activists. The analyses of these relationships has tended to focus on Black men's sexism, Black men's lust for White women, and Black women's racism toward White women.

McAdam and Rothschild, in particular, and Evans, to a lesser extent, have focused attention on the sexual relationships of Black men and White women. They contend that White women were sexually exploited in SNCC. This, along with women's relegation to household and clerical labor, supports their thesis of sexism within SNCC. They do not, however, sufficiently consider the gender relationships of Black women and Black men in the movement except within the context of Black male and White female relationships. None of the authors in question considered the relationships between Black men and Black women as important to their gendered analyses. Thus, they are left with only a partial analysis of the gender relations as they relate to sexism in SNCC.

Likewise, Evans and McAdam and Rothschild have taken up the thesis that

Black men seduced, raped, and exploited White women. During the Women in the Civil Rights Movement Conference held in Atlanta in 1988, Rothschild presented her thesis, whereby many Black women, who had been active in SNCC, asserted that White women came to the South to experience a sexual encounter with Black men. Both theses—of the Black man as sexual beast and the White woman as sexually loose—are culturally symbolic and fraught with political implications. As in much of the Old South, the former thesis suggests that Black males, if allowed to do so, actively seek to exploit White women. For example, Rothschild notes:

> Black men "in search of their manhood" were persistent and aggressive. If a woman refused them, they called her a racist. . . . Accusations and verbal abuse were not the only pressure that women volunteers faced. Some White women were raped by Black men in the movement.[2]

This approach reinforces the racist view that Black males are sexually driven beasts, a theme that has resonated in America for centuries. Ida B. Wells addressed this issue in her research, challenging White assertions that lynching was justified on the grounds that Black men were beasts with the uncontrollable desire to rape White women. Wells's research on 728 lynchings showed that only one-third even alleged rape. Moreover, Wells found that facts were often distorted and White women's advances ignored. In many cases, the lynch victims were even women and children. Wells also noted that several Black men who were lynched were independently wealthy and that lynching was a means of keeping Black men in their place.[3]

Likewise, the portrayal of White women as delicate, innocent victims and Black women as hostile and strong is not new, as it provided part of the rationale for slavery. In accounts of Black women in SNCC, they are characterized as the feared Amazons. Evans states.

> A white woman asked whether she experienced any hostility from black women, responded, "Oh, tons and tons. I was afraid of black women, very afraid." Though she admired them and was continually awed by their courage and strength, her sexual relationships with Black men placed a barrier between herself and black women.[4]

Evan's concludes that "the rising anger of Black women would soon become a powerful force within SNCC, creating a barrier that shared womanhood could not transcend."[5] Here these strong Black women are blamed for the barriers between themselves and White women. Throughout the texts, White women are portrayed as victims of their own guilt, as well as the aggression of Black men. Evans, in quoting Nan Grogan, a White volunteeer, states that "women found it 'much harder to say no to the advances of a black guy because of the strong possibility of that being taken as racist."[6] White women are portrayed as victims of Black men's own racism and of their desire to prove themselves to be nonracists.

Black women are portrayed as standing on the sidelines, filled with anger toward White women. The authors ascribe this anger to Black women's feelings of inferiority. We are not told about the positive intimate relationships between Black men and Black women. We are led to believe that most Black men in SNCC sought the company of White women. Can this be true? How many alleged instances of rape existed? Although even one instance should be considered tragic, it is unfortunate that these few cases of rape and sexual exploitation became the basis for a feminist analysis of SNCC. Moreover, it is the relationships of White women that have taken center stage in the feminist analyses of a Black organization. As Dinky Romilly, in critiquing existing accounts of SNCC, notes:

> We were in an organization that was led by Black men and women predominantly. It was a Black organization. And that was another thing, you know, that was, I think . . . been much misunderstood. The White people in SNCC were always there as participants, not taking leadership from the Black leaders of the organization. There were very few white people in SNCC that were really in any kind of leadership position. Therefore, I always felt as if I had an incredibly and unique privileged opportunity that most White people in this country have never had. And that is to work in a situation where there was dedication, love, commitment, and incredible success in the completely Black-led organization. So, I guess, the thing that I'm left with after all these years and looking back on it is: the bottom line is really racism . . . that people have made a big deal out of this issue of the Black men and the White women because it sells, and it's exciting or titillating or something. I think the reason is because the culture is still, or society is still, so unbelievably racist.[7]

Unfortunately, the approach of such researchers has provided but a glimpse of the complexity of race, class, gender, and culture in these relationships. The failure to do so has led these theorists to fall into the trap of supporting culturally defined stereotypical images of Black men, White women, and Black women.

Also problematic has been the focus on Freedom Summer. The Freedom Summer program was designed by SNCC and other movement organizations to develop a cadre of voter registrants, largely with the calculated use of White volunteers chosen because they could draw greater media attention. Evans, who does interview a broader range of participants, lumps Freedom Summer participants with more long-term workers without distinguishing their experiences. While Freedom Summer represents a portion of SNCC's history, it is not representative of the organization's gendered relationships because the volunteers came to SNCC long after the organization's inception and were there on a temporary basis.

Even more troubling is the fact that the voices of Black women participants in SNCC have been muted. What these studies have not done is to examine the relationships between Black men and Black women, a relationship which was and is profoundly influenced by their shared experiences in a racist society. Then, as now, racism shaped all relationships in some way, including those between Black men and Black women. And it was within this context of pervasive racism that the relationships between Blacks and Whites, men and women, were formed in SNCC.

SNCC, as has already been discussed, was an organization whose primary task was to bridge the masses to the movement. In doing so, SNCC's community bridge leaders often bypassed those formal local leaders who were reluctant to participate in the movement and cultivated the informal local leaders, creating a strong indigenous bridge leadership tier in the movement. SNCC, more than any other organization, worked in the pockets of the Deep South, attempting to bring the message of the movement to those who were uninformed or resisted participation for fear of their lives. In this context of a deeply racist environment, men and women, Blacks and Whites, sought change. Yet their experiences were necessarily shaped by their identities. Thus, women community bridge leaders' experiences differed significantly based on their culture, class, and race; previous, narrowly defined analyses of gender relations in SNCC are therefore only partial understandings of these dynamics.

Interpersonal Relationships in the Student Non-Violent Coordinating Committee

To clearly understand the gendered relations in SNCC, one must first understand that this organization was primarily led by Black activists. Whites, regardless of their sex, were neither primary nor secondary formal leaders. The highest level of leadership for Whites was either the community bridge leadership tier, of which there were very few, or the mainstream bridge leadership tier, which comprised the majority of White participants. The tasks of the latter were to provide a bridge to the mainstream, primarily through White institutions—for example, universities, service organizations, and affiliates. As Casey Hayden, a White woman and a mainstream bridge leader whose participation was central to SNCC, states, "this was really the coming to the fore of Black men—young Black men. . . . Black women had always been strong in the local community. . . . Now men could come forth. . . . It was a rising up of Black men."[8]

The White women who came to SNCC prior to 1963 tended to respect the position of SNCC as a Black organization in which they, as well as White males, could provide support as mainstream bridge leaders. Casey Hayden adds:

> I felt that my role was primarily a supportive role. I think that white women mostly felt that way. . . . That it was important for the leadership image to be Black. . . . That it was important for blacks to own that. My sense was that Black women also felt that about the men. They were not that assertive and aggressive.[9]

Though it was the time for young Black men to come forward, Black women's positions were of equal importance and differed significantly from that of White women's. Many Black women were viewed by SNCC participants as leaders. Cynthia Washington, a secondary bridge leader and Black project director in Bolivar County, elaborates this point:

> I didn't realize then that having my own project made a lot of difference in how I was perceived and treated. And I did not see what I was doing as exceptional. The community women I worked with on projects were respected and admired for their strength and endurance. They worked hard in the cotton fields or white folks' houses,

raised and supported their children, yet found the time and energy to be involved in struggle for their people. They were typical rather than unusual.[10]

Previous accounts of women's movement participation have emphasized the degree of sexism within the organization.[11] Both Evans and McAdam highlight, as a source of conflict between men and women in SNCC, sexist treatment of women within SNCC and its incongruence with the organization's philosophy. This, they conclude, provided much of the impetus for Casey Hayden and Mary King—both White and longtime SNCC mainstream bridge leaders—to produce a paper outlining sexism in SNCC.[12] The paper was presented at a group retreat in Waveland, Mississippi, and is generally referred to as the Waveland paper by scholars. This paper, in fact, was not a product of their concerns over their status in SNCC. Both women have acknowledged that they had little difficulty with their treatment as women in SNCC. As Mary King recalls, "our status in the movement was never the issue."[13] Casey Hayden agrees with this: "I was in the interworkings. I had really privileged status. I didn't have any real argument about my place in SNCC."[14] "What I recall experiencing in SNCC was the great lifting of sex role expectations and the freedom that ensued."[15]

Her ideas regarding feminism did not evolve from sexist treatment within SNCC. To the contrary, she was empowered in SNCC in ways that she never would have been in mainstream society. This personal sense of mastery gained from experiences in SNCC fused with other influences in her life, particularly her participation in YWCA activities and books by feminists, to create her feminist consciousness. Many leaders in the YWCA had been active in the fight for women's rights since the 1930s. During a conference, they developed a workshop on sex roles that Hayden attended. Around the same time, she began reading Betty Friedan's *The Feminine Mystique* and Simone de Beauvoir's *The Second Sex*. These influences, as well as her close association with Miss Ella Baker, led to an emerging consciousness of women's various statuses in society.[16]

After the summer of 1965, SNCC was in a state of turmoil. Casey Hayden felt that the timing of the Waveland paper was inappropriate because the issue at the SNCC conference centered on the organization's structural difficulties. Hayden elaborates this point:

> At the Waveland meeting it was in the question of SNCC's overall direction that the issue of nonviolence in style and substance as reflected in internal structure and in program, was being raised. In my mind, given the nature of SNCC heretofore, this issue was the issue of feminism and patriarchy. While there were, as I said before, many new and complicating elements present, I believe the two biggest were the size of the meeting (and of SNCC) and the crisis in sense of direction once the summer project ended.[17]

Judy Richardson, a Black activist, agrees and felt that dealing with this issue could only create more divisiveness in an already crumbling organization. Casey Hayden further emphasized that the problem was not one of sexism but of feminism and patriarchy, as manifested in SNCC's emerging hierarchical structure and the proposed shift from a nonviolent philosophy. In short, SNCC was debating whether or not to develop a centralized power structure with a clearly defined hierarchy, a reorganizing which those known as the "Freedom Highs" opposed. Hayden saw this as a clear step toward a patriarchal organization much like that of the SCLC. This certainly would have created a situation in which women would lose a great degree of power since, as already discussed, the decentralized, nonhierarchical nature of SNCC provided more free spaces and thus more leadership mobility for women.

In the summer of 1964, SNCC had begun the Freedom Summer project in which volunteers, mostly White, spent time in the South and assisted in voter registration and the Freedom School. This had not only increased the number of SNCC workers but also created a situation in which the majority of SNCC participants were White. Unlike the original White volunteers, the majority of new workers were unaware of the social mores of the South. They were college educated and possessed some organizational skills that many rural volunteers lacked. Moreover, it was the first time that more than a very few Whites were asserting themselves as community bridge leaders. Mary Lane, a Black field secretary and indigenous bridge leader in Greenwood, Mississippi, states:

> Summer of '64 people came from the North and could do the job better than those who were there before. This made people who were learning withdraw. Eventually those inferior workers were moved out into the field and the ones who did it better stayed on staff with positions.[18]

Many of the SNCC workers resented the presence of the volunteers regardless of their sex. Mary Lane, who helped recruit her peers to the movement, viewed the summer project as "destroying the indigenous base of SNCC." She and those in her project had not wanted an influx of White volunteers. Additionally, the media tended to focus on acts of violence against the White volunteers as opposed to the Black activists. Lane explains, "We've been getting beaten-up for years trying to integrate lunch counters, movies, and so-on, but nobody ever paid us no attention or wrote about us."[19]

With the large influx of volunteers, structural problems emerged. SNCC was founded on a decentralized structure in which group consensus was required. With the large number of volunteers, this became impossible. The Waveland meeting focused on these issues. Much of the debate centered on the need for SNCC to become a totally Black organization. Within this context, the Waveland paper on sexism was presented by two White women. Though sexism within SNCC may have been an issue for some Black women, it was viewed by most as divisive. It did, however, gain a modicum of support from Black men and Black women such as Bob Moses, Donna Richards, Jean Wheeler Smith, and Stokely Carmichael. Despite Stokely Carmichael's oft-cited joke that "the only position for women in SNCC is prone," both Hayden and King acknowledge that Carmichael was very supportive of the points the women presented at the retreat.[20] They situate his joke within the context of his frustration over sexual liaisons interfering with activism during the summer of 1964.[21] However, in the final analysis, given the internal difficulties and the divergent positions of Black and White women within the organization, the priority for Black women and Black men was the salvation of SNCC. Though Black women within SNCC operated under some gendered constraints, they did not share the same position as White women.

There were practical reasons for the primary positions of White women's leadership as mainstream bridge leaders. Though Faith Holsaert and Penny Patch were field workers in Mississippi, and they operated as community bridge leaders in ways other White women did not, most White women before 1964 occupied staff positions. One of the central realities within the South was that the presence of a White woman in a Black community provoked anger among local Whites. In a 1966 report on "The Stresses of the White Female Worker in the Civil Rights Movement in the South," Dr. Alvin F. Poussaint writes:

> The white woman stands at the very center of the "Southern-way-of-life" and for the Negro is the tabooed . . . object. It has been in her name and for her glory that the white South has oppressed, brutalized, lynched and mutilated the black man for centuries. Violation of the socio-sexual taboos surrounding the white woman has meant instant death for the Negro, particularly the black male.[22]

Of course, most of the alleged violations of sociosexual taboos were trumped up. Nonetheless, the reality was that even the accusation of such violations could result in the death of Black male workers. Thus, except for a few, most White women were not accepted in the field. And the field was where one's acts of courage and relative autonomy as a community bridge leader gained Black women secondary formal leadership positions. Likewise, most of the White females were coming south from northern Universities or colleges. Their knowledge was often used for fund-raising or for offering information or support to the Friends of SNCC groups outside of the South. All three northern Coodinators—Casey Hayden, Constancia (Dinky) Romilly, and Betty Garmen—were White women. Such positions, which served as a mainstream bridge primarily to White institutions and students, often necessitated office duty. Thus, while the bridges Black community bridge leaders built were between the politics of the movement and potential constituents in rural isolated communities, the bridges White mainstream bridge leaders constructed were primarily to other Whites or college students. Of her position in SNCC, Constance Curry, a White mainstream bridge leader who came to SNCC at its inception, states:

> It was clear that my role had to be different from the SNCC workers. And they said, "You don't need to be arrested, you don't need to go to jail. Someone has to stay on the outside to tell what is happening." So I was an observer all over the place. I went to Nashville and saw the brutality at Woolworth's, and the same thing . . . in Augusta, Georgia. Then I would call the National Student Association in Philadelphia and tell them what was happening or I would call the press. Here in Atlanta I would call the NAACP Legal Defense Fund about bail and bonds. I was an observer for the outside world and a link in telling what was going on.[23]

Moreover, most White women's leadership emanated from the Atlanta office, where women's leadership potential was more regulated because it was the center of operations for many of the male primary bridge leaders. Dinky Romilly was a White mainstream bridge leader and northern coordinator who came to SNCC in 1962. Her job was to raise money, coordinate support activities such as demonstrations, notify leaders when people were arrested, and get the media involved. She explains:

> Well, I was in the national office [Atlanta], so Jim Forman was there, Ruby Doris Robinson was there, Julian Bond was there, Mary King was there . . . the printing press was there. The newspaper was published there. We called it the "Student Voice." So . . . many of the big heavies were there and they were articulating the goals of the organization. . . .
>
> [SNCC] had a loose, decentralized structure, but it had a kind of a hidden central structure. In fact, in '64 and '65 . . . what we called a sort of "Freedom High" movement [a push to keep hierarchy out] within SNCC became so prevalent. One of the reasons was that people were criticizing this [structure]—what they perceived to be this little cadre of people who really ran SNCC. But of course out in the field on a day-to-day basis, it was such a huge organization and it sprang up so quickly. And there were very little formal structures in place. People could run around and kind of do what they wanted, and they would get called on the carpet at a staff meeting, but it was decentralized in that sense.[24]

Racism not only influenced Black male and female relationships but also defined the interactions of Black men and women to White men and women. Thus, White women with power were in the Atlanta office, a place where gendered norms were more closely maintained and monitored. Black women had greater movement and were able to occupy the free spaces in the field and therefore to act upon their leadership skills in this context.

Race, Class, Gender, and Culture in SNCC

Significant differences existed among SNCC participants based upon their race, class, gender, and culture. These constructs contributed to their experiences and positions in the movement. Whites from the North came to the movement largely ignorant of the social mores of the South. But early White participants in SNCC were mostly from the South, and because of this they understood the need to refrain from taking over or perceiving themselves as leaders. Dottie Zellner, a white mainstream bridge leader, explains:

> I was always very conscious of the fact that this was a *Black* movement led by Black people, and I don't want to give any impression that I'm taking away from that. They did not go into this to establish good relationships with White people. They went in to get their rights. And I knew enough, I was smart enough to know, that this was *the* central issue and by god I was going to get down there and be with them.[25]

Not one of the White women interviewed who had been part of SNCC's staff prior to Freedom Summer saw herself as a movement leader, though it is clear that these women often contributed as mainstream bridge leaders. Thus leadership was not simply a gender issue but also a cultural issue and a racial issue. Penny Patch, a White community bridge leader who more than others acted in a manner similar to Black community bridge leaders, acknowledges the limitations that race placed on her mobility. Explaining, she states that "race, class, everything influenced the roles that we played and the jobs that we did."[26] Prathia Hall Wynn, a Black secondary formal bridge leader, elaborates:

> The first White women that I met in the movement were southern White women. They were Mary King and Connie Curry and Casey Hayden and they were very strong and capable White women, but they came out of an entirely different ethos. They came out of that whole pedestalization and trivialization of women that the southern power establishment imposed on them.
>
> Now if you add to that the factor of race, then clearly they would not have been as comfortable asserting themselves in leadership positions as Black women. . . . so that they would have an appropriate deference for the community in which they had come to participate. And for the women that I just mentioned, I think that that was one of the reasons that they enjoyed tremendous respect also. . . . Dottie Zellner would be another woman who was northern, but was married to Bob, who was from Alabama. But what I am saying is that I never saw those women attempting to lead a Black movement.[27]

Wynn suggests that White women came to the movement out of a different sociohistorical context than did Black women. Certainly, cultural literacy and respect for the moral mandate of Black leadership account for much of the deference shown by White women participants, especially among those who joined earlier, since most of them were from the South. But in addition, Wynn believes that asserting leadership was more difficult for White than for Black women because White women's sense of themselves as capable in the world was weaker, owing to radical differences in experience. Black women asserted themselves daily, always faced with the strictures of racism and, in many instances, poverty. Wynn suggests that "there is a sense in which our social incubator in the Black community trained and nurtured Black women to do whatever was necessary."[28] This illustrates that only by factoring in race, class, and culture can the different experiences of Black and White women in the movement be adequately explained.

Before Freedom Summer brought an influx of non-Southerners into the movement, White women understood that their race and gender limited their actions. These constraints were not entirely imposed by the internal structure or leadership of SNCC, but derived from beliefs about White women encoded in Southern culture. Penny Patch believes that "there were always some limitations because I was White and particularly [because] I was a White female. My participation in certain kinds of activities would put the Black community at a lot of risk. There was some caretaking and some limitations because of it."[29] Still, Patch felt empowered by her participation in the movement.

I was a White woman and even given that I was able to do so much more than anywhere else in society. I worked on voter-registration campaigns, door to door. I helped organize the farmer's cooperatives, organized mass meetings. I was in demonstrations, and I also did a fair share of office work, but I did all those other things. There literally was a moment in time in Mississippi when I was one of the people that would drive out to plantations at night and visit people, sharecropper families . . . in their homes and talk about voter registration. Personally, looking back on that, I don't know if that was a smart thing to do at all [laughter] from any perspective. There was an immense amount of leeway and one would hope that we all exercised a certain amount of judgment and sometimes we did and sometimes we didn't.[30]

These White women understood that the limitations placed upon them came out of the culture they were working to change. Dottie Zellner adds, "This was the southern racist's worst nightmare . . . the Black man/White woman pair and to see a White woman at the head of a project working with a Black man? That would have been very difficult."[31]

Faith Holsaert, a White community bridge leader and another exception in that she too worked in the field, elaborates:

I mean when Greenwood, Mississippi, exploded in the spring of 1963, we sent, oh, actually we sent an all-Black male staff . . . and we didn't send the Whites because they would have created more problems than it would have solved.[32]

Of her own experience in the movement, Faith recognized the significance of her race and explains the differences between Prathia, with whom she eventually worked in the field, and herself:

So [Prathia] had a male role and skills that I certainly didn't have [laughter], and so she had the greater freedom of movement. And in terms of safety . . . the movement . . . wasn't just protecting me as an individual. . . . It was a rule, in order to protect local people and movement people, that no Black man should be traveling alone with me and some other things like that. And because [for White women the] movement was more circumscribed . . . my first few months in Albany I did a lot of stuff in the office. And I think that . . . was both gender and race determined . . . but I have never felt . . . that SNCC was a sexist experience [or that] my role was limited.[33]

Constance Curry, a mainstream bridge leader, recounting an experience she and Casey Hayden had at a civil rights conference, recalls:

Casey was there on a panel and pointed out that when you are engaged, like we were, in a fight for dignity, equality, justice . . . and plus the fact that feminism wasn't really defined back then . . . you don't really think about things in terms of gender or the male-female thing. . . . After Casey's presentation, a young Black woman stood up and said, "Well, my observation is that you were discriminated against and just didn't know it." Then I recall Casey saying, "Let me tell you something. You don't tell me what you think I thought or what I felt back then." It looks like there was male domination, but we didn't feel that, and it's really hard to explain. I would have known it. It just wasn't part of the ball game.... And a lot of people say, "Well, maybe the reason you felt so empowered was because of that old adage that behind every good man there's a good woman. Over the years that has been empowering in a sick crippling way." But it wasn't that. We never felt, "Here we are doing these things so that our men can go out there and have all the power and the glory."[34]

Thus, White women community and mainstream bridge leaders understood the constraints surrounding their participation and did not attribute their experiences to sexism in the movement. Their bravery and their support were greatly appreciated by those in SNCC. However, SNCC members often distinguished between the White women who were in SNCC prior to Freedom Summer and those who came during and afterwards. Muriel Tillinghast, a Black secondary formal bridge leader, suggests that "there was a big distinction. Those who had come prior to '64 were the family, those who came after were basically volunteers."[35] Dottie Zellner expands this point, "I think that, on the one hand, while there were a lot of clashes in the early days, there was also a profound trust that was established. ... Now later on, the racial issue became much greater in '64."[36]

Black women and White women sustained friendships throughout their participation in SNCC, and many still keep in touch. Penny Patch believes that "in the early years there were very close working relationships between Black and White women and there were some very close friendships."[37]

The major conflicts between Blacks and Whites in SNCC did not emerge until Freedom Summer. It was a difficult period for SNCC and perhaps for that reason is overrepresented in scholarly literature, but the period is atypical of most of the history of the organization. Dottie Zellner remarked that "some researchers are missing that there are really well-defined periods of time" in SNCC. She explains that "before the fall of 1963, [SNCC] was a rather small, self-enclosed group. Maybe thirty to forty people that we're talking about."[38]

This tight-knit group operated in a supportive manner. Black SNCC community bridge leader Jean Wheeler Smith Young describes the differences in SNCC's organization prior to 1964 and after Freedom Summer:

Now, I do see a difference in SNCC before '65 and after '65. After '65, I don't know what happened.... Before '65, it was very loosely structured, very equalitarian, an organization with easy entry and easy acceptance and a lot of respect for whoever was there, depending on whatever they were doing. Then after '65, it became more of a big organization with its own machine.... [Prior to '65 it was] very collegial and no problem. Then later on, like any distinction [referring to conflicts between Blacks and Whites], the distinctions became more established just because I think the central organizational structure was weakened after '65, and this business about conflicts between the Whites and Blacks and so on evolved out of that weakening of the structure of the organization.[39]

Prior to 1964, SNCC had conceived of the idea of encouraging a flood of White students from outside of the region to join the Southern struggle as a strategy to gain more media attention. The beating of White middle-class students would shift national sympathies toward the activists in a way that violence against Black students and local activists could not. Even earlier than the summer of 1964, SNCC conducted a massive number of interviews and processed numerous applications. But with the acceptance of over one thousand White students to the SNCC projects in Mississippi came a multitude of problems. As Jean Wheeler Smith Young explains, "White women and men who came late, 1964 and on, were not as distinguished a group of people, I don't think. I don't think they had the character and the commitment, in general, that the earlier group had."[40]

Many of the fears SNCC workers had about their actions triggering violent reprisals were borne out. Earlier, those who worked in Mississippi had opposed the Freedom Summer, in part expecting the huge influx and racial mix to cause racist attacks to escalate. Dorie Ladner, a Black SNCC community bridge leader in Mississippi, recalls:

> During the meetings when Bob, Hollis, Curtis, McArthur, Cotton, and others from Mississippi were meeting—Jessie Harris [too]—some concerns were raised . . . about the safety of staff with the state of Mississippi, the Blacks who may have lost their lives with White people coming in. Also, some people didn't feel that they needed that many people coming in to organize, for whatever reason. Some felt that they might be overshadowed by other people coming in. There were a variety of reasons.[41]

These reasons were not generally gendered, except as they related to the safety of Black male workers working with White women in the field. However, White volunteers, both men and women, were indeed a liability in many ways, as Prathia Hall Wynn explains:

> You had a massive project. You had extraordinary issues of safety. You had White students, male and female, who had never had to "take low," to use the idiom, for anything. They never had to not speak their mind. They never had to not do whatever they felt like doing. Now . . . whatever they did they were doing with Black people, which immediately put everybody's lives at risk . . . without the . . . period of proving themselves, of learning. . . . They had not had the learning period that the people who had been involved from the early sixties had. And those people had major responsibilities. You had younger students who had to be oriented in a hurry. And there is no way that you could give the same kind of responsibility to those people in that situation.[42]

The status of the Freedom Summer volunteers was greatly determined by a combination of their Whiteness, wealth, and education. Most of the volunteers were White, middle-class college students from regions other than the South. Their lack of experience and unfamiliarity with Southern mores were sometimes central obstacles to leadership within SNCC, as Joanne Grant, a SNCC participant, elaborates:

Frankly . . . there was less trust of, say, the northern White male student from Yale than [of] a local Black from McComb. Just normal common sense. And I would think that they would have used a White kid from Yale or Harvard in a nonthreatening way, although look what happened in '64 [the murders of three civil rights workers in Mississippi, two of whom were White, Michael Schwerner and Andrew Goodman, and one of whom was Black, James Chaney]. . . . So, you know, errors were made, but I do think they tended to protect the dopes from the North and also, you know, they didn't want a Yale kid walking up to a plantation and saying, "You know, 'why don't you register to vote?' " So they had to use their judgment, and they did.[43]

Muriel Tillinghast expands this point:

They were ignorant of southern protocal and in many cases ignorant of organizing skills and . . . those were the two chief problems. They had to be honed in order to be useful. In Mississippi, when you saw a Black person and a White person without an obvious [hierarchical relationship] you knew they were civil rights workers. And as such, both of their lives were in jeopardy.[44]

Constance Curry lends support to the view that some northern White women who came to work in the Freedom Summer project just didn't understand that their presence endangered the lives of other workers, especially Black men. She describes the problem:

When we would go to South Carolina, Casey [Hayden] and I were riding with Reggie Robinson, who was Black. He bought a chauffeur's cap and made Casey and I sit in the back seat. We had a wonderful time. On other occasions, when we would pull up in a filling station, we would make Reggie get on the floor in the back seat. It was a big risk factor and we were very conscious of it. That's what used to make us mad about some of the White women who would come from the North. This was all very new and very romantic and very titillating for them. And a lot of us resented the fact that they didn't know that they were putting these young Black men at high risk.[45]

For White women working in the cultural context of the Deep South, gender was salient in that their presence intensified the anger of southern Whites. Particularly in these rural communities, for a Black man to be seen with a White woman was a major breach of southern mores and sometimes laws. Moreover, any White volunteers stood out in Black rural communities. If young Whites and Blacks were seen together, southerners immediately suspected that they were civil rights workers. Such breaches branded the Black as a troublemaker and one who needed to be put in his or her place, in the form of beatings for women and lynchings for men. The level of community outrage was only made worse by any culturally insensitive behavior on the part of the White outsiders, acts which undermined the trust-building efforts of community bridge leaders and increased the likelihood of reprisals against all Blacks, locals, and movement activists. Veteran movement workers determined that the new civil rights volunteers required careful supervision and protection in order to minimize the potential damage of their blundering. This pragmatic strategy was essential to counteract the newcomers' lack of protest experience and ignorance of the cultural context in which the movement operated.

Northern Black women encountered this buffering strategy as well, since they were usually as abrasive to local cultural norms as their White counterparts, as Jean Wheeler Smith Young explains:

> Well, see, southern students were [at] first like Joyce Ladner. They had the Dixie level provision, so they . . . I think they were more . . . central to the functioning of the organization than the northern students. And I regard them as being more . . . I guess "tougher," 'cause they lived through all of this and I was new to it. [They] were doing it for eighteen years. I just got there.[46]

While Young, as a Black woman, eventually became a bridge leader in rural Mississippi, initially she had a lot to learn about southern culture. "When I went to Mississippi, there was this wonderful opening up of the culture . . . the music, everything was just so vital and alive."[47] Young explains that she began to identify more with Black culture, something she had not been as exposed to while growing up in Detroit.

Judy Richardson, a Black mainstream bridge leader who worked mainly in the Atlanta office, grew up in the predominately White New York City suburb of Tarrytown. She argues that the discouragement she encountered when she requested to join rural operations was based more on culture than gender.

> I was this innocent little thing coming out of college, so I'm not sure . . . it was because of who I was rather than the fact that I was female. . . . I used to say to Foreman, "I want to go to the fields," and Foreman said "Yeah-yeah-yeah". . . . So it wasn't so much . . . 'cause there were women in the field. . . . And . . . when Ruby Doris spoke, people listened. Certainly when Miss Baker spoke, *everybody* listened. So it was very hard to be a full-blown sexist for men in the context of the kind of women who were in SNCC. The guys knew Miss Baker . . . they called her the God-mother of SNCC. . . . The guys had a great, great deal of respect for . . . Ruby Doris. She really was their lifeline if they were in the field. They would talk to Ruby more than they would talk to Foreman. If they needed something, I think the sense was . . . [that] Foreman was essential to the organization, but he was not necessarily the field person. Ruby was the field person; Ruby was the organizer, a field kind of organizer.[48]

And while the Atlanta office adhered more closely to gender norms, the unique titles of Miss Baker as "outside consultant" and Ruby Doris Smith Robinson as "other"—neither precluded their leadership activities nor diluted the respect accorded them. Additionally, when the large influx of students met the decentralized structure of SNCC, problems developed in the organization's ability to monitor field activities. With over one thousand students, it was difficult to weed out the mentally unstable. Dorie Ladner describes the difficulties:

We got a lot of kooks from both races, Black and White. I knew a Black guy from Chicago who was a kleptomaniac. And one white guy who got off the bus who was burning himself with matches and cigarettes. So I'm saying you had extremes on both ends.[49]

The central leadership of SNCC attempted to monitor the situations as best they could. They were, however, preoccupied with survival. SNCC activities in the deepest pockets of the South were extraordinarily dangerous. Dorie Ladner and many other participants described feeling as though they were in a war. Muriel Tillinghast confirmed that she attempted to curb the behavior of one young man who was attempting to sexually exploit some White women.

Some of the project people had never had responsibilities like that before. For a few, it went to their heads. There was a young man in one of the areas who was holding checks to force young, White women to sleep with him. Well, when I heard that, I got in my car and drove to his site with another project director.[50]

Tillinghast believes that she was accompanied by Cynthia Washington, a powerful and strong secondary bridge leader, and that the two of them confronted the young man, instructing him never to pull a stunt like that again.

It didn't take us but a minute to straighten that out. I didn't have any indication that he had gotten his way with the women. . . . This issue never repeated itself there or any other place, to my knowledge. We cleaned that up fast.[51]

Still, Tillinghast and others who were a part of the leadership of SNCC had difficulty monitoring such greatly expanded movement activity. Most of those interviewed suggested that, while some abuses may well have occurred, neither sexual exploitation nor sexism ran rampant in SNCC; they are perplexed that so many researchers have focused on these aspects. My interview subjects concede that White women were more often relegated to office work, primarily because they were educated and skilled at writing. They also acknowledge that White women, even more than White men, found their movement work confined, attributing that to the dictates of the mystique that surrounded White womanhood in the South. By their presence, openly visible White women intensified the hatred aimed at all field workers. These constraints, however, mainly flow out of the various clashes of culture, class, and race. To reduce this complexity to simple gender bias does a disservice to the women and men of SNCC and to historical research.

Rather, for both the Black and White women interviewed, the problems in SNCC stemmed more from the huge influx of inexperienced workers, regardless of gender. Even Ella Baker suggested that "northern white kids" be kept out of the field. Jo Ann Grant recalls Baker saying, "Let's keep 'em out; let's let the less articulate people run this show, 'cause it's their show".[52] Northern Whites in general were clearly a liability in the field in any number of ways. During her recollections of White movement veteran Casey Hayden, Judy Richardson illustrated the centrality of complex interrelationships of race, class, gender, and culture:

I was thinking, for example, [that] Casey [Hayden] would . . . [know] the southern mores. She knew what to do and what not to do. She knew . . . and there were other White women who had been in the movement for a long time who just understood that there were just things that you did not do. The White women who were coming down from the North, I think, did not understand the rhythms of a southern Black community. And then some of the women who were there early on were women who had come out of the South. . . . They had a sense of some things that I think some of the northern White women did not have. And I think that was not . . . in terms of Black-White relationships but just in terms of general sexual freedom stuff. . . . For example, there was a young White couple who had come down during the summer of '64 in Mississippi and were living in the home of a Black family, and were living as a married couple. And in the middle of the summer they decided they were going to get married, and it was absolutely scandalous to the Black family because they [had] assumed they [were] living . . . in [their] home as a married couple, and it was a disrespectful thing to that Black family. Now, I think that a southern White couple would have known that. I think the problem was that they were northern. And that had nothing to do with White or Black.[52]

With the flood of Whites into the movement, and the passage of the Voting Rights Act, SNCC's course began to flounder. Many Black activists believed that their organization was being taken over by Whites and were advocating the expulsion of all White participants. At the same time, with passage of the Voting Rights Act, SNCC's usefulness in the South now needed to go beyond voter registration, and other types of alternative activisms were unclear. There were also significant divisions among the core activists, between those who felt a growing need for a more formal organization and those—the "Freedom Highs"—who wanted it to remain nonhierarchical and decentralized. Corresponding hostilities arose over these issues that extended beyond historical documentation of the conflicts between Black men and White women and between Black and White women. Judy Richardson clarifies that "there were these tensions between Black and White. . . . And that wasn't just White women. It was Black and White."[54] These tensions, she contends, existed prior to 1965 but were greatly exacerbated by the flood of Whites into SNCC. Bernice Johnson Reagon, a community bridge leader in the Albany, Georgia, movement, elaborates:

There was a growing energy in SNCC that had a growing hostility to White people. And I think there was just [such] a move as White people increased in participating. There was something that reacted against it, because it had been an organization headed up by Blacks that was integrated [and] never kept white people out. But there were tensions that occurred as the numbers shifted, especially around '64. . . . And I think this is a natural kind of tension, under the pressures of the movement, that would happen, so that SNCC evolved increasingly toward a move that would end up with a Black consciousness line, eventually asking all Whites to leave. And I think that White women were not only feeling increasingly something because they were women [but] . . . they were also picking up something because they were White. . . . There was a certain playing out of this Black man–White woman stuff. But it was,

like, part of the stuff that went on, not central to what the movement was and . . .
not central to the social experiences I had. So . . . I think there might be White
women who could tell you a very different story than what I'm telling you.[55]

Indeed, the data presented by researchers, containing the experiences of Freedom Summer White women, provide very different gender experiences from those
of Black and White women who constituted the core of SNCC. Black women, as
well as those who were active in SNCC prior to Freedom Summer, expressed dismay
at the research emphasis on sexual liaisons in the movement. While young people
at the peak of the sexual revolution certainly engaged in intimate relations, they
had little time to do so. Moreover, most of the long-term coupling occurred between those of the same race. Even more significant in the eyes of the respondents
was the fact that few of the researchers even mentioned the couplings of White
men and Black women.

In her fury over recent accounts of the civil rights movement, Cambridge,
Maryland, leader Gloria Richardson exclaimed, "They act like people had a movement so they could have sexual relations!"[56] Many of those interviewed expressed
feelings of exasperation which strengthened their frustration with existing research
and the claim that their story has not been told. Certainly, for all of the Black
and White interviewees, sexual relations were peripheral at best. Bernice Johnson
Reagon explains:

> A lot of the studies have dealt with the sexual activity and sexual partnering as an
> activity in the movement; you were dealing with teenagers and young adults who
> were sexually active. So you had partnering going every way you can imagine between
> people who were risking their lives every day. And I don't know if I have much more
> than that to say about sexual activity in the movement. . . . And I don't know about
> it because it seemed to me that a lot of it was nobody's business.[57]

Although some of the White women interviewed had either married or had
relationships with Black men, they did not feel exploited, as Dottie Zellner
relates:

> I actually think that most people . . . if you took a hundred people, I would say ninety-
> two went down there because they said this is a moral imperative. I think those
> ninety-two would say, "Of course, if I am down there and I find someone who is
> attractive and the opportunity arises, I may very well do something about it." But I
> think . . . those people would have said, "If the opportunity doesn't arise, that's not
> the main reason I'm going. . . ." I mean, lets face it, if sex is your motivation, why
> get killed? We had worked ourselves up into such a state that in the spring of 1964
> I was having nightmares hoping actually that I was going to get run over by a car
> and break my leg so I wouldn't have to go. . . . We knew that it was going to be
> extremely dangerous. When we were interviewing people to go down there we made
> sure that they knew that. So of the one thousand people who came down, I'd say
> 920 came down because this was something they felt they had to do. They had to
> do it for themselves and I think the sexual issue is minor, very minor.[58]

All of the respondents believed that the interracial couplings were few, simply because of the dangerous circumstances in which they lived, as Zellner explains:

> There were a few, but very few. When people talk about this frenetic coupling, they're not talking about even being able to walk down the street together. They're talking about what went on in the Freedom Houses. . . . But if you're talking about an open, stable, committed public relationship in Mississippi, that would be enough to get killed![59]

All of the women asserted that while some interracial relationships took place, the majority of Black men dated Black women. Moreover, they pointed out that some of the interracial couplings occurred between White men and Black women, ignored by the academic literature. Several of the Black women interviewed had dated White men. One early relationship resulted in a marriage between John Purdue and Amanda Purdue, he being White and she Black.[60] Bill Hanson, another White activist, also married a Black woman.[61]

Except for the marriage between Jim Forman and Dinky Romilly, the majority of the Black leaders married other Blacks. Bob Moses married a Black woman; so did Stokely Carmichael, Courtland Cox, Ivanhoe Donaldson, Curtis Hayes, and Hollis Watkins. And the majority of my interviewees had married within their own race: Diane Nash and James Bevel, Cordell Reagon and Bernice Johnson Reagon, Bob Zellner and Dottie Zellner, and many others.

Only three of my Black women interviewees indicated that they were disturbed by the union of Black men and White women, but they each objected for different reasons, none of which rested on interracial relations, per se. One respondent felt that such unions could interfere with the interworkings of SNCC. If leaders were busy having intimate relationships, then they could not be getting their work done. Another believed it was especially inappropriate for the leaders to have White partners, since they were the head of a "family." After Forman left his Black wife Mildred, the relationship he subsequently developed with Dinky Romilly, who was White, was resented mainly for its perceived disruption of the movement "family." This interviewee, however, maintained a friendly relationship with Dinky. In many ways, Dinky was like the stepmother who could not replace one's own mother. The third respondent resented such interracial relationships on the grounds that Black solidarity was broken, but she too developed positive bonds with the White mate. Nowhere was deep hostility toward White women articulated. Disappointment was evident, but it was equally directed at Jim Forman. Most of the older cadre of White men and women were also considered part of the "family," as Gloria Richardson explains:

> I have to tell you something about the movement. It's, whether you're Black or White, people from that time, if they see somebody, it's like [seeing] a long-lost family friend. So I don't see people that often, Black or White, but when I do, I'm really glad to see them. . . . I don't know that many White women . . . that were in the South. I knew some of them, but if I see them, it's like maybe twenty years have elapsed, but you don't have to start back [up] . . . where you left off twenty years ago.

It's like all that didn't happen in between. And then, too, regardless of who it is, it's very strange. It's almost like the same thing that happened to me with some cousins I hadn't seen for, oh, about fifteen years. And then we come together. We take up right where we left off. And that's true with SNCC people.[62]

Moreover, none of the women interviewed could be characterized as women who viewed themselves as inferior to White women. They were empowered by the movement and proud of their Blackness and their beauty. Of Black male activists' views of her, Jean Wheeler Smith states:

I think they thought I was great. They admired the fact that I was brave. They admired my intellect and they were glad to have me using my resources to help them do what they wanted to do. We've stayed together over the years [meaning she and other SNCC activists], and people are repeatedly, over the years, saying the same thing. So I don't have any doubt about that. And never, ever did I feel put down. There was really no problem! That's why the whole thing is kind of . . . a made-up problem.[63]

She continues, explaining her feelings about Black male activists:

I thought that they were brave and exciting. I think I overidealized them. But at the time I thought that they were brave and exciting, and that they had a handle on what it was all about, which is what you're supposed to do when you're twenty years old![64]

Day-to-day relationships between Black men and Black women were permeated with a deep respect and regard for their shared courage. The interviewees often described SNCC as a family and the men as their brothers. Dorie Ladner explains: "I got along with my comrades very well. They were like brothers to me. Closer than my blood kin at certain points in my life because we were bonded. We are still very close."[65]

Gloria Richardson characterizes the working relationships with men as "unisex," in that "they were collaborators in strategy." She "didn't see them as prospective boyfriends or anything." They "were people struggling toward a common goal."[66]

Dispelling Sexual Myths

None of my SNCC interviewees believe that sexual harassment or acts of rape were commonplace. None had heard of any cases in which Black men raped White women. This is not to suggest that sexual assault was completely absent, only that such acts never were endemic, either to SNCC relationships in general or to Black man–White woman relationships in particular.

There was evidence, however, of the widespread use of rape and sexual harassment of Black women by White men in the South. Muriel Tillinghast recounted a story of White men raping Black girls.

My first husband told me a horrendous tale of rape occurring in a small town in one of the Carolinas, in a CORE project where a farmer registered to vote. And his two daughters were abducted and raped by every White male in the town. The young women lost their minds. I had no proof of this, but it rang true to the cruelty of southern politics and those awful little towns with those despotic little minds bent on oppressing isolated Blacks. I know of no cases where White women were raped.[67]

Both Black women and White women activists were subjected to rape, sexual harassment, and humiliation at the hands of White police. On June 6, 1963, WNEW radio in New York reported that

teenage [N]egro and white girls, arrested during Freedom demonstrations, have been subjected to indignities in prisons in Mississippi and Georgia. Rape, sexual abuses and other indignities were reported by Dr. Jean Noble of New York University, and Dorothy Height, President of the National Association of Negro Women. Complaints are expected to be filed with the Justice Department.[68]

In the transcript of that radio show, Dorothy Height was quoted as saying, "There have been girls who have been raped. . . . We've had first hand reports from the women themselves. . . . They were raped by attendants in the jails."[69] Dr. Jean Noble, who was also on the radio show, then recounted the story of a twenty-three-year-old White girl who was arrested in a Freedom demonstration.

She has been on a hunger strike in jail for about two weeks. And when she was in jail she was asked to strip naked and stand before the male prisoners in the yard of the jail. Now there've been lots of rape and most of the girls who have been admitted to the Jackson, Mississippi jail have been subjected to unsanitary and unmedical vaginal examinations.[70]

These assaults were not uncommon during the civil rights movement. On May 21, 1963, in Albany, Georgia, Joni Rabinowitz and Joyce Barrett, who had been arrested and jailed for handing out leaflets, "were stripped in view of male prisoners."[71] The following day, Faith Holsaert, who was arrested for demonstrating in Albany, "was fondled while being searched."[72] Such tactics had been used to humiliate Black women for decades; now they were being inflicted upon White women activists as well.

On January 30, 1962, SNCC released the text of a sworn affidavit by Miss Bessie Turner of Clarksdale, Mississippi. She had been arrested for allegedly stealing money. When she was arrested and taken to the police headquarters, her nightmare began.

The short policeman told me to lay down on the concrete floor in the jail and pull up my dress and pull down my panties. He then began to whip me across my back with a wide leather strap, asking me all the time where was Luster P. Turner's money. He told me after I got sore he was going to whip me until I told him where the money was. He hit me several times and I could not tell him where the money was for I did not know. He then told me to "turn over an [sic] open your legs and let me see how you look down there." At this time, the tall policeman left the room. He hit me between my legs with the same leather strap he had whipped me with. He told me if he heard anything I had said about what he had done to me he was going to bring me back down to the jail and really whip me. He told me then to get up and fix my clothes and wipe my face, as I had been crying. He then told me to pull my dress down from my shoulders and pull down my bra and expose my breasts. He said he was looking for the money in my bra. The two policemen then brought me back home.[73]

The sexual humiliation of Black women extended beyond the confines of the sadistic local police and into the halls of the state legislature. On April 18, 1964, Jake Rosen, a writer for the newsletter *Freedom*, wrote an article entitled "Sterilization in Mississippi: A Plot to Wipe Out Negro People." The article explains that the Mississippi legislature intended to pass House Bill Number 180 authorizing the sterilization of parents of illegitimate children. The mother could either go to jail or consent to sterilization. Rosen wrote:

This bill actually legalizes the rape of Black women—if the rapist is a white man. According to Section 2 of the bill, no male can be convicted solely by the testimony of the mother. When it is remembered that the rape of Black women is now one of the most serious problems of Mississippi Negroes ("night-time integration" is what it is called) what threatens if this bill is signed into law ominous: bands of white hoods raping at will, knowing that they cannot be convicted if they take care to rape just one woman at a time (or one girl at a time), knowing that the police will let them alone because the State legislature has made it known it wants to get rid of the Negroes. And when the victims of the rape give birth—they either go to jail or are sterilized! A perfect criminal alliance between the government, the respectable members of the community, the police and the hoods.[74]

The brutality of sexual exploitation was not new to Black women who have endured it at the hands of White men since being torn from their native lands. For example, the Black women's club movement, which began shortly after a convention in 1890, was concerned with lynchings and the sexual abuse of Black women. Mary Church Terrell, Black civil rights activist and women's rights advocate, was the first president of the National Association of Colored Women (NACW) and served between 1896 and 1901. The antilynching efforts of the women's club movement inspired the development of the Anti-lynching Crusaders, a committee of seven hundred women in twenty-five states. It was established through the National Association for the Advancement of Colored People (NAACP) in 1922 and chaired by Mrs. M. B. Talbert.[75] The women's club movement also focused on the stereotypes of Black men as rapists and Black women as prostitutes. White southerners and media throughout the nation perpetuated the fear that all Black men were rapists. At the same time, Black women were routinely raped by White men and nothing was done to protect them. A Black woman, writing in 1904, states,

> It is commonly said that no girl or woman receives a certain kind of insult unless she invites it. That does not apply to a colored girl and woman in the South. The color of her face alone is sufficient invitation to the Southern white man—these same men who profess horror that a white gentleman can entertain a colored one at his table. Out of sight of their own women, they are willing and anxious to entertain colored women in various ways. Few colored girls reach the age of sixteen without receiving advances from them.[76]

When Black communities in the North or South were attacked by the Ku Klux Klan (KKK) or other White mobs, Black women were often raped. When their husbands, brothers, or sons tried to defend them, these men were generally lynched or beaten to death. For example, in 1914,

> Marie Scott of Wagoner County, a seventeen-year-old Negro girl, was lynched by a mob of white men because her brother killed one of two white men who had assaulted her. She was alone in the house when the men entered, but her screams brought her brother to the rescue. In the fight that ensued, one of the white men was killed. The next day the mob came to lynch her brother, but as he had escaped, lynched the girl instead. No one has ever been indicted for this crime.[77]

This incident graphically illustrates that the fate of Black men and Black women has been, and continues to be, intricately entwined. The legacy of slavery, the lynching of Black men, and the White man's unprecedented access to Black women's bodies were intolerable oppressions of Black people as a whole.

Consequently, when White women poured into the South to participate in the movement, they were exposed to the horrors of the everyday lives of Black people and to the treatment of Black women. In his autobiography, Cleve Sellers, a Black SNCC community bridge leader, graphically describes an encounter where he and a White woman were stopped by the police.

> The sheriff said, "He got a white girl in the back of tha cah. Take him back and git huh ovah heah. . . ." He was talking about Kathy Knustler, whose father—William Kunstler—was one of the lawyers working with COFO[78]

In the meantime, a crowd of White onlookers formed. Sellers continues.

> "Which one of them coons is you fuckin'?" The crowd roared its approval of the question.
> "Slut, I know you fuckin' them niggers. Why else would you be down heah? Which one is it? If you tell me the truth, I'll let you go. Which one is it?"[79]

Fortunately, Kathy did not single out anyone and eventually the police let them leave. Sellers explains that the sheriff said, "Take your white whores and get the hell out of Oxford [Mississippi]! If'n I ketch any one of you heah again, um gonna see to it that you get a quick trip to hell!"[80] They were subsequently followed by twenty-three cars, and met with a roadblock that they managed to dodge while speeding by at 105 miles per hour.

Sellers and those with him safely escaped, but many others did not. White women seen in the company of Blacks were viewed by the Southern White order as "fallen women"; they could then be treated as Black women had always been treated. Overall, the greatest threat to White women volunteers in the South were the White men who brutalized them for their transgressions.

Conclusion

Several factors have contributed to the misconceptions reached by previous researchers. First, they equated power with titled leadership. As has already been discussed, women within SNCC, though without the same titles as men, nonetheless operated as leaders and assumed a great deal of power. Second, while the authors acknowledge the organizational and structural difficulties SNCC was encountering at the time the Waveland paper was presented, they fail to tie this to Black members' reactions to the paper. Third, they do not sufficiently differentiate the positions of White women who came to the movement prior to 1964, from those who came during the Freedom Summer. Finally, and most important, McAdam and Evans and Rothschild focus on White women's experiences in SNCC. Such a focus, which ignores Black male-female relationships, shaped the empirical questions and does not provide a theoretical understanding of the relationships between Black men and Black women in SNCC.

Their studies of the gendered relationships in SNCC are often informed by the gender-focused feminist constructs of the seventies, and therefore pay little attention to such complicating factors as race, class, and culture. Such a view obscures the relationship complexities that existed in the civil rights movement.

Ironically, the actual daily actions of Blacks and Whites in the movement defied the classic stereotypes of the Black man as rapist, the White woman as fragile victim, and the Black woman as angry and ugly Amazon, which later researchers would unwittingly resurrect. Instead, what becomes clear is that Blacks and Whites, men and women, mainly shared positive, life-altering experiences. Rather than White women fearing Black men and Black women, they respected and loved them because they all shared an unwavering and life-threatening commitment to Black freedom. The greatest physical threat to all was not the Black man, but the southern White racist man, who was willing to murder, rape, and beat them to maintain the southern order.

Rather than feeling oppressed and sexually exploited, the Black and White women interviewed for this study felt empowered by their participation in the Student Non-Violent Coordinating Committee, seeing themselves as unhampered by sexist constraints. Though, given the times, gender norms certainly precluded the rise of women to primary formal bridge leadership positions, women—particularly African-American women—did rise to powerful positions in SNCC. Because of its decentralized, nonhierarchical structure, women in SNCC enjoyed leadership mobility more than in any other civil rights organization, as is evident in their rise to secondary formal bridge leadership positions. The decentralized nature of SNCC provided more free spaces, allowing greater individual autonomy and, therefore, increased leadership mobility for women.

A womanist/Black feminist perspective, which takes into account cultural context and the effects of competing oppressive forces, provides a more complete analysis of movement relationships. We have seen that gender overlaps with the constructs of race, class, and culture. Moreover, these constructs and their meanings shift over time and space. In the case of the civil rights movement, one's status as a woman was determined not only by one's sex but also by one's race, class, and culture. Gender was a significant construct in determining one's position in the movement, but it had very different meanings for the social construction of the positions of Black and White women in the Student Non-Violent Coordinating Committee. Moreover, the cultural milieu in which these women and men worked was significant in that White women's activities were more restricted because of southern social mores governing White womanhood.

While in general the participation of White women was more restricted than it was for Black women, race was not the only significant construct contributing to this outcome. One's class and culture significantly increased or moderated these restrictions. White women raised in the South approached the movement with a knowledge of the region's social taboos and norms. According to the interviewees, both Black and White northern newcomers were unfamiliar with southern ways of life and history. Southern racists were particularly incited by the appearance of White women in the company of Black men. Southern White women—more than those from the North or other regions of the United States—understood these southern strictures.

Most of the White volunteers came from middle-class and upper-class families; even if they didn't, as one informant commented, they had received a tremendous amount of formal schooling well beyond that available to local Mississippi workers. These skills were employed in the area most needed—the office. Therefore, White women and a few middle-class Black women, particularly those from the North, were more readily assigned to the national office as mainstream bridge leaders, where their activism generally involved connections to White institutions and White communities. The assignment to office work, however, also had the corresponding effect of placing them in more gender-normative positions with less access to the field, where free spaces were more abundant. Therefore, the experiences of White women differed significantly from those of Black women. It is clear that women's positions in SNCC were determined by a complex interplay of race, class, gender, and culture.

For White activists, one's understanding of the southern culture and Black oppression tended to correspond with one's understanding that SNCC was a Black-led organization. Those Whites who came to SNCC prior to Freedom Summer understood that they could not lead in the same way as either Black men or Black women. Moreover, they admired and respected the Black leadership, understanding the actual, as well as the symbolic, importance of Blacks as leaders of their own movement.

Later participants who came en masse on a temporary basis not only created difficulties based on their lack of knowledge but also strained the structure and organization of SNCC. While the strain created an increased need for more formal leadership, thus expanding the mobility of Black women leaders, it also served to undermine the nature of SNCC. Thus, in an effort to control their movement and to retain Black leadership, many members felt a need for a more centralized and hierarchical organization. While many Black women viewed this move as necessary, several White women and a few Black women and men saw it as a move that would threaten the free spaces, and not only for women. Even more at stake was the inherent threat to SNCC's goal, which had been to mobilize the leadership potential of those least connected to the politics of the movement. Centralization and hierarchy would destroy what was best about SNCC: the desire to leave a community with a strong indigenous leadership base. Such a base would serve to spread the message of the movement and strengthen its base in ways that the primary formal and secondary formal movement organizations could not.

EIGHT

Bringing the Movement Home to Small Cities and Rural Communities

Local Women's Activism Despite Minister Opposition

While the civil rights movement gained momentum in the upper South, it became increasingly clear that this heightened movement activity did not extend to smaller cities and isolated pockets of the rural South. Following the 1955 Montgomery bus boycott civil rights movement organizations—primarily the NAACP and the Congress of Racial Equality (CORE)—targeted southern cities for direct action—that is, sit-ins and organized protests. The Freedom Rides, precipitated by CORE, resulted in several successes in the upper South. In the Deep South, this challenge to segregation in interstate travel resulted in bloodshed and left the racist order intact.[1] Strategies were needed to link movement organizations to these otherwise isolated areas. Bridge leaders would fill this need.

What became increasingly clear was the need to penetrate the very core of these southern communities. Mobilization of Black populations in the deep pockets of the rural south and in smaller cities had been weak, yet their participation was critical for the demise of the powerful and ruthless southern order. Civil rights organizations, especially CORE, the SCLC, and SNCC, sought to mobilize these areas, but they were well aware of the dangers such tactics posed for both organizers and community members. Direct action in the rural south was a prescription for death. Even registering to vote was life-threatening. Still, the organizations formed an umbrella group, the Council of Federated Organizations (COFO), which was composed of SNCC, CORE, and the NAACP, to organize in the isolated pockets of the South.

The mobilization of smaller communities was more difficult in many ways than previous efforts in larger cities. Direct-action efforts in the latter, while certainly dangerous, were at least visible to the media. Violent reprisals in rural areas of the South were less likely to receive such attention. Moreover, in rural areas and in small towns, outsiders were more visible and the contacts between movement organizations more cumbersome and tenuous. Rural people tended not to trust outsiders and many wanted no part in "stirrin' up trouble." Mobilization of these sectors required recruitment tactics that built specifically upon trust and interpersonal community ties. Most rural people, no matter how inspired by the charisma of movement leaders or how impressed by an organization's financial resources, would not risk their lives without powerful motivation.

In large cities, a network of professional ties among ministers provided a powerful resource for mobilization; this was less often the case in rural communities or smaller cities. Muriel Tillinghast, a SNCC project director in Ruleville, Mississippi, illustrates:

> In my particular project areas . . . I did not get much support from the church. Greenville was the headquarters of our three-county project area, which was Washington, Issaquena, and Sharkey counties. We did not work with the church community consistently. I recall that in Washington County we met in people's homes, and the same occurred in Sharkey County. . . . Rural churches in poor Black areas did not have regular ministers. And, those that did, in my experience, tended to be conservative.[2]

Mrs. Boynton, an activist in Selma who traveled in her youth throughout rural Dallas County, Alabama, to teach homemaking and child-rearing skills, commented on her impression of the rural ministers:

> During reconstruction, the minister was mostly the black man's only leader. Often he was handpicked by the plantation owner and in most instances he was the only literate person in the black community. Few of the country preachers attended any of the political and cultural meetings because they felt it might conflict with what "Mr. Charlie" would like them to teach their congregations. . . . Some of these ministers have been conditioned to take their sermons to the plantation owner before they deliver them. If there is anything in them he doesn't like, they cut it out. The poor backwoods preacher, like a puppet on a string, preaches what he is told to preach.[3]

Yet the deference and caution were learned responses or realistic attempts to run the gauntlet between southern racist authority and one's people, outside the protection of much-vaunted liberal justice. Because of this, others also believed that mobilization could not come from these ministers. Gloria Richardson, who had been a student activist with Pauli Murray at Howard University in the early days of direct nonviolent action, and who was now the chair of a SNCC project in Cambridge, Maryland, echoed the belief that mobilization did not emanate from ministers, many of whom she felt were beholden to White officials and/or felt protest was sinful. Rather, she felt that women participated in spite of the church.[4]

While these are rather harsh pronouncements, they indicate the lack of support by many of the clergy for civil rights activities. Yet the fear felt by the clergy was realistic. Mrs. Boynton illustrated this reign of terror, recounting the story of Reverend Hughes, who dared to speak out from his pulpit against unjust wages paid to Black workers. Following his sermon, several White men called at his home and requested to see him. His wife, fearing the worst, told the men that her husband had gone to visit some sick church member. The White men pretended to leave and went around the back of the house, which gave the minister a chance to slip out the front door and into the church. Carrying knives, guns, and a rope the men proceeded to the church and searched, in vain, for him. Reverend Hughes hid in the belfry until they left. In the meantime, a visiting minister came to the church and offered him a ride to his town. As they traveled down the dirt road, they were pursued by several cars. Reverend Hughes jumped from the car into a ravine, where he rolled ten to twelve feet. He escaped on foot, never to return to his home. The White men continued to chase the car, not realizing that Hughes was no longer in it.[5]

Anne Moody, in her book *Coming of Age in Mississippi*, chronicles the horrendous conditions in which Blacks lived. Even when ministers allowed SNCC workers to give talks, Blacks were still afraid to participate. Moody, a SNCC and later a CORE community bridge leader who went to the Delta to assist with voter registration, described the ineffectiveness of SNCC:

> Things didn't seem to be coming along too well in the Delta. On Saturdays we could spend all day canvassing and often at night we would have mass rallies. But these were usually poorly attended. Many Negroes were afraid to come. In the beginning some were even afraid to talk to us. . . .
>
> On Sundays we usually went to Negro churches to speak. We were split into groups according to our religious affiliation. We were supposed to know how to reach those with the same faith as ourselves. In church we hoped to be able to reach many more Negroes. We knew that even those that slammed doors in our faces or said, "I don't want no part of voting" would be there. There would also be the schoolteachers and the middle-class professional Negroes who dared not participate. They knew that once they did, they would lose that $250 a month job. But the people started getting wise to us. Most of them stopped coming to church. They knew if they came, they would have to face us. Then the ministers started asking us not to come because we scared their congregations away. SNCC had to come up with a new strategy.[6]

The fear of reprisals and death was warranted. One Mississippi volunteer describes his shock at the treatment of Black citizens:

> Yesterday while the Mississippi River was being dragged looking for the three missing civil rights workers, two bodies of Negroes were found—one cut in half and one

without a head. Mississippi is the only State where you can drag a river any time and find bodies you were not expecting. And people wonder why we are here.[7]

People were so frightened of participating that one fifteen-year-old local youth leader, Joyce Brown, wrote a poem.

THE HOUSE OF LIBERTY

I came not for fortune, nor for fame,
I seek not to add glory to an unknown name,
I did not come under the shadow of night,
I came by day to fight for what's right.
I shan't let fear, my monstrous foe,
Conquer my soul with threat and woe.
Here I have come and here I shall stay,
And no amount of fear, my determination can sway.

I asked for your churches, and you turned me down,
But I'll do my work if I have to do it on the ground;
You will not speak for fear of being heard,
So you crawl in your shell and say, "Do not disturb."
You think because you've turned me away,
You've protected yourself for another day.

But tomorrow surely must come,
And your enemy will still be there with the rising sun;
He'll be there tomorrow as all tomorrows in the past,
And he'll follow you into the future if you let him pass.
You've turned me down to humor him,
Ah! Your fate is sad and grim,
For even tho' your help I ask,
Even without it, I'll finish my task.

In a bombed house I have to teach my school,
Because I believe all men should live by the Golden Rule.
To a bombed house your children must come,
Because of your fear of a bomb.
And because you've let your fear conquer your soul,
In this bombed house these minds I must try to mold;
I must try to teach them to stand tall and be a man
When you their parents have cowered down and refused to take a stand.[8]

Indigenous Bridge Leaders: Links Between
Community and Organization

While it is true that student volunteers, ministers, and movement halfway houses provided many resources for rural and small-town mobilization, that mobilization could not have succeeded without the efforts of indigenous bridge leaders, who facilitated the connection between these communities and movement organizations. Even Bob Moses, the SNCC leader who has been credited with initiating SNCC's movement into the deepest pockets of the South, relied on the contacts

Ella Baker had cultivated while traveling as the NAACP's director of chapters.[9] Still, many volunteers found it difficult to gain the trust of local people:

> It's the old case of having to prove ourselves. In their eyes we're rich middle- or upper-class Whites who've taken off a summer to help the Negro. We can't feel what they feel or live what they live—and of course they are right.[10]

Many of the volunteers were shocked by the conditions in which Blacks lived in the deep pockets of the South. One volunteer wrote:

> I have begun, finally, to feel deep inside me this horrible existence Negroes have to lead in both North and South . . . the strategies they must learn to survive without either going crazy or being physically maimed—or destroyed. Mr. Reese describes how a Negro [man] must learn to walk through a crowd: weaving, slightly hunched— shuffling helps—in order to be as humbly inconspicuous as possible.[11]

The extreme nature of oppression by Whites in the South necessarily placed a significant barrier between local Blacks and White volunteers. Yet the divide was not based on race alone, but on life experience. Even Black student volunteers, whose experiences did not include the extent of racist oppression in the deep pockets of the South, viewed themselves as novices rather than as leaders of the rural poor. Prathia Hall Wynn, a secondary bridge leader of SNCC, comments:

> In the beginning we were students, we were brand-new, we were from the North. We had a lot to learn, and I think our attitude was that of learners. We went to learn from the people who had already been there, the students who were senior to the southern movement, those who had begun the movement. We went to learn from the people in the communities, particularly the people in the local towns and in the rural areas where we lived. We were there; part of that work was doing some teaching in terms of literacy training and voter education, but we always felt—and I certainly felt very deeply that I was the student and that I was being given a great deal more than I was giving.[12]

SNCC workers from other parts of the country came to understand their limitations with regard to southern life—that in essence, they were living in a foreign country. Black SNCC workers from other parts of the country, while they did not pose a readily visible threat to the southern order, did not blend in with the locals. While Whites' very presence created a danger, Blacks from other areas did not always look or behave like locals. Mrs. Unita Blackwell, an indigeneous bridge leader, describes a typical encounter:

> And so they came walking down the street very fast and we knew; at that time people just didn't walk fast in the South. . . . They says "Hi." You know? Well, we knew something was going on then because people don't speak like that anyway in

the South. He talked New York style and at that time we didn't know what he was saying. We really hadn't heard too much of that kind of language.[13]

She continues with a story about a Black woman brought in later from New York.

So she came in with her hair looking funny. Well, at that time, it was Afro so we didn't know what to do with her. I didn't. I just told her that Louise that fixes hair was down the street there, and she kept saying, "Okay," and "I got to wash it. . . ." So she did wash it and she stood around. [She just let it dry naturally in front of everyone].[14]

Black women had been taught to be ashamed of the natural state of their hair. In resistance to this, young Black women, particularly in the North, were beginning to wear their hair in a natural fashion, a halo of hair called the Afro. In the South, pressing (straightening) one's hair was essential if one went out of the house. Such a shocking Afro presentation set these newer volunteers utterly apart from locals. Only fully trusted, indigenous leaders could bridge these gaps, thereby translating the message of the movement to the southern rural community or small town.

SNCC workers would enter a community and contact local, indigenous leaders, often one or more women or men, and sometimes a minister as well. Women such as Mrs. Julian Turner and Mrs. Thelma Leweller of Moscow, Tennessee; Julia, Beverley, and Delois Polk of Byhalia, Mississippi; Mrs. Ingram and Mrs. Wooten of Marshall County, Mississippi; Mrs. Dearworth of Lincoln County, Mississippi; Mrs. Reaves and Mrs. Willie Ruth Dougherty of Benton County, Mississippi—these are just a few of the contact women who bridged SNCC workers to the community.[15] While the focus of this book is on women, many men participated in this capacity as well. Anne Moody, who worked for CORE in Canton, Mississippi, describes her contact with Mr. and Mrs. Chinn, both of whom provided invaluable assistance. Of Mr. Chinn, who owned his own restaurant, she wrote:

The luckiest thing that happened to us was that we had succeeded in getting C. O. Chinn to work with us. He was a powerful man, known as "bad-ass C. O. Chinn" to the Negroes and whites alike. All of the Negroes respected him for standing up and being a man. Most of the whites feared him. He was the type of person that didn't take shit from anyone. If he was with you, he was all for you. . . . Because he was respected by most of the local Negroes, he was our most effective speaker in the churches.[16]

C. O. Chinn payed a heavy price for his involvement. His restaurant was shut down, and he was arrested and jailed on trumped-up charges. Still, he persisted in helping the workers and speaking his mind in a way that the activists could not. Anne Moody continues:

Often, when he was speaking, he would say, "Take me, for example, they have completely put me out of business. I have lost practically everything I have. These young workers are here starving to death trying to help you people. And for what? A lot of you ain't worth it!" Not one of us working for CORE could have talked to the local people like that. . . .

It was the middle of August now, and we had been working in the county for two months. Up until this time not one of the ministers in Canton had committed himself to helping us. When they did give us a chance to speak in their churches, it was only for two or three minutes during the announcements. The biggest Negro church in Canton was pastored by Canton's biggest "Tom." Most of his congregation were middle-class bourgeois Negroes. We all knew that if we could somehow force him to move, every other large church in Canton would open its doors to us.

We set up a meeting and invited all of the ministers, but since the number one minister didn't show up, all the others did was mumble to each other and tell us, "We can't do anything until Reverend Tucker says so." After that we decided to forget the ministers and go to work on their congregations. At this point the ministers started coming around. In fact they called a meeting to talk things over with us. But the talk was fruitless.

We had a surprise for them, though. We had made headway with several of their most influential members, and they put us right where we wanted to go—behind the pulpits for more than five minutes. Now we could hit the Canton churches hard.[17]

Much as Columbus did or did not discover the Americas, so movement organization workers did or did not discover local leadership. These men and women had been local leaders long before the arrival of SNCC or CORE activists.[18] Moreover, the strategy of community and secondary bridge leaders to bypass the formal local leadership in lieu of their assistance or resistance and instead to seek support from informal local leaders began to pay off. Unita Blackwell illustrates this as she describes the beginning of her involvement.

How I became an organizer was that one day I was out there trying to get registered to vote myself. And I spoke up and guess I was spotted as one of the potential leaders by [John] Lewis. . . . I could get up and stand in a church and tell people that nothing from nothing leaves nothing, and we're going to all have to get up and try to do something here by ourselves because none of us have anything.[19]

Absorption into SNCC provided local women with considerable support and direction, strengthening the organization's connection to the local community at the same time. That such women benefited from outside tactical support—a common enough practice among field commanders—should not be confused with deference. These women were the critical links, mobilizing the massive community support it took to effect change, and they would become movement bridge leaders in their own right.

Annelle Ponder, an SCLC activist and teacher, recalls the help she received in Greenwood, Mississippi, when

Mrs. Atlean Smith [a local beautician and later a dynamic leader in the Greenwood movement], in responding to our plea for meeting space, volunteered the use of her home, and I started a class there while recruiting local people who would eventually set up their own classes.[20]

James Jones and Noah Washington recount their experience in trying to find a place to hold their meetings: "We talked with a lady by the name of Mrs. Dearworth, about getting us a church and what date. She told us that the Pastor of her church didn't agree, and that there was going to be a vote on it." Later, they write, "she told us that she lost to her Pastor and that she was sure that she had another church for us."[21] Within three days, Mrs. Dearworth had secured a meeting place for the workers.

Women not only secured meeting places but provided outsiders with insights into the interworkings of the local community. In a report from the headquarters of Mrs. Annie Raines in Lee County, Georgia, an unidentified worker writes:

Mama Dolly [Mrs. Raines] is definitely a leader in this community and looked up to by the Negroes here. She has always remained dignified and a woman of high principal and sagacity. She has instincts about the "movement" and strategy which has [sic] not as yet proved wrong. In her own quiet way she trys [sic] to force her people to realize that "a new day's a come!" and for them to take action and take a stand. She talks with everyone and in her own way tries to educate and lift them to new heights. Her understanding of situations is unusual and her perception seldom equalled.[22]

Larry Rubin, in a 1962 Lee County report, writes:

In the first place, living with Mama Dollie Raines has been invaluable. She has given us much of the information about Lee county that we need to operate on. By living in her house and sharing her work, we have learned many of the assumptions, hopes, fears and beliefs upon which the people here base their lives. And, she has introduced to us local people we would have otherwise never met.[23]

Such women often maintained a degree of autonomy while cooperating with the movement organizers. Longtime local activist Annie Devine initially joined the Congress of Racial Equality and later the Mississippi Freedom Democratic Party. Matthew Suarez recalls:

She directed us to blacks who were trustworthy in the community, told us what blacks would do and what they wouldn't, how to address them. In many ways, she acted like a go-between with black male leaders [notably preachers] and young folks [who resisted their authority]. We were saying to leadership, "you ought to be ashamed not to be doing this and that for our people," and [Mrs. Devine] was saying "you ought to do this because of what has happened." She could draw on her lived experience. She was the backbone, a part of the strategists. She understood clearly how we should handle and conduct ourselves in Canton. We came in like we're here to save you folks and Devine instructed CORE that this was the wrong approach. You can't relate to people in this community using this approach. Mrs. Devine was a country diplomat.[24]

Winson Hudson had been active in the NAACP prior to the arrival of SNCC workers, and like other civic-minded rural women, she was one of the first indigenous leaders to be contacted. As did many other women in rural communities, she worked with several organizations in an effort to remain independent.[25] This independence is discussed by Victoria Gray, who considered herself a "local person": "I worked with every organization that was working in the state." She considered herself to be an interpreter between the old and the young. Many older people in the community believed in the local media, though they were "just distorting every thing." Negative media appraisals of the movement kept these people afraid to trust movement organizers. Victoria Gray convinced them that the organizers were the same "young people as your daughters and sons." In this way she could encourage them to trust the workers, and convince them to register to vote.[26]

Mrs. Blackwell, another indigenous leader, recalls doing the day-to-day organizing and footwork required to mobilize the local community:

Sometimes our contact would be just a friend in one county who knows somebody in another county. Then you go and talk to them and you go from house to house, and you knock on people's doors and you talk to them Black folks. . . . So that's the way you did it. It was a lot of footwork and we didn't have a lot of cars, and we didn't have no money so it was commitment, and so we had to go from door to door. . . . Right now, in any campaign anywhere, you will find women doing that legwork and that people work.[27]

These women were an inspiration to SNCC workers as well as to the community. Charles McLaurin, a SNCC worker wrote:

In 1962, I was in Ruleville to do voter registration work or to get Negroes to go to the courthouse to register to vote. I lived with a Negro man and his wife who for all of their family and lives had lived and worked on the plantation. The Negroes had already made attempts to register and the whites was upset. The police had started to harass the Negroes to keep them from trying to register to vote. Six brave ladies had taken it upon themselves to go to the courthouse to register and now they was like sore thumbs (meaning they were out there). These six ladies was the start of a fire that is still burning one year later.[28]

Mrs. Fannie Lou Hamer, the twentieth child of a Mississippi sharecropper, would become a civil rights movement symbol of "freedom". Her entrance into the civil rights movement began when she was extended an invitation to a SNCC meeting by Mrs. Tucker, an indigenous bridge leader who housed SNCC workers. Mrs. Tucker recalled:

I said, "Lord, I believe I'll go out in the country and get Fannie Lou. I want her to come in here and hear this because I believe it would mean something to her." So I did.[29]

Hamer was reluctant to attend the meeting at first, but her great respect for Mrs. Tucker led her to accept the invitation. She recalls:

I had never heard of a mass meeting in my life. So the next day, I asked my husband was it anyway possible that we could come out, you know, if we picked enough cotton that day then he would bring us that night. So we worked hard so we could come to the mass meeting.[30]

SNCC formal leaders John Lewis and Robert Moses benefited greatly from Mrs. Hamer's local ties; community confidence in her led to increasing trust in them, buttressing their community support efforts. They also noticed her potential for wider leadership, recognizing that Mrs. Hamer's prodigious talents were only hampered by her lack of familiarity with legal and political systems. To assist her, Lewis and Moses suggested she and Victoria Gray, another prominent indigenous leader, attended Septima Clark's SCLC-sponsored Citizenship Education Program workshops in Dorchester, Georgia.

Notably, both women had already been involved in voter registration work prior to their workshop participation. Charles McLaurin, a SNCC worker who came to feel like a son to Hamer, explains:

She told me that she had always wanted to get involved with something to help her people but she just didn't know exactly how or what to do. She had read about the Freedom Rides into Jackson and around the country, about various student sit-ins around the country, and she was really waiting for an opportunity.[31]

Hamer also spoke of what SNCC gave to her.

If SNCC hadn't of come into Mississippi, there never would have been a Fannie Lou Hamer. They treated me like a human being, whether the kids was white or black. I was respected with the kids, and they never told nobody what to say, nobody. Everything you heard us screaming and saying . . . nobody tell us to say that. This is what's been there all the time, and we had a chance to get it off our chests, and nobody else had ever give us that chance. . . . They brought every hope into the state of Mississippi.[32]

Mrs. Hamer, Mrs. Gray, and others worked at the local community level, encouraging others to register to vote. Although the church was a frequent organizing tool, it was not the only or even primary resource employed to recruit the masses. Mrs. Gray explains several ways to gain support:

If you had any organization to which you belonged or people you knew belonged to them, you used that. And of course, you used the old door-to-door, one-on-one. . . .

The young people were the foot soldiers, with people like myself acting as the local catalyst, if you will.[33]

Women such as Victoria Gray, Fannie Lou Hamer, Unita Blackwell, Annie Devine, and Peggy Jean Connors became the bridges between organizations such as SNCC, CORE, the SCLC and the communities they strove to serve. Additionally, they acted as bridges between the young local rural activists and reluctant ministers. They coordinated the activities of the young and developed strategies to achieve greater voter registration. But the greatest strength of these women may have been their responsiveness to specific community needs, tailoring the various organizations' voter registration efforts to the unique requirements of each situation.

Women and the Mississippi Freedom Democratic Party

On April 26, 1964, SNCC, whose philosophy was to build indigenous leadership within local communities throughout the Deep South, organized the Mississippi Freedom Democratic Party (MFDP). The MFDP was established to counter the efforts of racist southerners who continued to prevent Blacks from voting. For example, in the Second District of Mississippi, 52.4 percent of the population was Black, but only 2.97 percent of the Black population had been allowed to register to vote.[34] The conditions for Blacks living in rural areas of the South were abysmal, as described in a report compiled by COFO:

> Many deep south rural people live in housing unfit for human habitation. The 1960 census showed that in Mississippi over 50% of the rural occupied farm housing was classified as either deteriorating or dilapidated. Furthermore, more than 50% of the rural occupied homes have no piped water and more than 75% have no flush toilets, bathtubs or showers. For Negroes the housing situation is even more alarming. The 1960 census showed that in Mississippi, 66% of all Negro housing was "dilapidated or deteriorating"—71% in rural areas. More than 90% of rural Negro homes in Mississippi have neither flush toilets nor bathing or shower facilities.
>
> The infant mortality rate for the Mississippi Negro is more than twice as high as that of the white Mississippian. . . . Poor rural families, the under and unemployed fare as best they can—this in most instances means: tightening their belts, surviving off of one meal a day, adults going without so that children may eat—in short it simply means slow starvation. Even when food is adequate it is composed largely of starches and fats.[35]

Many of the local people who assisted movement organizations had experienced the poverty mentioned in the COFO's report. Fannie Lou Hamer, who has been described as a charismatic leader, as one who, "when she sings can make a church tremble," understood the pain of poverty. She described her life to a reporter for the *Nation*.

The family would pick fifty-sixty bales of cotton a year, so my father decided to rent some land. He bought some mules and a cultivator. We were doin' pretty well. He even started to fix up the house real nice and bought a car. Then our stock got poisoned. We knowed this white man had done it. . . . That poisonin' knocked us right back down flat. We never did get back up again. That white man did it just because we were gettin' somewhere. White people never like to see Negroes get a little success. All of this stuff is no secret in the state of Mississippi. . . . We went back to sharecroppin' halvin', it's called. You split the cotton half and half with the plantation owner. But the seed, fertilizer, cost of hired hands, everything is paid out of the cropper's half. Later, I dropped out of school.

So many times for dinner we would have greens with no seasonin' . . . and flour gravy. My mother would mix flour with a little grease and try to make gravy out of it. Sometimes she'd cook a little meal and we'd have bread. No one can easily say Negroes are satisfied. We've only been patient, but how much more patience can we have?[36]

In addition, Black people were routinely murdered, harassed, beaten, and intimidated even before the era of the civil rights worker. These acts steadily increased as more and more local people began to register to vote.

At the initial MFDP meeting representing four districts, a temporary State Executive Committee was elected that included nine men and three women. All three women—Mrs. Fannie Lou Hamer, Mrs. Annie Devine, and Mrs. Victoria Gray—were active indigenous bridge leaders within their respective communities. Throughout the history of the MFDP, women were often elected to be delegates; they were generally not elected as chairpersons. Women who served on the executive committee most often acted as secretaries. Even at the local level, men held most of the offices and were the committee chairs, though half the membership in the MFDP were women. Most of the officers in the MFDP were young men.[37]

Five of the three candidates running for office on the MFDP ticket were women, and though they did not hold offices within the organization, they were highly visible. This is in contrast to the patterns seen in the SCLC, MIA, and SNCC. The reasons for this pattern are not altogether clear, though some are offered. Victoria Gray's involvement in the MFDP offers one explanation:

I have always been doing something for as long as I can remember. . . . I began simply by agreeing to go to the courthouse and become registered to vote and that was my initiation into the movement proper. . . . Just about everything I did, I was always a community oriented person.[38]

Gray, like many other leaders in the MFDP, had been active in community affairs prior to her civil rights activism. She describes the early activities of the MFDP and how she was elected as a delegate:

We set up an alternative political structure and we went through the process as defined in the constitution of Mississippi and the United States. We actually went through every step of the process. We had our registrations, we had our different conventions, our caucuses, whatever they happened to be called. And we went step by step from the precinct, to the county, to the district, the state, and ultimately to the national level. That's how I got elected. . . .

Women in government were somewhat of a rarity, period. So certainly it was different, and the other thing was finding people who were willing to be nominated into that situation. There really was just a handful of us. We did not have a lot of competition, I assure you.[39]

Because of the dangerous circumstances in which these candidates would run for office, the women had little competition and the custom that only men should be visible leaders was temporarily displaced. Indeed, many believed that men were at greater risk than women. Constance Curry, a former SNCC worker who has written a book about a rural Black woman's life, explains:

When I was doing my book on Mrs. Mae Bertha Carter and her family, who were black sharecroppers in Mississippi, Mrs. Carter said she was always more protective of her sons. She knew that if she were in a dangerous position, there were a lot of ways that she could use her wiles to protect herself. She knew that, traditionally, she was in a safer place than Matthew, her husband, or her sons. They were the ones who needed the most protection.[40]

So under extremely dangerous circumstances, normative views about the acceptability of women's formal leadership broke down, allowing the mobility of Black women's leadership abilities. While the MFDP was not structurally similar to that of SNCC, its organization and philosophy of decision making came to parallel those of SNCC, creating an organizational climate more conducive for women's leadership. Similarly, the ways in which COFO coordinated action tended to decentralize power.

The efforts of the MFDP were coordinated through SNCC and the COFO. The COFO staff kept the records and coordinated the challenge to the convention. Women such as Mrs. Hamer, Mrs. Victoria Gray, and Mrs. Annie Devine were very vocal and were involved in the planning and strategy meetings.[41] Mrs. Gray often initiated discussions and proposed suggestions for strategies and tactics. In fact, in several meetings, she spoke more often than did the men. These women also took center stage in the MFDP newsletters, and they often wrote press releases.[42] Even at the local level, men and women seemed to have equal input.[43] Mrs. Gray describes the decision-making process as "no one person made the decision in the MFDP. Not ever. We insisted that whatever decisions were made, they were made by the body."[44]

That style of decision making is reflective of the influence of SNCC on the organizational philosophy of the MFDP. Many of those who worked closely with the MFDP espoused egalitarian values, such as Miss Ella Baker, who ran the Washington, D.C., office, and SNCC workers Bob Moses, Charlie Cobb, and Cynthia Washington.

During the campaign, many local women became involved in mobilizing the masses to support Black candidates. Mrs. Mary Belk, of West Point, Mississippi, who

> had gone from house to house almost every night for a month, getting people out of the bed who had spent the entire day picking cotton, talking about the elections, urging people to run, urging people to vote, reflected, "I work for the white folks in the daytime, and against them at night."[45]

Another member of the MFDP, Mrs. Ada Holliday of Clay County, in a November 26, 1965, letter to the Department of Agriculture, writes:

> We have worked on this election for two months now, canvassing, holding meetings, nominating candidates, getting petitions signed and campaigning. We have written and talked with every Negro farmer in the county. We do not intend to let this work and effort go in vain. But more important than the work is the fact that all the candidates have put their bodies in the line of fire, and we will support them with our bodies if necessary. . . . We will go to jail again if needed, to make our participation in the control of our livelihood a reality. We have risked the burnings of our homes and churches and the loss of our lives. We have been harrassed and intimidated by our white neighbors.[46]

Economic and Physical Reprisals

Those who provided local support for movement workers incurred terrible physical and economic risk to themselves and their loved ones. Annelle Ponder recalls that "many of them have experienced reprisals and intimidations either personally or through their families, friends, or students."[47] These reprisals took the form of jailings, beatings, and loss of jobs for themselves and/or their loved ones.[48] Miss Ida Mae Holland, one of eight Greenwood women who had completed training in Septima Clark's Citizenship Education Program, remembers when she, along with several other community people, attempted to register to vote. After being turned away at the LeFlore County Courthouse, she and local minister Reverend Tucker led potential voters in a march.

> A policeman came running from around the corner with a police dog. He said, "Break up, you black ass niggers, break it up." The officers told the dog, "Sic em.". . . . The officer then loosened the rein and the dog bit Reverend Tucker. Reverend Tucker stumbled into the street and fell. You should have seen the pain that was on that man's face, he was really hurt. I started toward him and an officer pushed me to the ground and tried to make the dog get me. The dog and I stared at each other, he bared his lips and I saw all those horrible teeth in his mouth, it was like a nightmare. Then I started crawling toward Reverend Tucker and the officer asked where I was going and I told him I was trying to reach my pastor. And he said, "get your black ass up and let the son-of-a-bitch die."[49]

Two SNCC workers helped Reverend Tucker to his feet. Miss Holland sensed that the crowd was frightened, so she got up and restored order. She and Charlie Cobb, another one of the SNCC workers, led the crowd safely to the First Christian Church. Throughout all of this, Miss Holland was clearly as much at risk of injury or death as any of the men. As well as demonstrating the shared danger that leveled many gender differences, this incident illustrates the special genius of bridge leaders. In moments of chaos and fear, it was these women who rose up to inspire and lead, over and over again throughout the South.

Fannie Lou Hamer was no stranger to harassment, physical violence, and economic reprisals. Mrs. Hamer had earned her position as "symbol of freedom." Several years before her participation in the MFDP, Mrs. Hamer had joined a group attending an SCLC voter registration workshop run by Septima Clark. While returning from the workshop, she and others stopped to eat at a restaurant. She remained on the bus, but others entered the White Only section. The police came and arrested them all, Mrs. Hamer included. June Johnson, Mrs. Hamer's friend, recalls the encounter:

> At night . . . they took Mrs. Hamer from her cell and began beating her. We could hear her screamin' and hollerin', just calling God for help. . . . On the way back she just fell out at our cell, just lay there cryin'. She said later they had two inmates sit on her and beat her on the leg she was crippled in.[50]

Mrs. Hamer spent two months recuperating, and she was to suffer all of her life from the injuries sustained from this beating. This incident among many others gained Mrs. Hamer her reputation as a courageous woman. She was also known for her charisma and was often sent to speak before crowds and church congregations. Mrs. Hamer could inspire others to stand up for their rights, regardless of the threats. Hamer, who had been a sharecropper and timekeeper on a plantation for sixteen years, had been thrown off the place when she registered to vote. Following the announcement of her MFDP candidacy, her husband was unable to get work at the cotton gin where he had been employed.[51]

All those who attempted to register to vote risked their lives and ways of living. Many were directly threatened, and some were either evicted or threatened with eviction from their homes. Victoria Gray describes a threat made on her life:

> I got my first direct threat at two o'clock in the morning, being told that I was on their list [a list of those who attempted to register and which was the equivalent of a hit list]. . . . [It was] shortly after the lynching of Mike Charlie Parker [a black man murdered for his participation], and they told me that I would be going like Mike Charles Parker and then they hung up. I guess initially it was the most frightening moment of my life.[52]

It was not unusual for the homes of those involved in voter registration to be bombed, such as the home of Mrs. Alberta Robbins near Canton, Mississippi, and Mrs. Dillion and Mrs. Alyanne Quin of McComb, Mississippi.[53] Many of these women feared for the lives of their family members, as well; all shared the risks whether directly involved or not. And knowing that the fates of their loved ones were inextricably linked to the daring actions they were taking was an added burden to carry.

As an example of this threat, in Ruleville, Mississippi,

> two young Negro girls were shot . . . by shotgun pellets from a speeding car as they sat in the home of Mr. and Mrs. Sisson, voter registration workers. Marylene Burks, 20, was shot in the head. Vivian Hillett, 18, was wounded in the arms and legs.[54]

Marylene was in critical condition. Mrs. Sisson was one of the the first women to attempt to register to vote in Sunflower County. And these were not isolated incidents. Registering to vote, housing SNCC workers, or becoming involved in any way with civil rights activities meant risking one's life.

Even young children who became involved in protest activities were beaten and arrested. In Gadsden, Alabama, "a 12-year-old girl, Lula Pollard, said a city policeman hit her in the stomach with a blackjack." Some of the five hundred demonstrators, children included, "were shocked by electric prod poles, both outside and inside the jail."[55] The following letter describes the conditions in which many of these young girls were jailed:

> [The photo] shows the 8' × 10' × 30' cell in which up to thirty girls were held for as long as a month, with no beds, mattresses, blankets, or springs. The picture of the shower shows the only source of water in the cell, for drinking or washing. An Affidavit from 11-year-old Lorena Barnum states: "The water was warm and sometimes hot. It tasted rusty and sometimes looked cloudy." The picture of the commode shows one of two commodes which were both stopped up so that there was no disposal of any kind in the cell.[56]

Economic reprisals were also not unusual. Peter Cummings, a SNCC worker, writes:

> Mrs. Reaves was a teacher at Old Salem High School until she lost her job this spring due to her civil rights activities. She was the only teacher in the school with an M.A. (from the U[niversity] of Chicago).[57]

In a field report, Bernice Robinson of the SCLC writes, "One teacher told of how she is continuing her class in spite of the attempts being made to force her father's employer and landlord to fire him and put him off the land (their only source of support)."[58]

Women of all ages experienced both physical and economic reprisals for their participation in the movement, just as their male comrades did. Many of these women became involved in the movement because they were already active local leaders. Their acts of tremendous courage inspired everyone around them, especially young men and women activists.

Conclusion

These indigenous leaders who risked their lives and the lives of their family members acted as crucial bridges between movement organizations and members of their respective communities. Without their day-to-day mobilization work and the trust that grew from their methods of operation, deeply frightened rural people could not have risked their lives. Although SNCC community and secondary bridge leaders provided the indigenous leadership with the tools to transfer their prefigurative politics to movement activism, they did not have the community connections and local know-how to motivate the rural masses to act. And in many cases, ministers as formal local leaders did not provide the leadership necessary to inspire their congregations or to assist the organizations' activists. The bridge between community and secondary leaders and indigenous leaders, the bridge between the latter and the rural community, and the preexisting community ties and networks nurtured by bridge leaders facilitated connections between rural life in the Deep South and the ideals of movement organizations.

Equally important is the fact that people in rural communities, in the face of extreme repression and violence, were able to overcome their fears through individual acts of courage, like that of Ida Mae Holland. It was the cumulative efforts of these emotionally charged, small but powerful, spontaneous, and sometimes planned responses that gave momentum to the movement. Local-level mobilization was the base upon which the civil rights movement rested, and it was no less important to the success of the movement than were the primary and secondary formal organizations and their formal leaders.

Cooperation and Conflict in
the Civil Rights Movement

Women as Primary Formal Leaders

Fannie Lou Hamer and the MFDP

The Mississippi Freedom Democratic Party (MFDP) continued its courageous effort to combat the entrenched Jim Crow laws that kept Blacks from voting. Despite increasingly violent reprisals, the MFDP succeeded in challenging the southern order through their alternative elections. With sixty-eight delegates and elected representatives, the challenge to the Democratic National Convention was well under way.

Upon their arrival in Atlantic City, the delegation was met by other Black civil rights leaders, including the Reverend Martin Luther King Jr., Bayard Rustin, and Roy Wilkins, as well as longtime White activist attorney Joseph Rauh. Rauh worked out the likeliest strategies for their challenge to the seats held by White delegates elected under Jim Crow laws. At the same time, political tension over the challenge reached the White House.

President Johnson, who had been in office only a year, was determined to win the nomination. He was well aware that his commitment to civil rights had alienated many southern Democrats, and that he could ill afford having his name linked to the Mississippi Freedom Democratic Party or their actions at the convention. Johnson was determined to control the MFDP challenge so that it did not endanger or overshadow his nomination. In addition to this concern, he planned to select Senator Hubert Humphrey as his running mate.

Humphrey had already alienated many White southerners by standing up to segregationists at the 1948 convention. His position as a potential running mate was further weakened because he had lost the 1960 presidential nomination. Under intense pressure to reshape his image so that he might be more palatable to south- ern Whites and with the political stakes high, Humphrey pushed the delegation to accept a compromise in committee rather than allow the seating decision to go to the floor. Had that happened and had it resulted in a successful challenge, the nation would have witnessed the removal of White delegates and their replace- ment by Blacks. Humphrey and Johnson understood that this powerful imagery would have signalled a shift of power and lost them the election.

To circumvent this possibility, a subcommittee of the Credentials Committee was appointed to seek a compromise. After this committee brainstormed for an entire weekend, Humphrey emerged and met with Dr. King, Attorney Rauh, MFDP chairman Aaron Henry, and Bob Moses of SNCC, urging them to accept a com- promise. At a subsequent meeting called by Representative Charles Diggs of Mich- igan, Hubert Humphrey met with Dr. King, Mrs. Hamer, Aaron Henry, Joseph Rauh, White MFDP activist the Reverend Ed King, and Congressional Represen- tatives Robert Kastenmeier of Wisconsin and Edith Green of Oregon. Ed King recalls Mrs. Hamer's confrontation with Humphrey, quoting her as saying:

> "Senator Humphrey, I been praying about you; and I been thinking about you, and you're a good man, and you know what's right. The trouble is, you're afraid to do what you know is right." She says, "You just want this job [as vice president], and I know a lot of people have lost their jobs, and God will take care of you, even if you lose this job. But Mr. Humphrey, if you take this job, you won't be worth anything. Mr. Humphrey, I'm going to pray for you again."[1]

The only tenable offer to come out of that meeting was made by Representative Green, who suggested that any of the delegates willing to take a loyalty oath ought to be seated. Hamer consulted the MFDP delegation, which decided that the com- promise was unacceptable. Mrs. Hamer's steadfast position during these negotia- tions—that the delegation should not accept any compromise unworthy of their cause and their constituency back home—resulted in her deliberate exclusion from future meetings.

Meanwhile, Rauh continued to lobby delegates and became increasingly aware of the power of President Johnson. While many of the convention's delegates supported the challenge, they were unwilling to publicly show their allegiance. Any support of the challenge now would be construed as a vote against the John- son-Humphrey ticket, since they had succeeded in distancing themselves from the MFDP cause. Frustrated, and with waning support, Rauh agreed to a meeting with Walter Reuther, a union leader and negotiator whom Johnson had persuaded to hammer out a deal.

At yet another meeting with Dr. King, Bayard Rustin, Aaron Henry, Bob

Moses, and Reverend Ed King, a final compromise was offered. The MFDP would be given two seats as at-large delegates. Aaron Henry and Rev. Ed King were chosen to fill those seats. The subcommittee would also make a public declaration that future state delegations would not be accepted if they were not legally elected or racially representative of their constituency. Rauh was horrified that the two seats were to be taken by a White minister and a Black middle-class druggist, while the majority of the delegates—the sharecroppers—remained unseated.

Even before Rauh had time to report back to the delegation, pressure to accept the compromise mounted. Walter Mondale, an aspiring politician and legal assistant to Senator Humphrey, presented the compromise to the Credentials Committee. Rauh recalls his experience: "I don't know if you've ever been in a lynch mob but this is one. They started hollering vote, even while I was still talking."[2]

Bowing to the atmosphere of near panic, Rauh and Mondale told reporters that a compromise had been reached. Bob Moses, meanwhile, had returned to the delegation, and the decision to accept or reject this latest compromise was debated. Some members worried that their representatives in the negotiation were too eager to surrender, that Moses was pressing the delegation to accept the compromise, and that Aaron Henry agreed because he felt beholden to Dr. King and Roy Wilkins for their support. But Henry recalls:

> I would have been perfectly willing to accept the two seats if they had permitted us to fracture these votes, shall we say in $\frac{1}{34}$ths, and give all of our delegates the same kind of rights to go on that floor and to take our seat and to participate in what was going on.
>
> I think we could have worked this thing out. I think that Bob [Moses] forced us into a hasty decision. I don't like to be critical of Bob, but I wonder really if he really wanted to win the situation. Now you know sometimes many of us feel more liberal every time we lose a battle. And because of the pressure that Bob was putting on so many of the delegates . . . move now, not later, now, now, now, now, now, I wonder, you know, really if he felt that we might be able to work something out that would be amenable to the total delegation rather than to be panicked into an immediate decision. Certainly the two votes were completely unacceptable to me and to everybody else. . . . I don't want nobody hand picking me.[3]

Despite the pressure exerted on the delegation by Bob Moses, he and James Farmer of CORE were the only male formal leaders to encourage the delegation to make its own decision. In private, Dr. King did not feel satisfied with the compromise and confided to Ed King that if he were a sharecropper, he would not have accepted the compromise. But King was swayed by Humphrey's private promise to wage war against racism in Mississippi.[4] Others, such as Roy Wilkins and Bayard Rustin, also accepted the compromise. During a heated argument, primarily with the women in the delegation, Wilkins told the women that they were ignorant of the political process, should listen to their leaders, and just return home.

In an interview, another of the delegates, Mrs. Unita Blackwell, recalls the event. She says that Mrs. Hamer just sat there in the back . . . and she said "Girl, I'm going to tell you the folks didn't send us up here for no two seats. When we left Mississippi, we said that we wanted all of the seats or half because we wanted to be represented in our state. . . ." So the three of us were just sitting there . . . and she said no compromise. "We been compromisin' all our life." I can feel it right now. Yes, honey, you could just feel the power of it. And, honey, they looked at us and told us we were ignorant. . . . The rumor went around that we was sixty-eight ignorant folks from Mississippi and didn't understand politics . . . and we looked at them and said, "We do understand more than you understand. We understand what we come out of."[5]

The delegation felt betrayed. Originally they had come to combat the Mississippi system of disenfranchisement, and now they found themselves battling their own. They no longer felt the sense of optimism and empowerment that had characterized the days leading up to the challenge. Many of the leaders were claiming a moral victory, but Hamer saw it as a defeat. Later, she remembered herself saying

"What do you mean moral victory? We ain't getting nothing."[6] [She continued]: What kind of moral victory was that, that we'd done sit up there, and they'd seen us on the televison. We come on back home and go right on up the first tree that we get to because, you know, that's what they were going to do to us. What had we gained?[7]

Unita Blackwell concurred:

Them people had not been talking to us poor folks. They had a certain clique that they'd talk to. The big niggers talk to the big niggers, and the little folks, they couldn't talk to nobody except themselves, you know. They just goin' to push the thing on through and have us there for showcase. But we tore that showcase down. That's for sure. We told them what we think.[8]

Despite their loss of power at the convention, the women aired their anger to other MFDP members. Hamer, in tears, made a plea to the delegates not to go along with the other Black formal leaders. She and Annie Devine convinced Henry Sias, a sixty-nine-year-old farmer who was chairman of the Issaquena County Freedom Democratic Party in the western part of Mississippi to change his support for the compromise. Sias recalls:

Now I seen Mrs. Hamer cry 'cause I got up on the floor; they wouldn't accept no two seats. . . . I changed my mind right there. Those two women just shamed me right there. When they got through talking and whoopin' and hollerin' and tellin' me what a shame it was for me to do that, I hushed right then. See, I backed off and drew way back in that corner.[9]

Through emotional and impassioned pleas, the women were able to persuade many of the delegates that they had a responsibility to their constituents at home. They continued to debate, and when the vote was taken, the delegation decided to reject the offer. However, Rauh and Mondale had already announced the unanimous acceptance of the compromise by the delegation. Hamer and others were furious. In response, she and the other women leaders, holding "guest" tickets to the convention forced their way onto the convention floor. They all stood in a circle for two hours, in silence.

The split between the formal male leaders of the movement organizations and the formal female leaders and most of the delegates further illustrates the degree to which women and men without the status of a minister's title were not considered formal leaders. Regardless of Hamer, Devine, and Blackwell's preeminent positions as formal leaders within a civil rights movement organization, they were not acknowledged as formal leaders within the social movement sector. Their locations within the movement did not require a conciliatory relationship with White political leadership at any level, allowing them to maintain their affinity to the poor Mississippians back home.

Gloria Richardson and the Cambridge Nonviolent Action Committee

This split between formal male and female leaders was also evident in the case of Gloria Richardson, co-chair and eventually chair and adult advisor of the Cambridge Nonviolent Action Committee (CNAC), in Maryland, whose conflicts with the social movement sector preceded those of women formal leaders of the MFDP. Richardson served as a formal leader of CNAC between approximately June 1962 and August 1964. Her position as chair occurred by default. She explains:

> Initially it was under a co-chairmanship. A man and a woman; the man was my cousin and ultimately resigned because he always was a bail bondsman and he felt that it was a conflict. The woman's health was temporarily impaired, which left me there, so by default I became chairman. Also, because there were community meetings and people really asked me to . . . I guess, bear the brunt of that—to represent them because they felt that I was furthest removed from economic reprisals at the time because my uncle and my mother would support me and my family at that period, whereas other people . . . [had] to, I guess, moderate their lives.[10]

As with many other women with primary formal and secondary formal bridge leadership positions, Richardson received her title because no man was willing or able to do the job. However, Richardson first became involved in movement activities while a student at Howard University between 1938 and 1942. Through her NAACP involvement, she and her fellow students picketed local stores in Washington D.C., protesting racial discrimination. Richardson characterized Cambridge as ripe for protests. By her own account, it was a place with a "disproportionately high unemployment rate for Blacks, unreliable seasonal employment, and blatant segregation [which] contributed to the feelings of anger and resentment [that] eventually led to the mini-wars on the street."[11] So when SNCC came to Cambridge to mobilize the community and to cultivate leadership, Richardson became involved. She had been frustrated by the local NAACP and its leadership, claiming that "I could never work with the NAACP; it took them too long to make decisions."[12] The CNAC operated similarly to SNCC with much of its "decision making [taking] place in bull sessions. Their protests and other actions often took the form of spontaneous responses to moves taken by local officials."[13] Moreover, as Richardson states, " 'We emphasized . . . that while you should be educated, that education, degrees, college degrees were not essential. If you could articulate the need, if you knew what the need was, if you were aware of the kinds of games that white folks play, that was the real thing.' "[14] SNCC's cultivation of local leadership led to Richardson's position as a formal local leader in SNCC's Cambridge affiliate.

Unlike other formal local leaders, such as Daisy Bates, who operated as community bridge leaders, Richardson became a high-profile and highly controversial formal leader by refusing to compromise with city officials challenging primary formal national leaders, and for not openly denouncing violent tactics. Initially the CNAC was concerned with integration of public accommodations. Subsequently, however, it solicited responses to a questionnaire aimed at assessing the concerns of the community. The results indicated a strong desire for better health care and low-income housing. Richardson sought changes in all of these areas, so

on July 22, 1963, at the invitation of Assistant Attorney General Burke Marshall who was in charge of the Civil Rights Division, a conference was convened in Washington. The government representatives were State Attorney General Thomas B. Finon; his deputy, Robert C. Murphy; Brigadier General George M. Gelston; and Governor Tawes's top aide, Edmund C. Mester. The civil rights leaders included Gloria Richardson, John Lewis, Reginald Robinson and Stanley Branche. The sessions included Attorney General Robert F. Kennedy and Robert Weaver, head of the Housing and Home Finance Agency. A prime issue in the Cambridge situation was the construction of a million-dollar housing project in the Negro section of the city (twice postponed by white authorities). On the morning of July 23, 1963, the mayor and other city officials arrived, and with Kennedy and Marshall as witnesses, the five-point Treaty of Cambridge was signed by Black and city officials in Attorney General Robert Kennedy's office.

The points of agreement called for:

1. Complete and immediate desegregation of the public schools (with integrated busing) and hospitals in the county.
2. Construction of 200 units of low-rent public housing for Negroes.
3. Employment of a Negro in the Cambridge office of the Maryland Department of Employment Security and in the Post Office.
4. Appointment of a Human Relations Commission.
5. Adoption of a Charter Amendment which provided for desegregation of places of public accommodation.[15]

Subsequently, despite the fact that those who took part in the conference did not want a referendum vote on the last point, citizens signed referendum petitions forcing a vote. A referendum to ratify the town charter that would make it illegal to refuse service to Blacks in restaurants, motels and other places of public accommodation was now up for a vote.[16] In addition, the mayor and city council were calling for a moratorium on demonstrations, pickets, and protests until after the vote was completed.[17] Richardson and the CNAC refused to endorse the measure and called upon the local Black community to refuse to vote. The NAACP and its leaders were appalled at CNAC's lack of support and blamed the subsequent defeat of the measure on the latter. Richardson believed that the issue of equality for Black people required an amendment to the U. S. Constitution rather than local and state-level amendment ratification. Moreover, such an amendment would not address the other issues so salient to the Black Cambridge community.

Following the demise of the amendment, violence in the streets escalated. Cambridge became a battle zone, and many leaders, both Black and White, local and national, blamed Richardson. Since she refused to renounce the violence and to compromise, the NAACP broke all ties with the CNAC in general and with Richardson in particular. In response to her acceptance of violence, she replied, "When a mad dog is after you, you don't run."[18] And she placed her beliefs as more in line with Malcolm X than Mohandas Gandhi or Martin Luther King Jr. Moreover, she criticized White liberals, who distanced themselves from the movement, and national leaders, whom she described as presenting "meaningless smiles." At one point, she was arrested and an attempt was made to have her institutionalized as mentally incompetent.[19]

In keeping with many Black female bridge leaders, Richardson's position was much more uncompromising than that of the formal Black male leaders. When city officials decided to name the Black leaders with whom they were willing to negotiate, Richardson responded:

> We wish to make it unalterably clear that we will determine, and not the political structure of the city, who shall speak for the Negro community. The day has ended in America when any white person can determine our leaders and spokesmen.[20]

The White media as well as President Kennedy, began to attack Richardson's position and leadership. Kennedy noted that Cambridge was a town that had "lost sight of what demonstrations are about because of violence."[21] Richardson quickly sent a letter protesting his statements, and later, at a rally, Richardson said that

> unless something is achieved soon in Cambridge, then no one is going to be able to control these people who have been provoked by generations of segregation, by countless indignities—and now by uncontrollable white mobs in the streets. . . . Instead of progress we have anarchy. The white men who have power . . . sit in their comfortable houses, undisturbed by events until it is too late.[22]

The White media, such as the *Washington Evening Post*, and the *New York Times*, portrayed her as fiercely ambitious and a liability to the movement. The *Post* relied on an anonymous Negro informant.

> The informant depicts Richardson as a college-educated social snob who really wanted to be accepted by whites and who responded to their personal rebuffs by

starting a race war between Whites and Blacks. The *New York Times* also seems to identify Richardson as a central catalyst of race hatred, identifying her as having made the most bitter statement of the entire desegregation campaign.[23]

Richardson was attacked not only by the White media but also by formal Black male leaders. Anita Foeman, who has researched Gloria Richardson's life and activism, writes:

In the day-to day movement, apparently Richardson's role as a female leader was challenged more directly. According to Giddings (1984), although Richardson was among the most radical and outspoken of the movement's leaders, the most radical Black male activists rejected her most vehemently. She was shouted down at one rally as "castrator." In perhaps another paradox of the times, the most radical Black *male* activists tended to be most conservative in terms of gender roles. Thus the men who were most consistent in their activist views with Richardson rejected her due to what they perceived as inappropriate gender behavior. . . .

More moderate activists were consistent in their views and found Richardson's style *and* her politics distasteful. So although Richardson was a leader in the sense that she held an organizational post, negotiated agreements, organized activities, articulated needs, and was courted by the media, she had no true constituency. Perhaps this explains the powerful but short-lived nature of her era and the willingness of activists on all sides to turn from her. Notably, as Richardson reflects on the times, she downplays any gender conflict, stating, "We were fighting for our lives. . . . There was lots of role flexibility, there had to be.[24]

Interestingly, the Black media, notably *Ebony* magazine, wrote about Richardson in positive terms, noting her personal attributes, as well as her controversial personality. Of her analysis of the Black media's treatment of Gloria Richardson, Foeman writes:

In each case, the posture of the publication was respectful, even reverent. As was typical of the publication, the stories focused on Richardson's individual persona and presented a positive profile. *Ebony* described both volatile and calculating qualities in Richardson and made little effort to reconcile any tension that might be implied between the two. The July 1964 article describes a 5-foot 7-inch, 138-pound woman (others describe this as slight), an only child born to a woman who says that, if she had had another child like Gloria, the mother probably would have been dead years ago. The same piece describes the leader as a woman who allured her fiancee by wearing a pink chemise to a protest demonstration. The article describes Richardson as perhaps overdramatic on the one hand and a witty, cunning "general" on the other. The writer allows all of these images to stand side by side and, in effect, challenges the reader to reconcile any inconsistency that might be felt.[25]

This inconsistency typifies the ambivalence of women's positions as primary formal leaders in the civil rights movement. They were women, but their leadership capabilities as strong and courageous leaders were needed. Yet when they acted entirely of their own accord, they often conflicted with formal male leaders, particularly those of the secondary and primary organizations, whose need to remain credible with the state necessarily influenced their decision making. As Foeman, points out, Richardson did not have a constituency. Unlike educated ministers, there was no traditional group for which she would have been considered a primary formal leader. As a woman, she was already outside of the inner-circle. Her failure to comply with the wishes of the primary formal and secondary formal leaders, and her assertiveness in questioning their philosophy, tactics, and strategies, further alienated her from the core of movement sector leaders. According to Foeman,

> The local NAACP would break with Richardson. . . . Later, King privately questioned her political stance. A number of Black churches created distance from her movement, and some local civil rights activists avoided associations with her. Her caustic and, to some, erratic political approach confused and disturbed people. Richardson's movement began to falter. Demonstrations became more infrequent and more sparsely attended.[26]

A year later, Richardson and her family would move to New York, and the Cambridge movement would never regain its former strength. Gloria Richardson, much like Fannie Lou Hamer, stepped beyond the bounds of her ascribed and gendered position to lead in the movement. However, when women as formal leaders were faced with the dominance of the formal male leaders in primary and secondary formal organizations, their ideas and desires were overridden or discouraged. Of course, the women were not faced with the pressures of national credibility and the need to compromise. They were not part of the inner circle and had the luxury of remaining true to their constituents. Women primary formal leaders who stepped outside the bounds of women's leadership risked alienating the very constituency they purported to represent. Both Fannie Lou Hamer and Gloria Richardson's rise to positions as primary formal bridge leaders was uncommon and by default. Hamer's rise to power was in an atmosphere of fear, where formal male leadership would likely result in death, and Richardson's leadership developed by default as well. They were needed, so as primary formal bridge leaders they remained credible as long as they occupied the free space of localized and nonthreatening organizations and complied with the wishes of the primary formal and secondary formal organizations.

Women as formal bridge leaders often operated semiautonomously in what Evans and Boyte term a "free space."[27] Here, women controlled their day-to-day activities and kept in touch with the desires of the community and the movement's constituents. This is not to suggest that the formal male leaders of primary and secondary formal organizations were out of touch with the masses, only that the requirements of their pivotal relationships with the state necessarily shaped their decisions. Yet when these women took on a title as formal leader and exercised their power to the fullest, they were either ignored and overridden or lost their credibility.

Women Bridge Leaders and Formal Male Leaders in Conflict

Women, Collective Styles, and the SCLC

It is clear that the dynamics at the Democratic National Convention were not an anomaly. Bridge leaders and formal leaders were often in conflict, and that conflict often took the form of clashes between hierarchical and collective styles of organization. An example of this was the earlier challenge to power relations within the SCLC brought by Miss Ella Baker, Mrs. Septima Clark and Miss Diane Nash, all believers in group-centered leadership. In her usual direct manner, Miss Baker recalled that she was not afraid to question Dr. King and that this irritated him.[28] In general, she disagreed with his approach to the movement. She recalls:

> I set up the office of the Southern Christian Leadership Conference in 1958, but you didn't see me on television, you didn't see news stories about me. The kind of role that I tried to play was to pick up pieces or put together pieces out of which I hoped organization might come. My theory is, strong people don't need strong leaders.[29]

She did not believe that a "leader-centered movement" was in the best interests of long-term civil rights activism. It was important to "try to develop leadership out of the group and to spread leadership roles so that you develop. . . . In other words, you're organizing people to be self-sufficient rather than to be dependent upon the charismatic leader."[30] Miss Baker was dissatisfied with the lack of effort to organize the SCLC for action. Instead, the SCLC relied on local groups to organize themselves; then Dr. King would appear and become "the center of attention . . . with this world-wide charisma that he had obtained, or the charismatic state he had reached."[31] She did not believe that one leader was the best for the movement.

Septima Clark echoed this view:

> I sent a letter to Dr. King asking him not to lead all of the marches himself, but instead to develop leaders who could lead their own marches. Dr. King read that letter before the staff. It just tickled them; they just laughed. . . . If you think that another man should lead, then you are looking down on Dr. King. This was the way it was.[32]

In a similar vein, following the bombing of Birmingham's Sixteenth Avenue Baptist Church in which four young girls (Carol Robertson, Cynthia Wesley, Addie Mae Collins, and Denise McNair) were murdered, Diane Nash, a key founder of SNCC and an extremely courageous civil rights activist, generated a plan of action that she submitted to Dr. King and other local leaders. While attending the funeral of one of the girls, she had noticed the anger of those attending and their desire for action. Her plan was to harness this fury and shut down Montgomery. King and the others read the plan, but as Birmingham minister John Porter states, Dr. King "looked at her and laughed."[33] He later agreed to review the plan. The philosophy of leadership espoused by these women clearly conflicted with that of the ministers in the SCLC and, if adopted, would have severely diminished the ministers' power and dominance.

Women Bridge Leaders and CORE

Similar problems beset CORE and were part of its ongoing struggle for identity. CORE was besieged with conflict between leadership from the national headquarters and initiatives taken by field workers and affiliate chapters. Because of its commitment to integration, and thus its integrated leadership, CORE was less attractive to potential Black supporters. Moreover, its National Office was located in New York and its national formal leadership lived in the North. Despite the fact that its central leader, James Farmer, was a well-educated Black Methodist minister, CORE as an integrated organization never gained the mass support of southern Blacks and constantly struggled to define itself within the context of the wider movement. Although it gained recognition through the Freedom Rides, CORE's mobilization influences were greatest in areas neglected by the SCLC and SNCC.

CORE-sponsored mobilization did occur, however, in a few southern states, especially Florida and Louisiana, and later in Mississippi as a part of COFO. Many of the leaders of the more activist local chapters were Black women such as Patricia Stephens Due, who single-handedly mobilized sit-ins in Tallahassee, Florida, and Oretha Castle of New Orleans, who organized and sustained that chapter. Due would be awarded the 1960 Gandhi Award for her efforts in Tallahassee. Zev Aelony, a CORE worker, recounts the strength of her leadership:

> In Tallahassee, demonstrations had stopped, largely because of the combination of the students being gone for the summer, and fatigue on the part of Pat Due. The situation reminds me of the bible story of the battle in which the People of Israel would win as long as Moses held his arms high, but as he became fatigued, the people lost heart and fell back. So it is in Tallahassee with Pat.[34]

CORE was organized hierarchically, with the work of local chapters monitored by the Office of Organization. Men constituted the majority of the officers, and its advisory committee consisted of Ralph Abernathy, King's right hand man, and Dr. King himself.[35] Few women served on the national field staff, most notably Genevieve Hughes, Joyce Ware, Lois Chaffee, Mary Hamilton, and Oretha Castle.[36] More women came to work in field operations with the development of COFO during the summers of 1964 and 1965, and many others came to head local branches. Although many women gained formal title at the national level, as well as at local levels, women never possessed the power held by men. Their national-level activities, field activities, and local leadership were continually overseen and coordinated by the male-dominated National Office.

In CORE more than any other organization, women's titles were not synonymous with power. While titles reflected exclusion from the primary and secondary national level of power, they did not exclude women from actual leadership. Moreover, when women did have titles, this often resulted in less power, since such titles or the work associated with them adhered more closely to gender-based norms. For example, Catherine Raymond was CORE's national treasurer, but she was also Executive Secretary George Houser's secretary.[37] She clearly did not have the power that one would assume from simply looking at her title. Another example is Gladys Harrington, chair of the New York CORE, who was at odds with the national headquarters and its officers precisely because James Farmer, national director of CORE, and Marvin Rich, executive director of CORE, asserted power over the affiliates.[38] Gladys Harrington's position as chair was rigorously challenged by Blyden Jackson, a Black male who was supported by Norman Hill, an individual very much a part of Farmer's inner circle.[39] Moreover, Harrington's position was challenged by Marshall England, another Black male, who was supported by Roy Innis, a proponent of Black male leadership who would later become CORE's national director.[40]

While many women served as chairpersons in CORE at the local level, this in no way suggests that women had national power. While the wives of James Farmer, Norman Hill, and Marvin Rich—Lula Farmer (who worked at the national level as the bookkeeper), Velma Hill, and Evelyn Rich—occupied positions on the National Action Committee that governed CORE, their status as independent powers was questioned even by Harrington, who pushed for an amendment to bar family members from participation.[41]

Bernice Fisher, a White female activist who served as secretary-treasurer, was active in CORE during its early years, primarily when there was a critical need for someone to organize CORE while working without a staff or office. She recalled that in "Those first three years, there was no money, no salary, no office of our own, and actually no desire on our part to get institutionalized."[42] This was not unlike the position of Ella Baker as the acting executive director of the SCLC, who in the latter's infancy worked tirelessly with little material or financial support.

Another example of a woman who was an essential leader in CORE but whose title does not reflect her contribution is Ruth Turner, who worked as a leader in the Cleveland chapter. She later developed CORE's Black Power philosophy and was subsequently appointed assistant to the national chair, Floyd McKissick.[43] Her position in CORE was not unlike that of Diane Nash's, who co-authored the philosophy of SNCC but who never served as SNCC's chair. Turner, in keeping with many women bridge leaders, advocated a grassroots mobilization strategy, one which Ella Baker put into place in the SCLC and SNCC. Many CORE women were in regional (really more often local) leadership positions, but this did not change the fact that at the national level, they did not hold formal positions with power. Their lack of national power often manifested itself in conflicts with CORE's national-level leaders.

Genevieve Hughes was a young White woman who quit her job with Dun and Bradstreet to work for the movement.[44] She was the first woman field secretary in CORE, but Charles Oldham, one of its founders and a previous national chairman, did not think highly of her. In a March 9, 1961, letter to Field Director Gordon Carey, Oldham discusses both his discontent with her performance and his approval of Joe Perkins, another new field worker:

My reaction to Perkins is favorable. However I have not had any opportunity to observe his work in the field, but I felt that he did a good job at council meeting, and while his field reports tend to emphasize the "I," I don't think this is a serious drawback.

In regard to Genevieve, I have serious reservations about her abilities to do an effective job for CORE. I am making this observation from the field reports that she has submitted and from the reaction various delegates at the council meeting expressed to me about her personality. The thing which concerns me in her field reports is the great deal of analytical material relating to the thought process and character analysis of the various individuals with whom she is working. She definitely goes overboard in this area, and her field reports read sort of like a miniature Kinsey report. By that I mean she is not reporting upon their sex activities, but rather upon their CORE activities in a psychiatric examination of their motives, impulses and behaviour patterns. I am not sure what her previous experience was, but she must have been a psychiatric social worker.

I agree with you in your observation that if we have individuals who will not contribute to CORE that we should definitely make arrangements for severance of relationships in order to get more competent individuals.[45]

Despite this rather scathing assessment of her abilities, Hughes did continue her work for CORE in both the North and the South, eventually organizing in California.

Conflicts continued to arise between the local field leaders and those in the National Office. In a letter to Norman Hill, who rose from field secretary to program director of CORE, Lois Chaffee, "speaking for the Mississippi Task Force Workers," describes the conflict:

While I am sympathetic to the special problems of the North, I do not feel that Mississippi is a blue-jeans operation, which lends glamour to the serious business up North. This situation is grown up. We write this letter in the shadow of the murder of Louis Allen. Allen was the only witness willing to speak out after the 1961 murder of Herbert Lee in Amite County. He never publicly testified because the Justice Department would not offer to protect his life and family. He was threatened repeatedly during the two and a half years he lived after the Lee murder, his jaw broken last summer by a deputy sheriff, and finally the threats upon his life were executed. That takes care of the possibility that the Lee case could have been settled with justice. We feel that we, too, are working with no outside protection in Canton, that we have only each other. We can't mess around with petty organizational disagreements and with separate loyalties when the OUT THERE aspect is so pressing. We must work together, and those are not just words. We would like you to try to understand and sympathize with this attitude we have (that we have to have), and try to communicate the feeling to other people in the National Office. It is very demoralizing when one of our fellows, a dedicated worker and a leader of the Canton project (and Canton is supposed to be a CORE Project) is excluded from the staff meeting because it is a "CORE staff" meeting by a representative of the National

Office. We cannot define staff in terms of payroll. Such ridiculous divisions lead to a breakdown of the tightly-knit "community" feeling we have to have. . . .

We have the impression that somehow we're not really true CORE people if we operate on a basis different from that of the New York Office. . . . We want a willingness on the part of the National CORE to approach staff problems differently. There can be no artificial division between salaried CORE workers, local volunteer workers and workers with other groups. . . . A person's work and leadership distinguish him as "staff," not the weekly $25.[46]

Such conflict also existed between the National Office and the New Orleans chapter headed by Oretha Castle. Mary Hamilton, a Black woman from the West Coast who formerly was rural central Tennessee's chairperson and organized fearful local communities in the South, was not unlike many of the bridge leaders of other organizations. Subsequently, however, she was sent to oversee local southern chapters by James McCain, director of organization. Of the conflict between the National Office and Oretha Castle, Hamilton wrote:

New Orleans CORE has turned out to be even a larger problem than I ever imagined at the first. In one of my earlier reports I stated that what was needed was new blood in their chapter. I then set as my task the solving of this problem. During the following weeks, after I first arrived, I attempted on several occasions to discuss with Oretha what steps could be taken in getting the chapter back on its feet. I met nothing but a stone wall in this effort. I have found it quite difficult to work with this group. To me there seems to be a general atmosphere of un-cooperativeness and a hostility towards anyone whose task it is to be assigned to them.[47]

Here the conflict and tension manifests itself between a woman as professional bridge leader and a woman as community bridge leader. Mary Hamilton was acting as a mediator between the desires of the National Office and the local chapter. Although she traveled throughout the South in a seemingly autonomous position, unlike professional SNCC bridge leaders or even leaders in the SCLC, she was very much accountable to the National Office. This fact impeded the effectiveness of CORE to mobilize in the South.[48]

Conclusion

The tensions between bridge and formal leaders were not as acute in SNCC and the MFDP. In the MFDP, though the structure was hierarchical, decisions were made through consensus, just as they were in SNCC. As Victoria Gray, a candidate in the organization, recalls, "No one person made the decisions in the MFDP. Not ever. We insisted that whatever decisions were made, they were made by the body."[49]

Thus, what seems to differentiate the positions of women within the SCLC, MIA, CORE, and the NAACP from those in SNCC and the MFDP is the centralized versus decentralized nature of power, the latter developed from a philosophy of group-centered leadership. Where the organization had centralized power, women were less likely, is spite of or because of their title, to *participate* as primary or secondary formal leaders. Though there were restrictions on SNCC and MFDP women, they had greater access to such positions. In organizations in which the power was decentralized and in which titles did not necessarily bring power, women chose autonomous positions. These positions, however, could be titled, untitled, or uniquely titled.

Within the MFDP, women were able to lead as primary and secondary formal bridge leaders. Their positions as formal leaders with power can be attributed to the dangerous circumstances in the South, which many of the interviewees pointed out were more likely to lead to death for male leaders than for female leaders. In this context, Fannie Lou Hamer became the symbol of Freedom for the movement, overcoming her aforementioned painful beating and asserting her charismatic appeal through song and speech. In a 1966 article, Joseph Gusfield noted:

> The public may accept as the leader of a movement someone whom the organized segments of the movement rejected. The "popular hero" may perform a considerable amount of articulating or even mobilizing functions without having the imprimatur of an official position. Such a person is able to perform functions in one area without being subject to the controls of the other parts of the role set.[50]

In looking at the civil rights movement as a whole—that is, the movement sector—it is clear that Fannie Lou Hamer held the position of popular heroine. She was a powerful figure within the Mississippi Freedom Democratic Party, both an articulator and a mobilizer at the formal level of leadership. Her power was not received as legitimate among the primary formal movement leaders, however, because she was a woman and lacked formal education. Like other rare women who were primary formal bridge leaders, this symbol of Freedom served as a steady voice of conscience for other poor people, articulating the sensibilities of those whose wisdom and vision remained behind the scenes and were often compromised.

In parallel fashion, both SNCC and one of its primary formal bridge leaders, Bob Moses, encountered great difficulty in being accepted as a legitimate voice for the movement. Although Moses was an educated formal leader, he led in a bridge organization that was student driven, decentralized, and direct-action oriented. SNCC was a crucial bridging organization within the broader movement sector, while women performed similar bridging activities at the internal organization level. In either case, such essential bridging functions were the backbone of the movement, yet they did not, and still do not, receive their rightful due.

The differences in allegiance and action among leaders from all three forms of movement organizations and the special mindfulness of bridge leaders to the desires of their constituents were exhibited during the MFDP challenge to the 1964 Democratic National Convention. Men who were primary formal leaders in their respective organizations were swayed by the power of the primary formal leadership in the primary and secondary movement organizations. Aaron Henry debated in favor of the compromise, as did Ed King. While James Farmer and Bob Moses left the decision to the delegation, they did not take a strong position in support of the delegation's decision not to accept the compromise. Women leaders in the

MFDP, having no hope of positional enhancement or of becoming part of the fraternal order within the movement sector, were more autonomous with respect to movement allegiance. Their activities were unlikely to be rewarded with increased status and power, as national-level, primary formal leaders, or even as members of the inner-circle.

The effects of the decision to accept the compromise were to have profound consequences for the movement. In many ways, the process by which the delegation was sold out led to the beginning of the end of SNCC, and to grassroots empowerment in general. Although Hubert Humphrey kept his promise and the the Voting Rights Act of 1965 was passed, the conflict between formal and bridge leaders resulted in feelings of disempowerment and hopelessness on the part of SNCC, COFO, and MFDP activists. Scores of volunteers who had expended immense energy on this project began to leave the state, and SNCC entered a crisis of self-definition. Although many scholars have attributed the decline of active mobilization in the Black community to a crisis in leadership following the assassination of Dr. King, the movement had already begun to unravel from the bottom.

The Movement Unravels
From the Bottom

Primary Formal Leaders, Compromise,
and Disillusionment

The events at the Democratic National Convention were to have profound consequences for the future of the civil rights movement and for the Black struggle
in general. They signaled the beginning of the deterioration of movement solidarity. Although relations had always been strained, the disillusionment of those
in the lower ranks, as well as among many SNCC and CORE activists, particularly
those working in Mississippi, led to a fractured movement and the loss of its
bridging tiers.

In his autobiography, Cleve Sellers describes the beginning of the movement's
descent:

> The national Democratic party's rejection of the MFDP at the 1964 convention was
> to the civil rights movement what the Civil War was to American history: afterward,
> things could never be the same. Never again were we lulled into believing that our
> task was exposing injustices so that the "good" people of America could eliminate
> them. We left Atlantic City with the knowledge that the movement had turned into
> something else. After Atlantic City, our struggle was not for civil rights, but for
> liberation.[1]

Dottie Zellner agrees:

> When the liberals completely betrayed SNCC, this is what . . . was SNCC's high point and its low point at the same time. Because this is where SNCC got the most visibility, and it actually was the beginning of the end. It was when people began to realize that society was not going to adapt. In other words, the doors looked like they were opened and they weren't. And SNCC then had to develop new, different strategies. And I think looking back thirty years later, I now see that people couldn't do it, weren't prepared to do it, didn't know how to do it. But at the time this great disillusionment set in, and I would say it started in the fall of '64. People felt they had been close, and that the doors had been slammed on them again. They felt that the people that they had traditionally relied on, the White liberals, had betrayed them, which they had. It was time for something new. How could they just keep on registering people to vote for . . . who? Lyndon Johnson. You know? I mean [these were] some very serious, profound questions and at the same time, and maybe not so coincidentally, the racial issue became much more severe.
>
> And then you had the . . . separatists, who were advocating it openly for the first time: an all-Black organization. And that had *never*. . . . The first time I ever heard those words come out of anyone's mouth to me, either publicly or privately, was in the winter of '65. This was said in a meeting, in a formal, official way. Up until then—now, I would say the whole year of '65—there were a lot of discussions like that going on, but until the winter of '65–66 I don't think that was articulated as a viable thing until then. And then it was. So it was sort of, to me, like, "Oh, someone has said the unspeakable." Once they said it, of course, it became much more a possibility.[2]

The teachings of Malcolm X began to resonate with many SNCC activists. After the disappointment at the convention, SNCC activists and MFDP leaders—Fannie Lou Hamer, Bob Moses, Donna Moses, Julian Bond, James Forman, John Lewis, Ruby Doris Smith Robinson, Prathia Hall Wynn, and others—traveled to Guinea. The trip was arranged by Harry Belafonte, who was a staunch SNCC supporter and who had traveled to Mississippi to personally witness the conditions. The group was astounded to see a country run by Blacks and to meet its president, Sekou Toure. The trip caused the group to ponder the fact that they could have been descendents of some of the people in Guinea, but because of slavery, they had been ripped from their roots. They experienced a country of Black people who were proud of their culture and heritage. Guinea had just gained its independence from France, and was deeply committed to the preservation of its culture. For the first time, Ruby Doris Smith Robinson and the others saw women wearing cornrows in their hair. Robinson let a Guinea woman braid her hair in this fashion. The group experienced a growing sense of identity that was rooted in one's Blackness, one's dark skin, one's kinky hair, and one's culture.

When they returned from their trip, SNCC was in a crisis over its identity, and Malcolm X's view of American society began to ring true in the hearts of many of its leaders. He appealed to the frustrations of the Black masses and began to tie the struggle of Blacks in the North to those in the South. Mrs. Hamer and the

SNCC Freedom Singers were to appear at rallies with Malcolm X in December 1964. Here, Malcolm X drew his parallels:

America is Mississippi. There's no such thing as a Mason-Dixon line—it's America. There's no such thing as the South—it's America. If one room in your house is dirty, you've got a dirty house. . . . You have authority over the whole house; the entire house is under your jurisdiction. And the mistake that you and I make is letting these *Northern* crackers shift the weight to the Southern crackers. . . .

The head of the Democratic Party is sitting in the White House. He could have gotten Mrs. Hamer into Atlantic City. He could have opened up his mouth and had her seated. Hubert Humphrey could have opened his mouth and had her seated. [Robert] Wagner, the mayor right here [in New York City], could have opened up his mouth and used his weight and had her seated. Don't be talking about some crackers down in Mississippi and Alabama and Georgia—all of them are playing the same game. Lyndon B. Johnson is the head of the Cracker Party.[3]

Whereas, previously King was able to draw northern Black activists and sympathizers from the North to the southern movement, Malcolm X began to draw such support from the South to the North. On one occasion in which he and Hamer shared a platform, she told of her brutal beating when jailed in Winona, Mississippi. Following her moving account of the events, Malcolm X began to speak, contextualizing Hamer's story of oppression in gendered terms:

No, we don't deserve to be recognized and respected as men as long as our women can be brutalized in the manner that this woman described, and nothing being done about it, but we sit around singing "We Shall Overcome."

We need a Mau Mau [a reference to Kenya's terrorist Mau Mau society led by Oginga Odinga]. If they don't want to deal with the Mississippi Freedom Democratic Party, then we'll give them something else to deal with. If they don't want to deal with the Student Nonviolent Committee, then we have to give them an alternative. Never stick someone out there without an alternative.[4]

Yet Malcolm X did not believe that women shouldn't be as fully engaged in the struggle as men. Of Fannie Lou Hamer, he viewed her as "the country's number one freedom-fighting woman" and believed that "you don't have to be a man to fight for freedom. All you have to do is be an intelligent human being. And automatically, your intelligence makes you want freedom so badly that you'll do anything, by any means necessary, to get that freedom."[5]

Malcolm X's pronouncements, which were at variance with the nonviolent philosophy of SNCC, appealed to the disillusioned members of SNCC. Although SNCC was shifting to a more radical politics and philosophy, it began a new project, the Mississippi Challenge, organized through the MFDP. The project involved a challenge to the congressional seats illegally occupied by White southerners. Much like the Atlantic City challenge, the law was on the side of the MFDP and their elected congressional officials. Yet when congress reconvened in January 1965, its members rejected the challenge. This defeat gave further credence to the view that even if Black people played by the rules, they couldn't succeed. Victoria Gray, one of the Black congresswomen challenging the seats, remarked:

> I guess the thing that hurt the most was the disillusionment on the faces of the young people. That hurt. That really hurt because many of them thought that when faced with the truth . . . our officials will do the right thing.[6]

And the loss left Mrs. Hamer in tears. In response to media questions about how she felt, she replied:

> What kind of country is it that is afraid to let the people know the truth? Why is the white man so afraid to let the people know? . . . I'm not crying for myself today, but I'm crying for America. I cry that the Constitution of the United States, written down on paper, applies only to white people. But we will come back year after year until we are allowed our rights as citizens.[7]

With a deepening disappointment with what working through the system could provide, the clash between SNCC workers and the SCLC reached its peak in Selma. In mid-January 1965, Dr. King and the SCLC announced a march from Selma to Montgomery to protest and draw national attention to voter-registration violations in several Alabama counties. The idea was actually the brainchild of Mrs. Amelia P. Boynton, an indigenous bridge leader who worked with both the SCLC and SNCC. SNCC workers had been in Selma for some time, organizing communities to help themselves and to fight for their rights. King and the SCLC, however, used a demonstration-march approach to draw national attention and to pressure local and state governments into compliance, which usually took the form of compromise. They would then declare a moral victory and move on. SNCC resented this approach and felt that it did nothing to gain real change, only lulling the masses to accept less than their full rights.

While King and the SCLC awaited court approval to march, they began small demonstrations, which SNCC felt detracted from their own efforts to mobilize and organize at the grassroots level.[8] Yet the SCLC was determined to make public the discrimination and repression of Blacks in Alabama. SNCC, recognizing that the march would take place, still voted against full participation, but did agree not to renounce it. Not all were against the march, however, the chief proponent being SNCC Chairman and member of the SCLC board of directors John Lewis. In the meantime, President Johnson exerted pressure on King not to march, and King's aides were concerned about the escalation of death threats. Eventually, King capitulated to the demands and fears, and Hosea Williams and John Lewis led the march.

It was one of the bloodiest and most violent encounters in the movement's history, with the notoriously racist Sheriff Clark deputizing hundreds of men and gaining the support of state troopers led by Major John Cloud. As the marchers crossed the Edmund Pettus Bridge, they were surrounded on both sides, teargassed, and beaten. The march descended into chaos and panic with men, women, and children fleeing for their lives while being pursued by men on horseback brandishing nightsticks, cattle prods, and chains. Seventy to eighty people were injured; among many others, John Lewis was hospitalized with severe injuries to the head. Mrs. Boynton was left unconscious from blows to the head and tear-gas inhalation. The media captured the events, and there was a subsequent public outcry against the brutality. Senators in support of the Voting Rights Act called for its passage as the least that could be done to honor the victims.[9]

Hearing the news, King immediately flew to Selma and conferred with local as well as national leaders. Many of the local people, as well as the bridge leaders in SNCC, supported a continuation of the march. The Johnson administration sought to block such a march with an injunction. King was torn. He had never before defied a federal judge, but his commitment to the masses, as well as the pressure exerted by indigenous and SNCC bridge leaders, prevailed. The evening before the march, LeRoy Collins, former governor of Florida and director of the federal Community Relations Service, which developed out of a provision of the Civil Rights Act, came to mediate the situation. He proposed that Sheriff Clark and Colonel Al Lingo, head of the Alabama state troopers, agree not to attack the marchers if they would turn around once they reached the troopers. King could lead the march, make a symbolic stop, and then turn around. This would avert bloodshed and allow King to support the masses and activists in favor of the march. King agreed to the plan. However, when King led the marchers, the troops cleared a path so that they could continue. King still turned the marchers around. They followed him, but upon returning to Selma, demanded to know why he had not continued on to Montgomery. King was forced to tell of his agreement with Collins.

SNCC bridge leaders and participants were outraged, and this served to widen the gap between the primary formal organization and the bridge organization. SNCC had now been betrayed twice. Once again, they possessed little or no power within the movement sector. In the encounter at the Edmund Pettus bridge, Jimmie Lee Jackson, trying to protect his mother from a trooper's blows, was killed. Reverend James J. Reeb of Boston was also beaten to death. SNCC felt that little had been accomplished. While King's actions displeased those in SNCC, he did gain the support of the federal government and mainstream Americans. Johnson had taken a stance insisting that Alabama's Governor Wallace ensure safe passage for the marchers to Montgomery. Moreover, he submitted a voting rights proposal to Congress. And in a televised joint session of Congress, Johnson voiced his support for equal rights and uttered the movement's slogan, "We Shall Overcome."[10]

King had finally gained the unprecedented support of an American president. In the days that followed, the marchers, led by King and other movement leaders, continued their journey from Selma and this time they reached Montgomery. Joyous and hopeful, King delivered one of his most famous speeches stating,

"a 'season of suffering" still lay ahead, but eventually "a society at peace with itself, a society that can live with its conscience," would be won. He asked the crowd, "How long will it take?" "However difficult the moment, however frustrating the hour, it will not be long." He repeated the question "How Long?" and his answer,

"Not long," buil[t] to a rousing climax that drew a thundering ovation from the thousands of listeners.¹¹

That evening, Mrs. Viola Liuzzo, a mother of five who had come to the South from Detroit to assist with voter registration, was shot to death by four Klansmen. She was on her way to pick up marchers from Montgomery and to drive them back to Selma. This event, as well as the deaths of Reverend Reeb and Jimmie Jackson, made it apparent that even if the government supported civil rights, it could not eradicate the hate and racism so endemic to southern life. Moreover, with the passage of the 1965 Voting Rights Act came the realization that Blacks in the South were now in the same position as northern Blacks, and that all the laws and legislation in the world would not bring equality and justice. A new approach was needed, one that did not try to appeal to moral imperatives for justice but took equal rights by force.

The Rise of the Black Power Movement

Joyce Ladner, a community bridge leader, divides Black Power advocates into locals, or those who only look at local problems, and cosmopolitans, or those who connect local problems to the world. She describes the circumstances that led many SNCC activists to change their philosophy and approach to civil rights.

As time went on, the cosmopolitans became more and more discouraged about their organizing efforts. They began to seriously question the feasibility of their strategies and tactics. By the end of 1964, after the historic Mississippi Summer Project, the cosmopolitans began to feel that their organizational methods were just not effective. For roughly a year and a half, they groped and searched for more effective strategies. Frequently they felt frustrated; sometimes they despaired. A number of them returned to the North and got well-paying jobs or went to graduate and professional schools. Others were alienated from some of basic values of American society. Some students developed a strong interest in Africa and began to look to various African states as possible havens. Still others, after deciding that they had accomplished all that was possible through organizations such as SNCC, associated themselves with radical leftist groups. . . .

[T]wo position papers were written by the cosmopolitans. One was by a group that insisted that Negroes expel whites from leadership roles in civil-rights organizations, and that Negroes develop "black consciousness" and "black nationalism." "Black consciousness" refers to a set of ideas and behavior patterns affirming the beauty of blackness and dispelling any negative images that black people may have incorporated about blackness. "Black nationalism" is a kind of patriotic devotion to the development of the Negro's own political, economic, and social institutions. Black nationalism is *not* a racist ideology with separatist overtones, however, but simply a move toward independence from the dominant groups, the whites. This paper states:

If we are to proceed toward true liberation, we must cut ourselves off from white people. We must form our own institutions, credit unions, co-ops, political parties, write our own histories. . . . SNCC, by allowing whites to remain in the organization, can have its efforts subverted. . . . Indigenous leadership cannot be built with whites in the positions they now hold. They [whites] can participate on a voluntary basis . . . but in no way can they participate on a policy-making level.[12]

Ladner's interviewees noted that black consciousness included saying, "I'm no longer ashamed of my blackness". In the same vein, the very definition of Black needed to be reassessed.

These young people firmly believe that even the term "black" has to be redefined. To one of them, "Black has never had any favorable expression in the English language." To another, "American society has characterized black as the symbol for strength, evil, potency and malignancy. . . . People are afraid of the night, of blackness."

Most cosmopolitans feel that black people must acquire black consciousness before they can successfully develop the tools and techniques for acquiring black power.[13]

Embracing this new philosophy of Black Power was to have far-reaching consequences. It was to become a positive base for Black identity, race pride, and self-respect. As Ladner notes, Dr. King felt it was positive as well. He wrote:

One must not overlook the positive value in calling the Negro to a new sense of manhood, to a deep feeling of racial pride and to an audacious appreciation of his heritage. The Negro must be grasped by a new realization of his dignity and worth. He must stand up amid a system that still oppresses him and develop an unassailable majestic sense of his own value. He must no longer be ashamed of being black.[14]

Although King supported the central message of Black pride, he did not agree with the means by which many Black nationalists wished to seize power. Rather, he felt that a nonviolent stance was more productive. Moreover, King and the SCLC had gained the unprecedented support of the federal government. At the same time, the base upon which the movement rested, the bridging tier, began to erode.

COFO began to disband, and scores of activists left the Deep South. In the summer of 1965, rioting broke out in major cities throughout the United States. Accordingly, King and the SCLC began to shift their focus to the North. And SNCC, as well as CORE, ejected Whites from their organizations, electing new chairs—Stokely Carmichael and Floyd McKissick, respectively, both more radical than either John Lewis or James Farmer. Both organizations developed a Black Power philosophy, outwardly rejecting nonviolence and inclusionary agendas. Rather, they proclaimed a Black nationalist philosophy and embraced the teachings of Malcolm X, some calling for separatism and using whatever means necessary to gain power. The movement had begun to erode, but not from the top—rather, from the bottom.

Women and the Loss of Free Spaces

SNCC's shift was to have powerful consequences for women, as well as for the movement as a whole. Its tranformation into a Black Power movement organization brought a corresponding shift in organizational structure and a collapse of the bridging nature of the organization. This left many local communities bereft of movement organization representation and Mississippi's rural bridge leaders without a means of resources, resulting in a weak mobilizing base for the movement. Moreover, the change to a Black Power philosophy also brought the development of a hierarchy and fewer free spaces for women's leadership. Prathia Hall Wynn, a secondary bridge leader in SNCC, reflecting on Black male-female relationships before 1965 and after, states:

> I really think that there was a collegiality and a kinship between Black men and Black women. I had good friendships with some of the men of the movement and I felt that they were solid. I think that, for instance, there was tremendous sharing of ideas, wrestling with the issues, and I never felt that my mind was not respected and this, of course, is not across the board. But some of the Black women that we're talking about—I remember . . . Joyce Ladner saying, "You know that if men had really gotten out of line or been demeaning or whatever, that women would have told them where to go! And in short order." And I think that that is true. However, I draw the line between the kind of relations that existed in the pre-1965, I guess, or 1966 SNCC and the later SNCC.[15]

While her reaction to the 1965 Waveland paper was ambivalent, and she saw herself as "among the Black women of the generations before [her] who wanted to see Black men in leadership," her reaction to the Black Power movement differed:

> If you ask me how I felt a year later or two years later after all of the Black macho rhetoric and "the best thing women can do for the movement is have babies," and all the women walking—I've forgotten how many steps behind, but that whole [business] . . . my reaction to all of that would be different.[16]

Hall left SNCC in 1965 to work for the National Council of Negro Women. Activist Jean Wheeler Smith Young, a community bridge leader who remained in SNCC until 1968, offers a similar response to the changes in SNCC after 1965.

> I wasn't interested in the leadership that had evolved at that time. I thought there were a lot of strangers that I knew nothing about, and I wasn't about to follow them anywhere. Because so much of why it worked in the beginning was [that] the people all knew each other and we knew that we could depend on each other. After there became so many new people that you couldn't know or depend on because of the way they came in or you'd never worked with them, it wasn't the kind of thing where you'd want to put your life on the line with somebody you never even met before, or you met ten minutes before.[17]

Others felt that the new shift was unfair and that many of the early White participants had sacrificed a great deal for the movement. Muriel Tillinghast suggests that the large influx of Whites during the Freedom Summer project pushed many Black participants into fighting for control of the organization, which resulted in the expulsion of all White activists. Tillinghast, as well as Gloria Richardson, felt that many of the new Black SNCC workers were agents who infiltrated the organization in order to destroy it.

I enrolled at Howard in the fall of '66. I had left SNCC. I left around April or May of that year, and I left because I couldn't tell the agents from my friends. I was getting fairly nervous about all these new faces and their pushiness. Some of the people I knew sounded peculiar, that is, their position seemed circular. It was difficult to follow some of the logic. I'd say about one-fourth of the organizing base was highly questionable. I became very paranoid; we were being destabilized by agents—that wasn't even an argument! I felt that the organization was going to explode and I no longer wanted to be there.[18]

Of the expulsion of Whites and the shift to Black nationalism, Gloria Richardson offers her doubts about the origins of these changes:

I didn't even know anything about that until about 1965, and I was here in New York by that time. I had resigned and left. In retrospect, and after talking to Cleve [Sellers] and some other people over the last couple of years, I'm not sure that there wasn't infiltration that accelerated that. Because shortly after that was effective and White people were "thrown out," and then you had these Black nationalists moving in who thought they could organize around Black nationalism alone, when people were concerned about bread-and-butter issues—you have to talk about voting, you have to talk about housing, you have to talk about education, you have to talk about jobs—and I think that that killed it. And I think that was by design. Because I think that Cleve told me that when he came out of jail and went down there, he didn't know anybody in the office.[19]

Whether by design or a shift of power, SNCC was no longer recognizable as the organization that was so loved by Black and White activists alike. Penny Patch describes her feelings of rejection and pain.

At the time I was more overwhelmed by what I was personally losing in terms of the work that I was committed to, the community that I had perceived as my community, close friends that I was losing, I don't know that I had a clear vision that this was an essential. . . . Later on I could look at it and say this was probably a necessary step, even though it may not have turned out to be a very successful step, that there was objective reasons why it was happening and why it needed to happen. . . . In the initial years after I left, I [felt] . . . enormous grief and a certain amount of bitterness, yet there was this loyalty and I know I never opened my mouth to the press. The loyalty is very strongly there.[20]

Many Whites such as Bill Hanson, who withstood beatings by racist Whites, had also been disowned by their families for their participation in the movement. It was a difficult time in SNCC's history. With the expulsion of Whites and the infusion of hierarchy, SNCC was irrevocably changed. However, Ruby Doris Smith Robinson, who died in her twenties, fought to keep the organization together. Bernice Johnson Reagon explains:

I think she kept the organization together. With her life she kept SNCC together. And I think it took her life. That's all. I don't think it's complicated. You have to have glue and you have to get it from some place. And Ruby Doris Robinson was SNCC's glue, and it cost her her life.[21]

Paula Giddings, a well-known Black historian, concludes:

In the beginning, the civil rights movement had served to confirm masculine as well as racial assertiveness, but when it began to break down, that old nightmare of impotence resurfaced. The evidence of this was found even in SNCC. In 1966, Doris Smith [Robinson] was elected executive secretary of the organization. The election of Smith, touted for her leadership skills and toughness, at a time when SNCC was on the verge of dissolution, was believed by many to be the last hope for the organization to pull itself together. Even so, she was plagued by chauvinistic attitudes. As James Foreman [Forman] asserted, "She endured vicious attacks from the SNCC leadership. They also embodied male chauvinism in fighting her attempts as executive secretary to impose a sense of organizational responsibility and self-discipline, trying to justify themselves by the fact that their critic was a woman."

A year later, Smith succumbed to a rare blood disease—though there were those in SNCC who believed she was deliberately killed. Kathleen Cleaver saw her death in other terms:

Ruby Doris died at the age of twenty-six and she died of exhaustion. . . . I don't think it was necessary to assassinate her. What killed Ruby Doris was the constant outpouring of work, work, work, work with being married, having a child, the constant conflicts, the constant struggles that she was subjected to because she was a woman. . . . She was destroyed by the movement.

By 1966, the movement had taken a decided turn—to the North. There, manhood was measured by wages, oppression had no face, and powerlessness no refuge. And in the North, the exhibitionism of manhood was not mitigated by the strength of Black institutions whose most vital resource was women. Both Black men and radical-chic white men-women, too applauded the machismo of leather-jacketed young men, armed to the teeth, rising out of the urban ghetto. The theme of the late sixties was "Black Power" punctuated by a knotted fist. It caught a common ethos between northern and southern Blacks. Although it may not have been consciously conceived out of the need to affirm manhood, it became a metaphor for the male consciousness of the era. As Floyd McKissick, who replaced James Farmer as head of CORE, explained: "The year 1966 shall be remembered as the year we left our imposed status as Negroes and became Black men."[22]

With the corresponding shift in philosophy and organization, the position of Black women in the struggle for equality and justice took an unprecedented turn. Never before had Black women been required to "step back." While previously women had voluntarily done so, always knowing that the step was really to the side, they were now explicitly receiving messages that dictated their positions were behind their men. Angela Davis, one of the few women leaders in the Black Power movement, said:

> I ran headlong into a situation which was to become a constant problem in my political life. I was criticized very heavily, especially by male members of [Ron] Karenga's [US] organization, for doing a "man's job." Women should not play leadership roles, they insisted. A woman was to "inspire" her man and educate his children. The irony of their complaint was that much of what I was doing had fallen to me by default. . . .
>
> Some of the brothers come around only for staff meetings (sometimes), and whenever we women were involved in something important, they began to talk about "women taking over the organization"—calling it a matriarchal coup d'etat. All the myths about Black women surfaced. (We) were too domineering; we were trying to control everything, including the men—which meant by extension that we wanted to rob them of their manhood. By playing such a leading role in the organization, some of them insisted, we were aiding and abetting the enemy, who wanted to see Black men weak and unable to hold their own.[23]

This view would be echoed by Kathleen Cleaver and Elaine Brown, both leaders in the Black Power movement. Even longtime leaders such as Gloria Richardson would experience the wrath of the new male activists, who at a rally shouted her down as a "castrator."[24]

And Ella Baker had some harsh words regarding the position of Black women in this movement.

> You know this new dialogue that has emanated out of the business of the male having been emasculated by his woman has put an extra burden on the black female, young black female, to not be party to continued emasculation. So she has begun to take even a much more of a retiring role within the movement than she did in 1960.[25]

The backlash against women's leadership was further fed by the literature that proliferated in the middle 1960s to the early 1970s, which served to support the myth of the Black matriarch in low-income households.[26] Such a myth has been soundly refuted by scholars, many of whom argue that the findings are erroneous and are based on the false assumption that the earning power of poor Black women gave them more power in their relationships.[27] Sociologist Robert Staples notes that "in reality wives in poor black families contribute less to the total family income than do wives in nonpoor black families because they are much less likely to be employed among the low income group."[28] Scholar Bonnie Thornton Dill makes a similar observation. Black women worked as household domestics, some of the lowest paid work in America, because they were black, poor, and women.[29]

Many of these scholars suggest that what is important is access to power within society, which most researchers asserting the matriarch thesis failed to acknowledge. The more significant factor contributing to the difficulties of African Americans was the racial barrier erected to prevent their access to power. Yet the movement to exclude women from leadership positions and to place them in the background further undermined the sustenance and slowed the momentum of the movement.

The Collapse of the Bridging Tier Within the Social Movement Sector

The new hierarchical form of power so vividly described by Elaine Brown in *A Taste of Power* led to the erosion of the very qualities that had propelled the movement earlier. And SNCC was no longer mobilizing to bridge the masses to the movement.

Ladner characterizes the Black Power cosmopolitans as philosophical, "urbane, educated, highly skilled young civil-rights activists" whose disillusionment with the system led to a newfound identity and political orientation.[30] This disillusionment, born of the MFDP's failed challenges and the subsequent eviction of sharecroppers who pitched tents on the White House lawn and occupied an inactive Air Force base in Greenville, Mississippi, in an attempt to gain funds for inadequate housing,

> even caused a large number of locals—like the cosmopolitans—to pause and question the effectiveness of their traditional organizational tactics and goals. Indeed, many even came to seriously question the Federal Government's sincerity about alleviating the problems of the Negro. A number of the participants in these events stopped being active in the movement. Others began to express strong anti-white sentiments.[31]

For many of the locals, Black Power meant voter registration, political power held by Blacks, Black solidarity, and power over the Black community.[32] Ladner concludes, "For both the Mississippi cosmopolitans and locals, then, it was mainly frustration that drew them to the concept of black power."[33]

SNCC's ideological shift to Black consciousness and Black Power led liberal financial supporters to stop contributing.

> In terms of practical considerations, however, urging the white volunteers to leave the black communities has had negative effects. SNCC and CORE, which at one time directed most of the grass-roots organizing, have always depended upon the economic and volunteer resources of liberal white individuals and groups. These resources are scarce nowadays.[34]

Faye Bellamy, a community bridge leader and participant in SNCC until the early part of 1969, explains:

Really, it was dissolving then as far as I'm concerned. Because there are a couple of things that we did in the process of those last few years. And we knew that it was going to be a detriment to our money-making capabilities. One of those was a statement on the Middle East crisis. The first one was '66 on the Vietnam War, which at that time most people in this country did not know . . . was even going on. They called it, at the time, the Vietnam conflict. There were supposed to be some advisors in a place called Vietnam. And I remember we used to get the *Congressional Record*, and I used to go, because I had never seen a *Congressional Record* before and I was always fascinated by them. And I remember reading one [speech] of a congressmen who was on the floor. He was just haranguing Congress and saying, "When did these bases get built in Taiwan?" They already had bases and troops and planes there. And, like, I was stunned that Congress wouldn't even know that a base had been set up to help coordinate a war effort. I said, "Well, if they don't know, who the hell knows? Who's running this place?" So when we did the Vietnam thing, we knew the government was going to start harassing us more, was going to do some things and interrupt us, [though] we didn't know what forms it would take. We had read enough history of other struggles in the world to know the kind of things that can occur. We also knew, based upon our own experiences in this country, the kind of things that did occur. So you just say, "Well, okay. Now we know if we do this, these things are going to happen, possibly." But with [the] system, you say you're either for it or against it. We either make a statement or we don't.[35]

Bellamy felt that these stances, for better or for worse, lost them the support of previous benefactors. She explains why, in part, she left SNCC:

I really think because we didn't have the funds, we were not able to spend as much time putting organizers into the field, which was our mainstay before. . . . You have to have some consistency, you have to have people out there on a regular basis finding people, and you have to have new people coming into your organization. But you can only do that by going out there and getting them, and I didn't see that happening. And I learned early by being in SNCC, and I guess as a result of learning about other organizational systems, that the healthiest environment is one where new blood is being pumped in constantly. And for the first number of years I was in there, that was happening and there seemed like there were groups of people coming in.[36]

SNCC had ceased to operate as a bridging organization, as Ladner explains,

[the cosmopolitans] are widely read and widely traveled. They are also artistic: Writers, painters, photographers, musicians, and the like. . . . Their general orientation toward life is an intellectual one. They are associated with SNCC, the Freedom Democratic Party, and CORE. Although a few are actively engaged in organizing black people in the various counties, much of their work in the state is centered on philosophical discussions, writing, and so forth.[37]

Later she notes that the cosmopolitans emphasized the global nature of oppression and the connection to people of color all over the globe, while locals were more concrete, focusing on "black-power programs . . . registering to vote, running for political office . . . building independent political parties . . . building cooperatives and small businesses, and on almost exclusively patronizing black merchants in an effort to keep the money in the black community".[38] Ladner calls for a partnership of the two orientations.

> Through the development of such unity, there is a great possibility that black-power advocates in Mississippi will again turn to creative, large-scale organizing that would incorporate the major emphases of each group; black consciousness and immediate gains.
>
> The key question, of course, [is] what are the prospects for Mississippi Negroes' developing black-power institutions in the near future? Clearly this will depend to a great extent upon the number of organizers in the field, on adequate economic re-sources, and on commitments from major civil rights organizations to the Mississippi scene.[39]

SNCC's loss of financial resources and the subsequent crumbling of its infrastruc-ture left indigenous bridge leaders and local organizations without the power of a national bridging organization. Clay Carson, in *In Struggle*, meticulously documents the fall of SNCC:

> Carmichael and other SNCC workers roused the racial feelings of blacks through verbal attacks on the existing leadership and prevailing strategies of the civil rights movement, but their own organization was weakened in the process.[40]

Powerful women bridge leaders Ella Baker, Muriel Tillinghast, Ruby Doris Smith Robinson, and Faye Bellamy were openly critical of SNCC's recent failure to focus on programs, to develop indigenous leadership, and to build political power. All believed that individual aggrandizement had supplanted SNCC's course. In a late 1960s interview, Ella Baker, when asked "In what way has SNCC fallen short of its goal?" replied:

> It has not been successful in developing basic leadership in Mississippi, Alabama, Southwest Georgia. Its greatest difficulty has been in reconciling its genius for indi-vidual expression with the political necessity for organizational discipline. I myself approve of group discipline in general. The trend is more toward discipline, because the members of SNCC are a smaller and smaller band. This is because SNCC is no longer "the thing" and the civil rights movement is no longer "the thing."[41]

Exactly what Ella Baker meant by "the thing" is unclear, but what is clear is that SNCC had begun to fall apart, and its changes in organization and philosophy were at the core of its collapse. SNCC's new chairman, Stokely Carmicheal, was becom-ing increasingly uncontrollable, making statements as *the* representative of SNCC without regard for the executive committee or SNCC members. Even Ruby Doris Smith Robinson, who supported the Black Power philosophy, criticized Carmi-chael. As Carson reports:

Executive Secretary Ruby Doris Smith Robinson wrote that SNCC's staff had not decided, as had Carmichael, to advocate "the destruction of Western civilization." Referring to Carmichael's public image as the "architect of Black Power," she asked other staff members, "How could one individual make such a tremendous impression on so many people in such a short period of time . . . so much so that to some people SNCC is only the organization that Carmichael has at his disposal to do what he wants to get done?" Answering her own question, she asserted that Carmichael had been "the only consistent spokesman for the organization, and he has had the press not only available but seeking him out for whatever ammunition could be found— FOR OUR DESTRUCTION." She conceded that "at his best, he has said what [the masses of black people] wanted to hear," but added that "cliché after cliché has filled his orations."[42]

Muriel Tillinghast also noted that prior to Carmichael's election, chairs did not dominate the organization and its decision making, but after he became chair, "the chairman began to determine policy autonomously and the rest of us had to make a decision as to whether we were going with the chair or not."[43] In a meeting, Robinson, Bellamy, and Ralph Featherstone, as well as others, talked to Carmichael and convinced him to stop making speeches that included declarations and positions not approved by the rest of SNCC. He agreed to the request and decided to focus more on "developing programs and working on internal structure."[44]

The programs, however, shifted from the Deep South to urban areas. As Carson notes,

By October 1966 only a third of the staff were in these areas; the other two-thirds were gathered near SNCC's Atlanta headquarters or scattered in cities outside the South.

A comparison of SNCC's staff in the fall of 1966 with the period prior to 1965 reveals that few of SNCC's officers and project directors in the fall of 1964 remained in SNCC. . . .

Even more damaging to SNCC's southern effectiveness . . . was the deterioration of its field operations. SNCC's ability to rebuild its southern projects was hampered by the departure of its most experienced organizers. Several staff members in Arkansas also resigned rather than adjust to SNCC's new ideological thrust. Other projects were also weakened by resignations and declining morale among organizers. . . .

Yet, SNCC's problems in 1966 were more serious than ever before, because it no longer served as a catalyst for sustained local struggles. Rather than encouraging local leaders to develop their own ideas, SNCC was becoming merely one of many organizations seeking to speak on behalf of black communities. Instead of immersing themselves in protest activity and deriving their insights from an ongoing mass struggle, SNCC workers in 1966 stressed the need to inculcate among urban blacks a new racial consciousness as a foundation for future struggles.[45]

SNCC's philosophy and organizational shift away from the teachings of Ella Baker and the methods developed by Septima Clark destroyed the foundation of the movement. And SNCC, which had been the grassroots mobilizing force for the movement, collapsed in the early seventies.

Approximately fifteen years later, on July 17, 1985, at a convention, the Reverend Jesse Jackson addressed his speech to President Reagan, outlining the problems still faced by many Black Mississippians:

> Tunica, Mississippi, just thirty miles south of Memphis on highway 61, is the poorest county in America. The county has 9,600 residents, including 1,300 in the city of Tunica. The county is 75 percent black and 25 percent white. The city is 75 percent white and 25 percent black. Sugar Ditch is located in Tunica. Sugar Ditch is a group of shanties housing about two hundred poor people, mostly women and children, located between a new downtown business district and $50,000–$100,000 homes. Thirty-eight millionaires live in Tunica. Rich farmers are paid not to farm, while the average per capita yearly income in Tunica is around $4,000. There is no indoor plumbing in Sugar Ditch. Feces and other waste matter are thrown into an open ditch—their sewer just five to seven feet from the houses where children eat, sleep, and play. One mother testified that roaches and other rodents eat as many potatoes as her children. I saw thousands and thousands of roaches in the houses and on the food with my own eyes. Residents pay between $25 and $85 a month to live there. They are charged for sewer services they never receive.
>
> Five state health agencies are charged with the responsibility of protecting the health and safety of its citizens. Yet never has there been a formal investigation into the health conditions or status of Tunica or Sugar Ditch residents. The public school has 2,064 students, less than twenty of them white. The white children go to an all-white, private, Christian, segregated academy called the Tunica Institute of Learning. Public officials divert funds for the public school to the private school. The public school has a chemistry *room* but no equipment or chemicals. Tunica County has the highest rate of substandard or deteriorated housing of the 82 counties in Mississippi, the poorest state in the union.[46]

Jackson continued to explain that most of the Black residents live on plantations because "plantation owners join together to block new industry and new jobs from coming to Tunica in order to preserve their cheap seasonal labor." This and the fact that there is a paucity of decent low-income housing keeps Blacks from living in the city, where their vote could change the face of political officials. He elaborated:

> Thus, politically, urban blacks are disenfranchised and left powerless through at-large election and dual registration schemes. Never in the history of the city of Tunica has a black been elected or appointed to any public office. Rural blacks are disenfranchised and left powerless because of economic intimidation on the plantation and the lack of job alternatives beyond the plantation. Blacks are 40 percent of Mississippi's population, therefore a potentially potent political force. There is a conspiracy in Mississippi to leave blacks uneducated, with poor health care, few jobs or job training, and politically disenfranchised so they will leave the state—and leave the power in the hands of a white power elite.[47]

Reverend Jackson's words could have been written in the 1950s, before the civil rights movement began. The loss of the bridging tier left local Black Mississippians and their indigenous leaders to fend for themselves without the power and support of a movement organization. While SNCC's philosophy and mobilizing structure required the development of local leadership, the organization had really only begun its work in Mississippi. Indigenous bridge leaders could not break the back of racism and disenfranchisement on their own. Their efforts required continued association with a bridging organization that had a working relationship with the primary and secondary formal organizations and their leaders.

Conclusion

What is abundantly clear is that the bridging organization and its bridge leaders were central to the mobilization and sustenance of the civil rights movement. The conflict between women bridge leaders in bridging organizations and primary formal leaders marked the beginning of the movement's erosion at its base. The compromise so necessary to the relationship between the state and the movement's primary formal leaders created disillusionment in the bridging tier of the movement sector. The interplay of race, class, gender, and culture served to mark that moment, with White male elites having the most power, educated Black male formal leaders having a bit of power, and poor, uneducated Black women having the least power to decide the fate of Mississippi and Black representation in the political arena.

As previously mentioned, because they could never possess the power of primary formal leaders within the movement sector, women took a position much more in line with that of the masses they represented. On the face of it, the challengers had achieved an unprecedented victory; but to those rural activists who suffered daily, who were to return to impoverished conditions and oppression, the compromise marked a monumental defeat.

With the rise of Black nationalism came a corresponding shift in SNCC's organizational form, mobilizing frame, and structure. Rather than the open organization that had sought to empower indigenous leaders, SNCC's new ideology narrowed its organizational power. While the new leadership shared many of the views of people in the rural South, it abandoned this population and sought instead to mobilize in northern cities. SNCC's new dogmatism and its attempt to develop new cultural beliefs through rhetoric rather than dialogue served to destroy the organization's ability to mobilize the masses. Likewise, SNCC embraced patriarchy, thus shrinking the free spaces once occupied by women leaders, whose bridging work was critical to movement recruitment, mobilization, and sustenance. The subsequent loss of many of its longtime activists, coupled with its failure to develop educational programs aimed at community empowerment, signaled the beginning of the end of the civil rights movement.

ELEVEN

Theoretical Conclusions

Black Women as Leaders, Not Just Organizers

What is abundantly clear is that movement participants cannot be conceptualized in a dichotomous fashion as simply leaders and followers. Neither can it be suggested that women's civil rights movement participation was primarily of an organizing nature, as has been suggested by previous scholars. For example, Charles Payne, in his earlier work on Black women's activism in the Mississippi Delta, has suggested that "men led, but women organized."[1] In a later analysis, which clearly enriches our knowledge of movement organizing in Mississippi, he labels them leaders but describes their work as that of organizers.[2] Bernice McNair Barnett, who also studies Black women in the civil rights movement, agrees with Payne that women organized and that their organizing was an important aspect of leadership.[3]

The present study illustrates that African-American women's activism included much more than organizing. While formal networks, leaders, institutions, and movement centers were significant factors in the recruitment process, they do not adequately reflect who, on a daily basis, provided the local leadership necessary to bridge, extend, amplify, and transform the movement's message to potential recruits.

It is clear that central to the success of a social movement is an intermediate layer of leadership, whose tasks include bridging potential constituents and adherents, as well as potential formal leaders, to the movement. Women as bridge leaders performed these tasks. Certainly, men such as Esau Jenkins, who assisted with the SCLC's Citizenship Education Program, and many others also participated as bridge leaders. It is not the case that bridge leaders were exclusively women; rather, this was the primary level of leadership available to women. While women were generally excluded from formal leadership on the basis of their sex, men seemed to be excluded on the basis of their education. In the case of the civil rights movement, the exclusion of most women from formal leadership positions created an exceptionally qualified leadership tier in the area of micromobilization.

The social location of African-American women, as defined by a gendered hierarchy, served the movement's need for a bridge between the prefigurative politics of small towns and rural communities, and the strategic politics of movement organizations. Within this context, potential constituents could be solicited by bridge leaders who had little or no direct access to the power politics of the formal organization. This resolved the problems faced by many movement organizations that lack an intermediate layer of capable leadership. Gender exclusion was particularly useful because the movement could draw upon the resources of well-educated and/or articulate women to act as carriers, as cultivators of solidarity, without the same set of leaders experiencing conflict between movement constituents and mainstream political compromise. In the case of the civil rights movement, these tasks were divided, though not exclusively, along gendered lines, thus providing the movement with a strong base of leadership.

This analysis of women's participation in the civil rights movement also provides examples of the ways in which mobilization does not always occur in a linear fashion—that is, formal leaders mobilize followers. Rather, women as bridge leaders recruited men as formal leaders. Moreover, they and the movement's followers extended and transformed the movement's message so that conflict sometimes existed between their desires and those of the formal leaders. Bridge leaders as the lead voices of the movement's followers were not afraid to challenge the power of formal leaders.

That African-American women, for the most part, did not share primary or secondary formal leadership titles should in no way obscure the fact that they were leaders. They were instrumental as leaders in the recruitment and mobilization process and were effective, influential leaders who elicited loyalty from their followers. Given the context of the times—the period 1954–1965—women who participated in the civil rights movement experienced unprecedented power. Their social location as Blacks, as women, and as economically marginalized people was empowered in a context in which they were the purveyors of political consciousness, in which they were able to lead relatively autonomously, and in which they were able to bring about group solidarity and social change. It is only in hindsight that we may observe their positions as limited by their gender. Ironically, it is this "now" perceived limitation that served to catapult and sustain the identity, collective consciousness, and solidarity of the movement.

Emotion and Spontaneity in Social Movements

By studying women's leadership, it becomes readily apparent that emotion contributed significantly to the success of the movement. Yet emotion was also central to men's leadership. Throughout the text, I have illustrated that emotions—feelings of anger and humiliation—were central to many women's decisions to risk their lives for the movement. It was these feelings that enabled them to overcome their fears in the face of violence and hatred. Mobilization of a movement requires strategic and spontaneous emotional responses. Emotion in social movement protests has been most widely written about by collective behavior theorists, and in this context emotions have been viewed as irrational actions that are not normative and are a result of contagious rebellion born of collective mass discontent. This theory is, of course, no longer the one to which most social movement theorists adhere.

In the United States, resource mobilization theory and its variants have, until recently, dominated mainstream sociological thought about social movements. Resource mobilization theorists suggest that emotion is a mere by-product of or an aside to the construction of collective action. They stress the importance of the availability of resources and the development of organizations as central to movement mobilization and collective action. Moreover, they emphasize the rationality of the actors and the planned nature of their activities. Conversely, new social movement theory, more prominent in Europe, has reinserted the actor into movement theory, and the focus is on the internal dynamics of social movements. Therefore, attention to how collective identity and group solidarity are developed has created an inroad to discussions of emotions in the movement context.

This book has reinserted emotion as a critical component of social movement recruitment and mobilization. Previous accounts of movements juxtapose emotions and rationality, as though the two are mutually exclusive. Yet acceptance of the centrality of emotion to the success of social movements implies acceptance of social movement behavior as sometimes unpredictable. Emotion may be the enemy of social movement theorists because it is difficult to predict, to qualify, or to quantify. The "problem of emotion" has been a thorn in the side of social movement theory, even though we no longer acknowledge the pain.

One way to get around the problem has been to discuss the importance of emotion in the context of organizational structure. For example, Morris has argued that charisma and the emotional appeals of ministers were a direct result of institutional training within the Black church.[4] While it is true that emotions were strategically and deliberately used by ministers to elicit particular responses from participants, this provides but one aspect of the importance of emotions in social movements. And it leaves unexplained the importance of emotions to all facets of social movements, including the origins of social movements, movement opportunities and successes, social movement action frames, and movement mobilization.

With this in mind, it is more useful to explain emotions in the context of social relations. While most social movement theorists would concede that Martin Luther King's speeches evoked emotion among constituents and potential adherents, they might not necessarily agree about their significance to social movement mass action. I, too, agree that formal leaders often manipulate the feelings and emotions of their audiences, as Patricia L. Wasielewski has pointed out in her discussion of the emotional basis of charisma,[5] but I argue that, their strategic emotional appeals were not enough to persuade the masses to act. As discussed, bridge leaders provide much of the emotional work needed to persuade the masses to join the movement and to act. The day-to-day interactions between bridge leaders and potential adherents and constituents provide the basis for the emotional intimacy so necessary for persuading the masses to take risks. Additionally, bridge leaders provide a leadership, not in the traditional sense of the formal charismatic leader, but as the trusted leader who constructs a kind of local charismatic authority.

As has been discussed in the previous chapters, bridge leaders often went unrecognized nationally and by the media. The loyalty of the bridge leaders remained within the confines of the constituency they developed and mobilized. For this reason, conflicts often developed between bridge leaders and formal leaders. Such conflict created a climate in which the trusted charismatic community bridge leader often acted in spontaneous and emotional, but not irrational, ways and remained loyal to the local constituency. This provided the foundation necessary to sustain the momentum and build a solidified and unified movement. The mobilization work required interpersonal relations between individuals, which included specialized and individualized appeals aimed at identity transformation, all of which required emotions. Moreover, the civil rights movement succeeded because these emotional processes were implemented not only through bridge leaders attached to formal and secondary movement organizations but also through bridging organizations.

Organizational Forms, Mobilizing Structures, and Charismatic Leaders

What is at once apparent is the need for such an organization within the movement sector. Interestingly, the bridging tier succeeded because of SNCC's organizational form, which did not conform to shared societal models or "repertoires of collective action."[6] How we understand how to organize is drawn from what Pierre Bourdieu terms "cultural capital" and Ann Swidler terms "cultural toolkit," or ways of knowing. How we come to understand what is normative and appropriate is learned through the *bricolage* process, which is influenced through cultural stock or a set of understandings about our world.[7] Obviously, how we come to "know" is, at least partially, constructed by the ways in which race, class, and gender are ordered in our society.[8] These "cultural toolkits" develop into activists' skills, beliefs, and ideologies that determine their approach to resistance. Here it is necessary to define several terms. Using Mayer Zald's definitions,

culture is the shared beliefs and understandings, mediated by and constituted by symbols and language, of a group or society; ideology is the set of beliefs that are used to justify or challenge a given social-political order and are used to interpret the political world; frames are the specific metaphors, symbolic representations, and cognitive cues used to render or cast behavior and events in an evaluative mode and to suggest alternative modes of action.[9]

Through an ideology of inclusion, cooperation, and individualism as opposed to self-interest, SNCC broke down barriers to participation, seeking not to indoctrinate but to engage. Consequently, its organizational form as created by its ideology was able to incorporate indigenous leaders into its leadership structure, thus providing a bridge to a variety of rural cultural scripts. This aided activists in their dialectical exchange with potential recruits. Such an engagement was born of an equalitarian, consensus-building, antihierarchical approach to leadership that created its mobilization structure. SNCC sought to empower, not to lead, and its allegiance and loyalty to local communities often set it at odds with primary formal leaders in primary formal and secondary formal organizations. This conflict, however, served to remind the latter of the desires of local communities and followers, thus reinforcing opposition to the wishes of the state.

Yet who provides the message, to whom it is provided, and how it is conveyed are equally important. SNCC bridge leaders, following the teachings of Miss Ella Baker and Mrs. Septima Clark, did not simply deposit a message to potential followers; rather, they engaged others in a dialectical relationship, allowing for individual reconstructions of identities and interpretations of action frames. As feminist scholar Joan Acker notes,

> differences in political issues and ideology, as well as differences in the sociopolitical climate of time and place, may create variations in the likelihood that people with disparate life situations will come together.[10]

While many movement organizations have difficulties transcending race, class, and gender differences, SNCC was able to weaken these traditional boundaries. SNCC was revolutionary not only in the political sense but also in terms of its widening of the socially constructed cultural norms surrounding race, class, and gender. In this regard, Penny Patch, a mainstream bridge leader maintains that "what was probably extraordinary was the degree to which people leaped out of, and I'm talking about all races and classes, prescribed roles."[10]

SNCC defied normative beliefs about these constructs and reorganized hierarchical lines into all-inclusive circles. While not completely successful, SNCC redefined the meanings of these constructs because everyone was encouraged to question the cultural norms governing life in the 1960s. Subsequently, SNCC gave rise to the women's movement as well as the Black Power movement, as progressive extensions of SNCC's open, dialectical mobilizing frame. Both movements sought, in part, to redefine the institutions of gender and race, respectively.

Of course, many scholars have written about egalitarian, antihierarchical, cooperative organizational structures as reflective of women's traits.[12] Alternatively, men's traits as manifested in organizational structures are hierarchical and competitive. Feminist organizations, much like SNCC, have been characterized as collectives that require consensus in decision making and nurture an ethic of care.[13] Some scholars attribute these distinctions in organizing to biology, suggesting that women's ability to reproduce predisposes them to cooperative patterns. Others suggest that the differences are socially constructed. While Ella Baker was responsible for the organizational structure of SNCC, it is clear that both men and women acted in accordance with this structure, thus lending support to the constructionist explanation. Whether or not these varied systems of organization are rightly characterized as masculine or feminine, it is clear that both were needed.

While SNCC's approach was clearly critical to the success of the movement, it is equally clear that the movement could not have succeeded without the other movement organizations and primary formal leaders. At least one movement organization needed to appear rational, in control, and able to engage the state in a dialectical relationship that necessitated compromise. The legitimacy of the primary formal and often secondary formal organizations rested on their organizational form, as well. In order to appear legitimate, these organizational forms needed to comply with normative societal repertoires governing collective action. For example, in contrast to SNCC, the SCLC drew upon mainstream templates and thus took the form of hierarchical organizations with a single primary formal leader. In extending Snow and Benford's analysis of frames to organizational forms, Elisabeth Clemens states:

Translated into the language of organization, to the extent that the proposed model of organization is believed to work, involves practices and organizational relations that are already familiar, and is consonant with the organization of the rest of those individuals' social worlds, mobilization around that model is more likely.[14]

Though many scholars highlight the importance of shared cultural scripts and models of collective action, it is clear that, while primary and secondary formal organizations must adhere to such forms, the success of bridging organizations depends on a less normative organizational form, at the same time incorporating familiar cultural repertoires.

Equally clear is that movements require a primary formal charismatic leader who has a goodness of fit with existing societal norms, as well as specific cultural norms for such leaders. In this regard, Dr. King was the perfect primary formal leader. Conversely, Fannie Lou Hamer, who has often been described as a charismatic leader, never received her place as a primary formal leader within the movement sector. Organizer Mike Thelwell describes her abilities:

Now you know all the people on the local level in the movement were special to us. We called them Mr.and Mrs.—Mr. Steptoe, Mr. Turnbow, Mrs. Hamer—so she looked like another local person to me. Then she started to talk. The room had been full of random conversation. Slowly it came to attention. She talked about what had happened in Winona. Now, there were not just Southern people there. There was SNCC staff from all over. We had college students who had come down from New York and other places. So, it was the first time they heard her too. There were tears in lots of people's eyes. And then she started singin' "This Little Light of Mine."

This little light of mine,
I'm gonna let it shine,
Oh, this little light of mine,
I'm gonna let it shine,
This little light of mine,
I'm gonna let it shine,
Let it shine, let it shine, let it shine.

All over Mississippi,
I'm gonna let it shine,
All over Mississippi,
I'm gonna let it shine,
All over Mississippi,
I'm gonna let it shine,
Let it shine, let it shine, let it shine.[15]

Mrs. Hamer had the ability to arouse listeners in a way that others did not. Civil rights activist and attorney Eleanor Holmes Norton, who worked in Mississippi and heard almost all of the orators in the movement, believes that Fannie Lou Hamer's skills were comparable to those of Dr. King. She explains that Mrs. Hamer had

> the capacity to put together a mosaic of coherent thought about freedom and justice, so that when it was all through, you knew what you had heard because it held together with wonderful cohesion. . . . She also, let us not forget, would break out into song at the end of her things, and I'm telling you, you've never heard a room flying [like one] that Fannie Lou Hamer set afire. Her speeches had themes. They had lessons. They had principles. And then when you had heard all that said with such extraordinary brilliance—like *wow*, that's what it is. She had put her finger on something truly important that all of us had felt but she had said. You heard that all the time. What really gets you is that person somehow concretizes an idea that you had never quite been able to fully form. And she did that in this extraordinary ringing style and then ended up singing "This Little Light of Mine." You never needed to hear anybody else speak again.[16]

In spite of Fannie Lou Hamer's charismatic appeal and her formal title as vice-chair of the MFDP, the fact that she was a woman and lacked a formal education precluded her acceptance as a primary formal leader within the social movement sector. As stated in chapters nine and ten, race, class, gender, and culture all operated to undermine the power of a poor, Black, charismatic woman from the Deep South. Yet she had still achieved unprecedented power as a primary formal leader, and this was a direct result of SNCC's conscious realignment of power relations.

Political Opportunities and Outcomes

Analyzing power relations within a social movement significantly increases our understanding of movement opportunities and outcomes. In considering political opportunities, Doug McAdam, a social movement scholar, calls for a distinction between "structural changes and power shifts" and "collective processes by which these changes are interpreted and framed."[17] While he and others who study political opportunities and mobilizing structures acknowledge radical wings of the movement as critical to creating political opportunities for the movement sector, they have not adequately addressed the distinctions made among the competing organizations and their participants in terms of the variance of interpretations regarding political opportunities or outcomes. Nor do they adequately address the culturally prescribed constructs of race, class, and gender that operate and mediate political opportunities, mobilizing structures (e.g., movement organizations, churches, Highlander Folk School), and framing processes (amplification, or the compatibility of the movement's values and beliefs with those of potential constituents; frame extension, or the incorporation of concerns not originally part of the movement's goals; frame bridging, or providing those already predisposed to one's cause with information sufficient to induce them to join the movement; and frame transformation, or the process whereby individually held frames are altered entirely or in part to achieve consensus with the movement's goals). In other words, how these opportunities are constructed, who constructs them, and who interprets their meanings are all affected by cultural stocks or the assemblage of a variety of cultural templates that order relations of power. For example, in our society, cultural stock consists of a set of cultural templates of organization that give more power to elite White males than to economically disadvantaged Black women. With similarly influenced "cultural toolkits," many scholars and politicians viewed the compromise at the Democratic National Convention as a monumental success. Others, such as primary formal Black male leaders, considered the outcome as marginally successful. Yet the decisions of poor rural Mississippians regarding both the construction of the "opportunity or outcome" and the interpretation of its meaning were disregarded by those with more power.

While McAdam has explained that "any event or broad social process that serves to undermine the calculations on which the political establishment is structured occasions a shift in political opportunities,"[18] it is clear that the objective reality of favorable opportunities or outcomes itself is subject to interpretation by one's position in society—a position as defined by one's identity as it is by the larger society's cultural stock. Given that these templates define one's identity, they also determine, though not completely, one's interpretation of political opportunities and outcomes.

While feminist women of color were the first to discuss power differences among women, current feminist scholarship also addresses these issues. Feminist scholars bell hooks and Elizabeth Spelman, in critiquing feminist scholarship, discuss the tendency of current feminist scholars to privilege the experiences of White, middle-class women as though the meanings of their lives are representative of women's lives in general.[19] Alison Jaggar and Paula Rothenberg point out that feminist theorists often develop theories based on the women who are the most privileged in society.[20] And, feminist Allison Tom, in her study of the organization and interpersonal relations in feminist banks, notes:

Other organizations that wish to work "as women" and "for women . . . have to struggle with problems similar to those facing this bank, particularly when power differences in their particular settings . . . are reinforced by structure inequalities of race and class in the wider society.[21]

While these feminists focus on differences among women in terms of race and class, and therefore power—a difference discussed in terms of women's participation in SNCC—the analysis may be extended to consider differences among movement participants within and between movement organizations. Clearly, as McAdam suggests, the interpretive aspects are most critical to our understanding of what triggers mobilization and how the opportunities are viewed by participants.

In applying a dynamic, interactive model of political opportunities, scholars have analyzed the ways in which states and movements interact such that, as Meyer and Staggenborg argue, "the relevant aspects of opportunity are a function of the particular challengers and the issues under concern."[22] Gamson and Meyer contend that "a movement is a field of actors, not a unified entity," and that opportunities are "relative" and a source of "contention within movements."[23] Yet in treating the interactions between a movement and political opportunities, scholars highlight distinctions in the latter that take into account stable aspects, such as its institutions and traditions, and elements that fluctuate, such as political discourse and public policy; but they do not sufficiently analyze power relations within a social movement. How these relationships affect the interactions of a movement and political opportunities and outcomes is understudied.

Nancy Whittier has noted the importance of understanding that social movements cannot be reduced to analyses of formal organizations, strategies, resources, and tactics. Rather, social movements require an understanding of identity, culture, and community.[24] Verta Taylor, as has Judith Lorber, calls upon us to view gender as an institution "whose manifestations are cultural, structural, and interactional."

Gender is an institution that serves its own particular purpose—just like other core institutions such as the family, religion, the economy, and politics. The purpose of gender as an institution is "to construct women as a group to be the subordinates of men as a group."[25]

Taylor has shown that in women's self-help groups, the institution of gender was challenged, so that what it means to be "female," "feminine," and "woman" was transformed over time. These challenges themselves shape and redefine action frames and therefore mobilizing structures. In expanding Taylor's notion of institutions, it is clear that race, class, and culture are also institutions. And it is quite easy to construct alternative sentences. The purpose of race as an institution is for "people of color" to be the subordinates of White people as a group. The purpose of class as an institution is for the "economically disadvantaged" to be the subordinates of the advantaged as a group. Of course, these are oversimplified statements with complex fluctuating meanings that need further study, but they nonetheless represent institutions that are intricately intertwined.

Neither is it enough to essentialize the meanings of the institutions themselves and to believe that they do not possess variance within each. Yet as they interact and overlap, these institutions form cultural templates that create "cultural toolkits," or ways of knowing. As has been discussed, women's positions and power varied depending upon their race, class, and culture (or the region in which they grew up), and an analysis of gender alone does not sufficiently explain their placement in the movement. An analysis of the interactions of these cultural templates helps to explain why Black women from the rural South viewed the compromise as a defeat. For them, little had changed. To determine that a particular event constitutes a political opportunity or a successful outcome, or alternatively to view it as a pittance or failure, requires an understanding of the relations of power and representation among movement subgroups.

The decision to offer two seats to the delegation was the result of a complex array of interactions between actors that embodied power relations as defined by the predetermined cultural templates of race, class, and gender that operate as structural institutions. But this dynamic not only is central to social movements and their actors but also impinges on the development, expansion, and retraction of political opportunities. During the civil rights movement, the successive administrations capitulated to many of the demands made by activists. But their responses were equally complex and often the result of public outrage, not at the deaths of Black activists but of White middle-class youths. And because of this, the interpretation of the ensuing expansion of opportunities may be variously viewed as more or less positive, depending on the social location of the interpreter.

This raises questions about our conceptualization of collective identity in social movements. While many scholars have shown the importance of collective identity to grievance interpretations, they have not sufficiently addressed distinctions among civil rights movement participants.[26] Sociologist Alberto Melucci analyzes social movement collective identities, arguing that more recent movements are formed through a coalition of other movement groups, and that the collective identity of the new movement is a result of its confrontation with the state. Yet out of the public view is this coalition of distinct groups or "submerged networks." Carol Mueller, in critiquing Melucci's analysis, argues that he does not sufficiently analyze the internal conflict and competition among these submerged networks. Yet Mueller's analysis of the emergence of the women's movement and a collective identity among contending groups does not sufficiently address the cultural templates that gave "the voice of the Women's Movement" to the more formal hierarchical organization, the National Organization for Women, which in effect excluded, among others, women of color and lesbians.[27]

In the civil rights movement, clearly race, class, gender, and other cultural templates operated, but they did so in a multitude of ways producing a multiplicity of "we" groups. As has been discussed, analyzing gender as a unidimensional institution is not enough. The meaning of "gender institution" or other templates for a particular woman in the movement differed, based on the extent of overlap with the race institution, class institution, and culture institution. And the meaning of all of these institutions shifted over time.[28] Early White women participants, steeped in southern mores, understood that SNCC was a Black movement, and this brought an acceptance of them as mainstream bridge leaders. As a new and larger influx of White women less knowledgeable about the South entered SNCC, White women's status and positions began to decline; therefore, the meaning of their gender participation as White women also shifted. Likewise, with the rise of Black nationalism, Black women began to experience a decline in their autonomy and free spaces, creating a shift in the meaning of their participation as well.

Given this, it is easy to see that the "we" in the movement was fluid. Action frames often shape the beliefs of participants and potential adherents. Embracing common action frames, however, does not erase differences among participants, though clearly it serves to build solidarity and political collective identities. However, political collective identities do not replace the identity of particular subgroups, as they are part of the larger cultural milieu. For example, most SNCC participants, both Black and White, saw themselves as a political collective "we," distinct from activists in the SCLC. Yet the degree to which SNCC activists constituted an aggregate "we" is an empirical question. In SNCC, prior to 1965, individualism was revered, and there was a conscious effort to break down race, class, and cultural institutional barriers. Even so, early White women participants repeatedly acknowledged their place in a "Black movement." The problem developed when Whites new to the movement assumed a definition of "we" that went beyond the political collective identity, thereby disregarding subgroup identities as defined by race, class, or other cultural distinctions. This leaves open the empirical question of how much "we," or acceptance of a collective identity beyond the political, is productive or even real.

Moreover, as the movement progressed, the notion of "we" became explicitly narrower, to the point of excluding longtime Black activists. Even a shared collective action frame was not enough to build a strong mobilizing base upon which the Black Power movement could build. As Ladner noted, it was mainly educated, young Black men who rejected the notion that the doors were opening to freedom and equality. Despite their agreement and shared collective action frame with poor, rural Blacks and many women bridge leaders, the potential coalition fell apart. Instead, these dynamic urban Black men left the rural sector behind and imposed more gender-based and race-based strictures on leadership.

The peak of the movement collapsed despite unprecedented political opportunities, such as passage of the 1965 Civil Rights Act and the 1964 Voting Rights Act. Scholars Steven Barkan and Herbert Haines have shown the importance of a radical flank of the movement.[29] While SNCC and the MFDP represented the radical flank, arguably SNCC became even more radical as political opportunities increased. In 1966, the social movement sector, or all of the movement organizations, still had political opportunities, a radical flank, a charismatic leader, resources, political elite alliances, and political action frames. The movement was still organized, with the SCLC and the NAACP continuing their work. Yet while King and the SCLC experienced greater effectiveness with the federal government, including passage of the 1964 Economic Opportunity Act, which corresponded with the government's War on Poverty, they did not share similar success in their efforts to mobilize the North. And mobilization efforts were weakened in the South.[30]

The heart of their mobilization difficulties, I argue, was at least in part the disintegration of the bridging tier. In addition to resources, primary and secondary formal organizations and leaders, bridging organizations and leaders, action frames, and mobilizing structures, what seems to be one of the most critical determinants of a social movement's ability to mobilize and sustain support is the ideology embraced by the bridging tier. Also crucial is the extent to which this ideology allows for individuality and simultaneously challenges existing cultural stocks, as manifested in the race, class, and gender cultural templates, through its framing processes and mobilizing structures.[31] In modifying Suzanne Staggenborg's three outcomes of social movement—political and policy, mobilization, and cultural— Verta Taylor concludes:

> Conventional social movement wisdom would probably lump gender changes in with the shifts in norms, roles, identities, behaviors, and consciousness generally thought of as a cultural change.[32]

Rather than limiting shifts in gender norms to cultural outcomes, Verta Taylor's analysis treats them as successful political outcomes. SNCC's challenge to existing cultural templates created successful outcomes that reached beyond narrow definitions of political success. Even if the explicit discussion of gender equity developed later in its history, the nature of women's participation in SNCC—even White women's—stretched beyond the cultural norms governing women's activities and, as has been well documented by numerous scholars, led to the 1970s women's liberation movement. Yet it was the antihierarchical, consensus-seeking, community-building ideology of SNCC that shaped its action frame, its mobilizing structure, its activists' interpretations of political opportunities and outcomes and the corresponding changes in cultural stocks, as manifested in the altered templates of race, class, and gender institutions.

For all intents and purposes, Miss Ella Baker, whether aware of Brazilian educator Paulo Freire's work or not, understood the philosophy and ideology behind a pedagogy of the oppressed.[33] Both Baker and Clark understood the need not to educate others by making ideological deposits requiring the student to memorize and repeat what has been learned. Instead, the organization and its bridge leaders served the students or potential constituents, allowing for a dialectical exchange that stimulated creativity in both the teacher and the student.

With the rise of Black nationalism and a corresponding shift in ideology came the imposition of hierarchy and the reinstitutionalization of gender and class normativity. It is not the case that the Black Power movement was negative in its entirety. On the contrary, it created a positive base for a dramatic shift in racial identity and pride. However, that shift in ideology created a narrow action frame and mobilizing structure that undermined the bridging nature of SNCC. Power became centralized and followers were now depositories for their leaders' ideological beliefs. Status was gained by a commitment to a narrow ideology rather than to community action and empowerment. And this undermined SNCC's effectiveness.

Movement leaders cannot simply preach or deposit a new repertoire for the creation of a mobilizing action frame; rather, such frames must evolve out of individual and subjective experiences of oppression, of specific community cultural stocks. Professional bridge leaders Ella Baker and Septima Clark understood that. Moreover, they understood that resources, charismatic leaders, hierarchical structures, deposited action frames, and political opportunities were not sufficient to sustain or even mobilize a movement. Professional bridge leaders brought to the movement a specific ideology of contention and, therefore, alternative templates for organization that shaped corresponding action frames, mobilizing structures, political opportunities, and outcomes. The bridging tier of leaders, as well as the bridging organizations, were critical to the success of the civil rights movement.

Epilogue

Lessons From Our Past

SNCC, MORE THAN ANY other movement organization, left us with a model for grassroots mobilization that sought to empower all and to encourage everyone to reach his or her potential. Yet in today's political climate, we find an unprecedented return to a legacy that was never our own. African-American women have been at the forefront of movement activism, from the ill-fated days on the slave ships to the peak of the civil rights movement. So what has happened? Why has the Black woman's invisibility once again been required?

In this regard, we have much to learn from the success of the civil rights movement and its subsequent abeyance. The civil rights movement began to decline, at least in part, because of the philosophical and ideological shift in its primary source for bridging the masses to the movement. Yet, ironically, the decline of this tier—because of its narrower, more militant stance, its infusion of hierarchy, its negative perception of women's leadership, and the domination of the movement by young educated Black men no longer seeking equality but power by any means necessary—reshaped the state's posture toward the demands of the primary and secondary formal organizations, the SCLC and the NAACP, respectively.[1] While Dr. King and the SCLC won the hard-fought battle to gain support of an administration, the movement had begun to deteriorate from below.

What we have seen is the necessity to build a mass base of support from the bottom up. Such a task requires the inclusion of all and a commitment to indigenous and local leadership. Yet in recent years we have seen an escalation of gender tensions between Black men and women, as played out in the Anita Hill–Clarence Thomas hearings and the Million Man March. Many African-American women scholars, activists, and writers have issued various opinions regarding these events. But what is common to all is the question of, To what extent should we, as Black women, support our men? and, To what extent should "Black" become synonymous with Black woman? For decades, this has been a dilemma for Black women, with suffragist and Black activist Sojourner Truth opposing the Fifteenth Amendment, which enfranchised Black men but excluded Black women.

For generations, Black women have led and fought for the struggle of Black people, which obviously includes themselves, their daughters, sons, husbands, mothers, and fathers. They have struggled, sometimes at the forefront but more often in the free spaces of movements, showing solidarity, loyalty, and support for Black men. This pattern has sustained the Black community and, as we have seen, provided a strong base for the civil rights movement. And this pattern carries us into the present. The question remains, however: What has been the consequence of Black women's acceptance of this pattern?

Today, 54 percent of African-American children live in woman-headed households, 68 percent of our children are born to unwed mothers;[2] only 40 percent of us are married;[3] of single male-headed families, 24.3 percent live in poverty, of single woman-headed households, 49 percent live in poverty;[4] for our children aged 15–19, males and females are more likely to die from a homicide than from any particular disease or an accident.[5] While these unsettling statistics cannot be attributed entirely to gender bias, they do require a reevaluation of who ought to lead in the Black community. In point of fact, impoverished Black women are raising most of our children, alone, yet they have the least voice in the political arena, while also remaining "behind the scenes" in most Black civil rights organizations. Moreover, in the last several years, we have seen Black women's voices increasingly muted in our struggle for freedom.

When Anita Hill dared to speak out with allegations that Clarence Thomas, an anti–affirmative action conservative, had sexually harassed her, African Americans, both men and women, castigated her for breaking ranks, for being a traitor to the race. She and other African-American women who speak for gender equality are cast as sell-outs, as anti-Black. As Black activist and writer Barbara Smith elaborates:

> It was demoralizing to see how the confrontation reinforced the perception that any woman who raises the issue of sexual oppression in the black community is somehow a traitor to the race, which translátes into being a traitor to black men. It is particularly disheartening knowing that probably a lot of black people took this stance despite believing Anita Hill. They who decided that standing behind a black man— even one with utter contempt for the struggles of African Americans—is more important than supporting a black woman's right not to be abused.[6]

And June Jordan, an African-American professor of African-American studies and women's studies at the University of California, Berkeley, asks:

How is it possible that only John Carr—a young black corporate lawyer who maintained a friendship with Anita Hill ten years ago—how is it possible that he, alone among black men, stood tall and strong and righteous as a witness for her defense? What about spokesmen for the NAACP or the National Urban League? What about spokesmen from the U.S. Congressional Black Caucus? All of the organizational and elected Black men who spoke aloud against a wrong black man, Clarence Thomas, for the sake of principles resting upon decency and concerns for fair play, equal protection, and affirmative action—where did they go when, suddenly, a good Black woman arose among us, trying to tell the truth? Where did they go? And why?[7]

Perhaps the answer lies in our willingness as Black women to want Black men to have the out-front positions. Perhaps it lies in our willingness to work in the "free spaces." Perhaps it lies in our willingness to wait while we focus on racism in society. Perhaps it lies in our willingness not to rock the boat. While the civil rights movement could not have succeeded without our willingness to put gender concerns aside, it has not served us well to continue this pattern. If there are lessons to be learned from the movement, it is that we must not stifle any segment of our community. More than any other organization, SNCC provided an alternative template, an all-inclusive empowering legacy, a legacy of community empowerment rather than personal aggrandizement. While SNCC was not completely successful, women were not subjugated to, nor were their contributions predefined by, men. In contrast, one of the strongest mobilizing forces in the Black community today has followed the legacy of Black nationalism. While I see the virtue in this movement, its relegation of women to the home, as a partner whose identity is defined by men, whose stability rests on male atonement and his motivation to do the right thing is not the legacy of successful mobilization.

I, like many of my sisters, viewed the Million Man March with conflicting emotions. Black journalist Julianne Malveaux expressed dismay over the support offered by many Black feminists and activists:

But when men are "taking control," we have to ask what control will they take, and from whom? These uncooperative words—taking, not sharing—not so subtly attack the women who now head almost half of African-American households. When men are "stepping up," we have to ask, will the first step be onto a woman's back? . . ."

A Nation of Islam publication titled "Women in Support of the Million Man March" offers a soothing message for women. "Were it not for our boldness, our courage, our intelligence and forthrightness, Black men would have very little. . . . We have been their leaders, their teachers, their nurses. We have patiently waited for our men to take up their responsibility. Now that they have made up their minds to stand up for us and our families, they want us to aid them in this march by staying home with the children."[8]

Malveaux explains that this message fails to capture the historical reality of African-American women's participation in leadership. And it sends a "terrible signal to young women and girls." She elaborates:

Not long ago, I met a high school junior who told me that she would like to travel and write, much as I do, but that she "needed" to find a man first. She had already assimilated the message that men's interests come before hers. I thought she needed a reality check about the meaning of family and partnership.

And so do the organizers of the Million Man March. Women like Dorothy Height [former president of the National Council of Negro Women and longtime activist] and Rosa Parks support this march in the name of love for black men. I say these men need challenge, as well as love. They need women marching beside them to provide that challenge. The African-American community can't build much momentum from the imperfect vehicle of an exclusionary march. If the march really belongs to us all, then women should be encouraged to join the Million Man March.⁹

Of course, many African-American women did not feel excluded. Many, such as myself, did feel excluded, but experienced a sense of joy in viewing the coming together of so many Black men making pledges to support their families and their communities. In view of the violence that so plagues our communities, the sight of Black men standing together, strong and in peace, was a sight to behold. Yet through my tears I felt that something was missing, that if the men wanted to clean their houses, they should have done it in concert with their women. Black writer and scholar Michael Dyson, who attended the march in spite of the objections of his Black women friends, comments:

I argued, and still contend, that there is a difference between acknowledging the pains and problems of Black men and downplaying the lives of black women. And the problems that black males face—drugs, homicide, gang violence—dramatically affect the health and character of their communities.

The peaceful march succeeded in countering various stereotypes of Black men— that they are violent, that they are bereft of mainstream values, that they have no interest in spiritual or moral matters, that they blame social structures or blind forces for their problems.

But the message of atonement, including Farrakhan's disjointed and esoteric disquisition on the subject, failed to address squarely the issue of black men's treatment of black women. No strong note was sounded of repentance for the misogyny, sexism, patriarchy—and homophobia that have plagued our communities, our churches and mosques.¹⁰

Dyson, who was slated to speak but did not have the opportunity because of the length of Farrakhan's speech, goes on to argue that Black women have suffered as well, and their issues also needed to be addressed. Not to invite women, he maintains, was a "brutal slap in the face, a graceless gesture of ingratitude for the constancy of companionship they have shown Black men from the beginning of our time together on American soil."¹¹ He like so many Black feminists such as former Black Panthers Angela Davis, a professor and activist, and Barbara Arnwine, executive director of the National Lawyers' Committee for Civil Rights Under the Law—feels that the march seemed to follow the disturbing template set by that movement.[12] And Black author and historian Paula Giddings remarked that "Farrakhan represents 19th-century solutions to 21st-century problems".[13]

My reaction has been much more complicated. While I am angered at being excluded, I could not help but feel joy that at last some of our problems are being addressed. It was uplifting to see groups of Black men from all walks of life, shoulder to shoulder, standing tall, in tears and in solidarity with one another. Daily, we are inundated with media images of Black men's mug shots. And even if the news weren't reporting the crimes, we cannot honestly claim that Black men aren't killing one another in record numbers, while women mourn their losses.

Interestingly, most of the attention has been shifted to a dialogue with Nation of Islam leader Louis Farrakhan, even though the march was also organized by former NAACP executive director Benjamin Chavis. The latter has sometimes been characterized as single-handedly destroying much of what it took the NAACP years to build. He was ousted from office for alleged improprieties that included sexual misconduct. I think that the attention has been placed on Farrakhan because he represents the greatest threat, with the Nation of Islam representing one of the few organized, self-sufficient Black movements. And this movement has a lot to offer the Black community, providing a viable alternative to those who would pursue a life of drugs, crime, and irresponsibility. It is an appealing way of life offering stability, love, and family. Commenting on the Nation of Islam and the Million Man March, one Black businesswoman who was interviewed on a radio local station explained that she was not upset by the march. Every day on her way to work she sees unemployed Black men hanging out, dealing drugs or taking them. They usually address her in a derogatory manner or ask her for money. However, just as she approaches her business, which is next door to a Nation of Islam enterprise, she is greeted with respect by the men and offered assistance with her packages. Which would you rather have, she asked the interviewer?

Had I not been fortunate enough to have a stable, loving family who encouraged my education, I might not have the luxury of spending my time criticizing the gender bias in an organization that clearly cares about Black people. Faced with poverty and the task of raising children alone in violence-ridden neighborhoods and in a culture that denigrates Black people, I would find the Nation of Islam extremely appealing.

Yet in my present privileged state I find much of what Louis Farrakhan represents reprehensible: his anti-Semitism, his homophobia, and his sexism. Unfortunately, his approach is a sign of the times. Many movements today, even our election campaigns, are built on platforms of hate—that is, the anti–affirmative action movement, the anti-immigrant movement, the Aryan movement, the anti-choice movement, the anti-government movement—and this has been the decade for an astounding upsurge of such movements and campaigns. Yet it is particularly unfortunate that the Nation of Islam has built a platform of exclusion, because in doing so, it has undermined its ability to empower Black communities.

I guess that what I find most disturbing is that there is such a paucity of formal Black leadership with know-how. It seems that all of the lessons of the civil rights movement have been lost. While, as I have discussed, a gendered and classed hierarchy existed among Black people in the movement, this in itself could have been a point of departure for change in this area and continued movement success. Had the movement expanded to empower all to reach his or her fullest potential, where might Black America be today? While it is almost impossible to separate the message from the messenger, Farrakhan has done a great service by calling Black men on the carpet, by uttering the unspoken that Black men must take more responsibility for themselves, for their loved ones, and for their communities. Yet what saddens and angers me is that women were not included. What might have been more empowering would have been a call not only for a Million Man March but also a simultaneous Million Woman March, followed by a procession through the streets to a central location where two million African-American men and women joined hands and sang our Black national anthem, "Lift *Ev'ry* Voice and Sing" (my emphasis added).[14] Together and in harmony, our voices should be heard singing James Weldon Johnson's first two stanzas.

> Lift ev'ry voice and sing
> 'Til earth and heaven ring,
> Ring with the harmonies of liberty.
> Let our rejoicing rise
> High as the list'ning skies.
> Let it resound loud as the rolling sea.
>
> Sing a song, full of the faith that the dark past has taught us.
> Sing a song, full of the hope that the present has taught us.
> Facing the rising sun of our new day begun,
> Let us march on 'til victory is won.[15]

An effective movement cannot be built on exclusion. While we have seen that hierarchical organizations and primary formal charismatic leaders are necessary, since they engage the state, we can also acknowledge that decentralized, consensus-building, antihierarchical organizations provide the basis for grassroots mobilization and solidarity. While the Reverend Jesse Jackson has called for coalitions and for organizing from the bottom up, his organization has been weakened by its multiplicity of foci, its relations with the state, its international focus, and its failure to develop a sufficient educational base or bridging organization. One of the strongest features of the Nation of Islam has been its focus on personal transformation and shifts in identity by combating stereotypes and negative imagery of Black people. Of course, this focus has been weakened by the narrowness of its definitions of Black identity, appropriate religious beliefs, gender relations, and sexual preference. Its movement seeks to deposit predetermined identity frames, and this undermines the action potential of this movement. Conversely Jackson, while aware of the problem of self-image and self-esteem, does not have a program that actively engages potential recruits in his platform. Jackson's Rainbow Coalition, which calls for solidarity among all those excluded in America—including African Americans, the poor, gays, lesbians, and other disenfranchised groups—is really more of an ongoing campaign than a movement.

To effectively seek change in America much more is required. Leadership must be fully developed in every Black community in America. Action frames must include a dialectical relationship between prefigurative politics and political agendas, each reshaping the other. Moreover, the mobilizing structures must be such that leadership is not impeded but, rather, raises the most able, the most gifted to bring about change. In response to Dr. King's refrain, "How long? How long?" I answer, "As long as it takes for us, African-Americans, to join together; as long as it takes us to empower *everyone* in our community, including the poor, the unlettered, gays, women, Christians, Muslims, Jews, and Atheists; as long as it takes us to realize that to uplift ourselves we must first love one another; and as long as it takes us to realize the old adage, which my grandmother Emma Williams always repeated to her seven daughters, 'A chain is only as strong as its weakest link.' " My brothers and sisters, we have allowed ourselves to be weakened. We have not learned the lessons from our history. As a people, we are in a struggle for survival. We cannot afford to exclude; we must link arms to strengthen all and to benefit from the strength of others. In replying to his own question, Dr. King answered, "Not Long." Let us extend our hands and help one another make that dream come true.

Appendix A

The Study

THIS BOOK PLACES African-American women at the center of the analysis and focuses on the movement within the context of their organizational participation. As much as possible, women's voices are used to illustrate themes that emerged during personal interviews and archival research.

The study used a number of qualitative data sources, including life histories, archival materials, secondary sources, and personal interviews. Multiple methods through triangulation were employed in an effort to discover which women were leaders. For example, names were located in several well-known accounts of the civil rights movement (e.g., Morris 1984; McAdam 1982, 1988; Branch 1988). The accuracy of these findings was verified through the use of archival data. Interviewees were also asked for names of women whom they felt were movement leaders, thus implementing the "snowball" method. Through this process, I could be relatively certain that my categorization of a particular woman as a leader was valid. Additionally, this allowed the participants to define leadership in their own terms.

Data from twenty-five telephone interviews were used for this study. Women were asked the same questions regarding their participation, as well as the participation of other women in their respective civil rights movement organizations. The method was to ask specific open-ended questions and to follow the interviewee's line of thought with additional questions. The remaining interviews were obtained from the Civil Rights Documentation Project, Moorland Spingarn Research Center at Howard University, the Oral History Project at the Martin Luther King Jr. Center for Non-Violent Social Change in Atlanta, and from secondary sources. These interviews, primarily of women who are now deceased, were especially suitable for the study, as the interviewers had focused attention on their participation in the movement organizations.

Women's activities in seven civil rights movement organizations—the Women's Political Council (WPC), the Southern Christian Leadership Conference (SCLC), the Student Non-Violent Coordinating Committee (SNCC), the Montgomery Improvement Association (MIA), the Mississippi Freedom Democratic Party (MFDP), the National Association for the Advancement of Colored People (NAACP), and the Congress of Racial Equality (CORE)—are discussed in this study. Special emphasis has been placed on the SCLC and SNCC women, for several reasons. The activities of both organizations were more concentrated, with most of their activism taking place in the South. Moreover, the oral history project at the Moorland Spingarn Research Center and the one at the Martin Luther King Jr. Center for Non-Violent Social Change, provided more interviews of women who were active in both SNCC and the SCLC. Also, the King Center hosted a reunion for women activists that consisted primarily of women in the SCLC and SNCC. Their names, addresses, and telephone numbers were already compiled for this event and I was given access to the list. Moreover, despite my efforts, I had difficulties locating women in the other organizations, since many of them had either moved or remarried, often changing their names. Thus, my focus in no way suggests that the activities of women in the NAACP or CORE were any less important than those of the women in the SCLC and SNCC.

This research began by examining scholarly accounts of the civil rights movement. Additional information was acquired from special papers and archival collections, as well as from secondary sources. Archival research took place in several locations. At the Martin Luther King Center in Atlanta, the Martin Luther King Jr. Papers, C. B. King Papers, Fred D. Grey Papers, Dexter Avenue Baptist Church Papers, Mississippi Freedom Democratic Party Papers, Montgomery Improvement Association Papers, Fred Shuttlesworth Papers, Southern Christian Leadership Conference Papers, Student Non-Violent Coordinating Committee Papers, Mrs. Johnnie Carr Papers, Mrs. Erna Dungee Papers, Mrs. Septima Clark Papers, Mrs. Hazel Gregory Papers, Montgomery Bus Boycott Inventory, Oral History Series, Reverend H. J. Palmer Collection, and the Charles Sherrod Papers were analyzed.

Additionally, the Dr. Martin Luther King Jr. Papers at Boston University supplied detailed information regarding the beginnings of the MIA and SCLC. All of these archives provided numerous written documents, as well as oral histories. Moreover, the MFDP Papers on microfilm and the CORE Papers on microfilm were examined.

The years 1954–1965 are the central focus of this study, since these were times of heightened civil rights movement activity. Moreover, concentrating on a narrower period facilitated more in-depth study.

Appendix B

Interviews

Interviewees:

Diane Bevel Nash   January 26, 1990
Fay Bellamy   February 7, 1990
Judy Richardson   August 7, 1990; July 10,1992
Unita Blackwell   January 30, 1990
Dorothy Cotton   January 20, 1990
Casey Hayden   January 12, 1990
Victoria Gray   February 6, 1990
Johnnie Carr   January 26, 1990
Mary Fair Burks   January 22, 1990
Thelma Glass   February 2, 1990
Anonymous SNCC Member   March 16, 1989
Hazel Gregory   February 15, 1990
Virginia Durr   February 1, 1990
Dorie Ladner   July 27, 1992
Penny Patch   August 10, 1992
Prathia Hall Wynn   November 9, 1992
Bernice Johnson Reagon   November 30, 1992
Gloria Richardson   August 8, 1992
Muriel Tillinghast   July 19, 1992
Dottie Zellner   July 27, 1992
Constance Curry   August 22–23, 1992

Joanne Grant   August 25–26, 1992
Jean Wheeler Smith Young   August 9, 1992
Faith Holsaert   September 1, 1992
Constancia Romilly   June 5, 1992

Interviews used from the Civil Rights Documentation Project, Moorland Spingarn Center at Howard University:

Ella Baker
E. D. Nixon
Fannie Lou Hamer
Mary Lane
Rosa Parks

Interviews used from the Oral History Project at the Martin Luther King Jr. Center for Non-violent Social Change:

Johnnie Carr
E. D. Nixon
Septima Clark
Virginia Durr

Steven Millner's interviews, included in Garrow 1989:

Jo Ann Gibson Robinson
Erna Dungee Allen
Johnnie Carr

Secondary sources used to obtain information and quotes for the following women:

Fannie Lou Hamer
Pauli Murray
Amelia Platts Boynton
Daisy Bates
Ruby Hurley
Rosa Parks
Ella Baker
Gloria Richardson
Joyce Ladner
Dorothy Height
Elenor Norton Holmes
Angela Davis
Kathleen Cleaver
Septima Clark
Jo Ann Gibson Robinson
Erna Dungee Allen
Ann Moody
Barbara Arnwine

Appendix C

Archives and Primary Sources

From the Martin Luther King Jr. Center for Non-Violent Social Change, Atlanta, Georgia:

The Martin Luther King Jr. Papers
C. B. King Papers
Fred D. Grey Papers
Dexter Avenue Baptist Church Papers
Mississippi Freedom Democratic Party Papers
Montgomery Improvement Association Papers
Reverend Fred Shuttlesworth Papers
Southern Christian Leadership Conference Papers
Student Non-Violent Coordinating Committee Papers
Mrs. Johnnie Carr Papers
Mrs. Erna Dungee Papers
Montgomery Bus Boycott Inventory
Oral History Series
Mrs. Hazel Gregory Papers
Mrs. Septima Clark Papers
Reverend H. J. Palmer Collection
Charles Sherrod Papers

From the Civil Rights Documentation Project, Moorland Spingarn Research Center at Howard University, Washington, D.C.:

See Appendix A.

From Boston University:

Martin Luther King Jr. Papers

On Microfilm:

Mississippi Freedom Democratic Party Papers, Congress of Racial Equality Papers, 1944–1968 Sanford, N.C. Microfilming Corporation of America.

Periodicals:

Montgomery Improvement Association Newsletter
Southern Christian Leadership Conference Newsletter
Student Voice
Freedom Newsletter

Notes

INTRODUCTION

1. See Robinson 1987; Payne 1989, 1990, 1994; and Barnett 1993.
2. Somers and Gibson 1994, pp. 37–99.
3. Ibid., p. 41.
4. Brown 1989, pp. 613–614. See also Ogunyami 1985 and Walker 1983.
5. Walker 1983, p. xi.
6. See Appendixes.
7. Taylor 1989.
8. McAdam 1982.
9. Evans 1979; McAdam 1988; and Rothschild 1982.

CHAPTER ONE

1. See, for example, the mass society approaches of Kornhauser (1959); Fromm (1941); and Hoffer (1951); and the Chicago School theorists, Turner and Killian (1957); Park (1967); and Lang and Lang (1961). These earlier approaches, including the work of LeBon (1960) and Blumer (1969), emphasized the irrational nature of social movement behavior. As noted by Lofland (1982), later collective behavior theorists such as Turner (1968), Couch (1970), Berk (1974), and Charles Tilly (1978) would take a more normative view of crowd behavior, while still

placing an emphasis on shared grievances and frustrations. This later emphasis, as Lofland notes, has led to a neglect of emotion in contemporary collective behavior analyses of social movements. Furthermore, he calls for researchers to develop studies that analyze the interactions between micro and macro forms of emotional expression.

2. See, for example, Zald and Ash 1966; Olson 1965; Lipsky 1968; Gamson 1975; Fireman and Gamson 1979; McCarthy and Zald 1973, 1979.

3. See McAdam 1982; Jenkins and Perrow 1977; Tarrow 1989; Tilly 1978.

4. See, respectively, Taylor and Whittier 1992; Robnett 1996.

5. Klandermans and Tarrow 1988.

6. Snow, Rochford, Worden, and Benford 1986.

7. Melucci 1995.

8. See, for example, Snow, Zurcher, and Eckland-Olson 1980.

9. For example, Jonasdottir 1988; Lawson and Barton 1980; Payne 1989, 1990; McAdam 1992.

10. See, for example, P. Collins (1990); Collins and Anderson (1995); Davis (1981); Zinn and Dill (1994); Moraga and Anzaldua (1981); West and Blumberg (1990) for a fuller understanding of differential experiences based on race, class, gender, and sexual preference.

11. For example, Melluci 1985, 1988; Pizzorno 1978; Cohen 1985; Klandermans 1986.

12. See Gamson 1992; Lofland 1981.

13. For example, Dyson 1993.

14. Calhoun 1994, p. 27.

15. Dyson 1993, p. xxi.

16. Hall 1996. Also note that scholar Joshua Gamson (1985) criticizes social movement scholars for placing too much emphasis on the role of social movements in forging "new" collective identities, arguing instead that there are multiple collective identities among participants.

17. Morris 1984.

18. Payne 1994.

19. While Payne does a good job of documenting the efforts of local leadership, his emphasis is also on male leadership. Moreover, while he acknowledges class and gender as important determinants of leadership, he does not sufficiently or systematically develop the interactions between movement participants as defined by their race, class, gender, and culture. Moreover, where gender is discussed, he has a tendency to title women's participation as leadership, but to define their efforts in terms of their organizing skills.

20. Sacks 1988, p. 121.

21. Ibid.

22. Victoria Gray, interview by author, February 6, 1990.

23. See West and Blumberg 1990, pp. 3–35; Jonasdottir 1988; Smith 1988; Siim 1988; Spender 1983; Bookman and Morgen 1988.

24. For example, Freeman 1975, 1979; Buechler 1990.

25. See Ferree and Hess 1985, pp. 94–103.

26. Taylor and Whittier 1992.

27. See, for example, Kanter (1977); Cockburn (1983, 1985); Connell (1987); West and Zimmerman (1987); Staggenborg (1991); and MacKinnon (1982) for a complete discussion. Also see Acker (1990) for a discussion of the need for the analysis of gender as an organizational construct in organizational theory. (The

concept of gender as an organizational category is not new. Many feminists have written about the theoretical insights gained from such analyses in several areas and fields of research. See Game and Pringle 1984; Scott, 1986; Fraser 1989; and Ferguson 1984.)

28. See page 13 for definitions of these terms.

29. See Breines 1982; Gamson 1992; Tarrow 1992.

30. See Payne 1994, p. 266. Also, Payne notes that Drake and Cayton's study of Chicago in the 1930s and 40s suggests that activist women were trusted more than men because "they could not easily capitalize off of their activism" (p. 275). This conclusion certainly reflects my findings. I disagree with Payne, however, who, in citing Arlene Daniel's work, suggests that women's work in the movement was devalued (p. 276). Rather, my findings suggest that while their work was not in the formal sector, it was appreciated, acknowledged, and viewed as important by men and women activists alike.

31. This phenomenon has been well documented by scholars. Women are often more visible and initiate movement activity only to recede into the background later. See, for example, West and Blumberg 1990.

32. Evans and Boyte 1986.

33. McAdam 1982, pp. 49–51; Piven and Cloward 1979, pp. 3–4.

34. Morris 1984.

35. Ibid., p. 91.

36. Gamson 1975.

37. Piven and Cloward 1979; Jenkins and Eckert 1986.

38. Gamson 1975.

39. Zald and Ash 1966.

40. Gusfield 1966.

41. Ibid., p. 142.

42. Zald and Ash 1966, as discussed in Jenkins 1983, p. 542.

43. The merging of these two categories as a result of SNCC's organizational structure and philosophy created an environment much more conducive to the leadership mobility of otherwise excluded groups, such as those without formal education and women. This is discussed at length in chapters 6 and 7.

44. McAdam 1982.

45. Morris 1984, p. 81.

46. *Congressional Quarterly* 1970, p. 33.

47. Morris 1984, p. 83.

48. Tilly 1986; Tarrow 1994; Also see Traugott 1979.

49. Ibid., pp. 7–8.

50. Ellis 1986, p. 6.

51. Ibid., p. 8.

52. As quoted in Ellis 1986.

53. Ellis 1986, pp. 8–9.

54. Wasielewski 1985, p. 209.

55. Ibid.

56. Ellis 1986, p. 13.

57. Seligman 1994, p. 5.

58. Bendix 1977, pp. 300–301.

59. Hochschild 1975, p. 285.

60. Morris 1984, p. 8.

61. Ibid., p. 10.

62. Wasielewski 1985.
63. Hochschild 1979, p. 566.
64. Wasielewski 1985, p. 211.
65. Ibid., p. 213.
66. McCarthy and Zald 1977.
67. Killian 1984; Freeman 1979.
68. Freeman 1979, p. 170.
69. See England (1989) and Jagger (1989) for fuller discussions of this phenomenon.
70. Weber 1968.
71. For example, Cohen 1985; Fireman and Gamson 1979; Marwell 1982; Klandermans 1984; Ferree and Miller 1985; Ferree 1992; Taylor 1995; 1996.
72. Mansbridge 1990, p. x.
73. Taylor 1995, p. 225.
74. For example, Hirsh and Keller 1990; Taylor and Whittier 1992; Whittier 1995; Taylor 1996.
75. Collins 1990.
76. Rosenthal and Schwartz 1989, pp. 46, 52.
77. For example, Pizzorno 1978; Touraine 1981; Melucci 1985, 1989; Habermas 1984, 1987; Cohen 1985.
78. For example, Jaggar 1989; Mansbridge 1990; England 1989; Ferree 1992; Rupp and Taylor 1987; Taylor 1989, 1995; Taylor and Whittier 1992.

CHAPTER TWO

1. See, for example, Evans 1979; King 1987; McAdam 1988; Rothschild 1982.
2. See, for example, Garrow 1986; Morris 1984; Adams 1972; Branch 1988; McAdam 1982; Meier and Rudwick 1973. This point, of course has been made by Pat Hill Collins (1986, 1990) and others who call for analyses that place African-American women at the center of research and theorizing. See, for example, Hull, Scott, and Smith 1982; King 1988; Brewer 1989, 1993; Dill 1979.
3. Bernice Johnson Reagon, interview by author, November 30, 1992.
4. Ibid.
5. See Gilkes 1985. See also Brooks, in Swerdlow and Lessinger (1983), pp. 31–59, for a discussion of African-American women and the church.
6. Reagon, interview.
7. Fay Bellamy, interview by author, February 7, 1990.
8. Judy Richardson, interview by author, August 7, 1990.
9. Bellamy, interview.
10. The phenomenon of gender norms changing during social movements has been widely documented by researchers, who note that afterwards men's and women's normative positions resume. See, for example, West and Blumberg 1990.
11. Bellamy, interview.
12. Anonymous SNCC member, interview by author, March 16, 1989.
13. Bellamy, interview.
14. Reagon, interview.
15. Dorie Ladner, interview by author, July 27, 1992.
16. Higginbotham 1992.
17. Victoria Gray, interview with author, February 6, 1990.
18. See, for example, Davis 1981, 1971; Gates 1988; Giddings 1984.

19. Hall 1995. Also see Lewis 1977.

20. See hooks 1981, chap. 3. Although I do not agree with several of her points regarding Black male-female relationships, hooks does point out difficulties with ignoring gender in a race-based struggle for freedom. She notes that although AA men may be subjected to racism, it does not mean they cannot act in a sexist fashion. And she is critical of those who view sexism in the Black community as only a by-product of White society. While I agree that it is not simply a by-product, but also has a life of its own, I disagree with her assertion that sexism binds Black and White men together. This, I believe, neglects the different power relations between the two. Moreover, her portrayal of Black men as unemployed, sexist, violent, and filled with self-hatred essentializes Black men and neglects a large portion of Black men who work, love themselves and their families, and are non-violent. While I agree that violence among young African-American men is a problem, her analysis does not tease out which men we are talking about and lacks demographic and class analysis.

21. I discuss this point, at length, in chapter 9.

Prathia Hall Wynn, interview by author, November 9, 1992.

23. Bellamy, interview.

24. See Deborah King 1988.

25. Unita Blackwell, interview by author, January 30, 1990; Bellamy, interview; Richardson, interview; Gray, interview.

26. Clark 1986, p. 78.

27. Dorothy Cotton, interview by author, January 20, 1990.

28. I hope that this brief and incomplete glimpse of the history of African-American women's activism and of movement continuity will stimulate scholars to do more research in this relatively neglected area.

29. White 1985, p. 63.

30. Ibid., p. 64.

31. Salem 1990, chap. 5.

32. Peare 1951, p. 149.

33. Giddings 1984, pp. 199–230.

34. Ibid., p. 233.

35. Ibid.

36. Ibid., pp. 236–237.

37. Murray 1987, chaps. 13, 14.

38. Ibid., pp. 172–173.

39. Ibid., p. 201.

40. Ibid., pp. 204–205.

41. Ibid., p. 176.

42. Ibid., p. vi.

43. Ibid., p. 212.

44. Meier and Rudwick 1973, p. 4.

45. Beverly Jones 1990, p. 71.

46. Ibid., pp. 72–79.

47. Higginbotham 1992, p. 254.

CHAPTER THREE

1. Bennett 1968, pp. 113–128.

2. Coleman 1990, p. 296.

3. As quoted in Coleman 1990, p. 296.

4. Coleman 1990, p. 296.

5. Sterling 1988, p. 72.

6. As quoted in Coleman 1990, p. 298.

7. Ibid., p. 298.

8. As quoted in Coleman 1990, p. 298.

9. Murray 1987, pp. 138–146.

10. Mary Fair Burks, interview by author, January 22, 1990.

11. Johnnie Carr, interview by Stephen M. Millner, in Garrow 1989, p. 528.

12. Robinson 1987, p. 25.

13. Burks, interview.

14. Branch 1988, p. 127.

15. Ibid.

16. Morris 1984; Garrow 1986; Branch 1988.

17. As quoted in Dallard 1990, p. 62.

18. Gloria Richardson, interview by author, August 8, 1992. It is clear that although Morris (1984, pp. 139–157) has acknowledged Highlander as an important movement "halfway" house, or a resource center for seasoned activists, he does not fully discuss the importance of Highlander to the beginnings of the civil rights movement.

19. Clark 1986, pp. 17–18.

20. Ibid., p. 19.

21. Johnnie Carr, interview by author, January 26, 1990.

22. Thelma Glass, interview by author, February 2, 1990.

23. Ibid.

24. Carr, interview.

25. Robinson 1987, p. 45.

26. Ibid., p. 53.

27. Carr, interview by Millner, p. 528.

28. Robinson 1987, p. 53. See also Gilkes (1985) and Payne (1990) for a discussion of women as the majority of church participants.

29. Burks, interview.

30. ibid.

31. Erna Dungee Allen, interview by Stephen M. Millner, in Garrow 1989, p. 522. See also List of participants in carpool, MIA papers, Box 6 I38, Martin Luther King Center, Atlanta. The carpool had 23 women and 29 men; mostly men owned cars. See also MIA minutes and agendas of three mass meetings, Box 1, File 15, Hazel Gregory Papers, Martin Luther King Center, Atlanta. Only one women—Carr—speaks at one meeting, July 11, 1956. She was allotted five minutes.

32. Dungee Allen, interview, p. 457.

33. Ibid.

34. Martin King 1958, p. 44.

35. Jo Ann Robinson, interview by Stephen M. Millner, in Garrow 1989, p. 570.

36. Carr, interview.

37. E. D. Nixon, Transcript, p. 13, Spingarn Center, Howard University.

38. Morris 1984, p. 44.

39. MIA document, Box 16, File 25, Hazel Gregory Papers.

40. See numerous documents of women's committee positions during the boycott and within the Dexter Avenue Baptist Church, Box 6 I 38 MIA Folder, King Papers, Boston University.

41. Carr, interview.
42. Ibid.
43. Robinson 1987, p. 71.
44. Hazel Gregory, interview by author, February 15, 1990.
45. Ibid.
46. MIA newsletters dated 1956–1960, Box 1, File 21, Hazel Gregory Papers. Martin Luther King Center.
47. Virginia Durr, Transcript, pp. 19–22, Oral History Project #66, Martin Luther King Center, Atlanta.
48. Carr, interview.
49. Gregory, interview.
50. Johnnie Carr, Transcript, pp. 10–13, Oral History Project #60, Martin Luther King Center, Atlanta.
51. Ibid., pp. 19–21.
52. Durr, transcript, pp. 19–22, Oral History Project #66.
53. Glass, interview.
54. See Payne 1990, p. 2.
55. Rosa Parks, Transcript, p. 25, Spingarn Center, Howard University.
56. Carr, interview by Millner.
57. Robinson 1987, pp. 130–140.
58. Parks, transcript, Spingarn Center, p. 25.
59. Millner 1989, p. 485.
60. Burks, interview.

CHAPTER FOUR

1. Note the use of Miss and Mrs. throughout the text. During the period 1954–1965, these titles were used as a sign of respect. Whites in the South often called Black women "Auntie" or by their first names as a sign of disrespect. This was also true for Black men—i.e., "Uncle," "Son," or first-name usage.
2. Dallard 1990, p. 70.
3. As quoted in Raines 1977, p. 136.
4. Ibid., p. 132.
5. Ibid., p. 133.
6. Ibid., p. 134.
7. Ibid., p. 133.
8. Ibid., p. 272.
9. Raines 1977, p. 327.
10. Greenberg 1994, p. 226.
11. Morris 1984, p. 31: "By 157, the NAACP was tied up in some form of litigation in the states of Louisiana, Texas, Virginia, Tennessee, Arkansas, Georgia, South Carolina, and Florida and was, of course, completely outlawed in Alabama.
12. Ella Baker, Transcript, p. 10, Spingarn Center, Howard University.
13. The Montgomery Story, p. 11, transcript by Martin Luther King Jr., Box 118, King Papers, Boston University.
14. Morris 1984.
15. Cantarow and O'Malley 1980, p. 54.
16. Branch 1988, p. 231.
17. Baker, transcript, p. 15, Spingarn Center.
18. Garrow 1986, p. 101.

19. Ibid., pp. 100–103.
20. As quoted in Garrow 1986, p. 99.
21. Greenberg 1994, pp. 226–227.
22. Bates 1962, p. 61.
23. Dallard 1990, p. 59.
24. Bates 1962, p. 47.
25. Ibid., p. 29
26. Calloway-Thomas and Garner 1996, pp. 623–624.
27. Bates 1962, p. 62.
28. Calloway-Thomas and Garner 1996, p. 623.
29. Ibid., p. 623.
30. Bates, 1962, pp. 65–66.
31. Ibid., p. 66.
32. As quoted in Dallard 1990, p. 59.
33. Bates 1962, p. 68.
34. Ibid., p. 92.
35. Ibid., p. 96.
36. Calloway-Thomas and Garner 1996, p. 624.
37. Bates 1962, pp. 162.
38. As quoted in Bates 1962, pp. 162–163.
39. Bates 1962, p. 169.
40. As quoted in Bates 1962, p. 169.
41. Calloway-Thomas and Garner 1996, pp. 624–625.
42. Bates 1962, pp. 214–215.
43. As quoted in Garrow 1986, p. 100.
44. Garrow 1986, pp. 106–107
45. Greenberg 1994, p. 226.
46. Ibid.

CHAPTER FIVE

1. Garrow 1986, pp. 109–110.
2. Ella Baker, Transcript, p. 18, Spingarn Center, Howard University.
3. Branch 1988, p. 231.
4. Memorandum from Ella Baker to Dr. King, November 14, 1958, Box 71A, King Papers, Boston University.
5. Garrow 1986, p. 118.
6. Ibid., p. 119.
7. As quoted in Garrow 1986, p. 119.
8. Septima Clark biography, Series D: IX Box 124:5, SCLC Papers, Martin Luther King Center, Atlanta.
9. For example, Morris 1984; Couto 1991.
10. Memorandum from Andrew Young to Dr. King, February 27, 1964, Citizenship Education Project, Box 29:13, King Papers, Martin Luther King Center.
11. Clark 1986, p. 49.
12. Ibid., p. 53.
13. McAdam 1983, pp. 49–51; Piven and Cloward 1979, pp. 3–4.
14. Clark 1986, p. 53.
15. Ibid.
16. Ibid., p. 50.

17. Ibid., p. 64.

18. Citizenship Education Project, King Papers, Martin Luther King Center.

19. Robert L. Green, SCLC 11/22/65. "Characteristics of Students at the Citizenship Education Program Workshop," November 22, 1965 report, Box 29:14, King Papers, Martin Luther King Center.

20. Annelle Ponder, Greenwood, Mississippi Report, March 1963, Box EI 141: 7, King Papers, Martin Luther King Center.

21. Clark 1986, p. 60.

22. Young memorandum to Dr. King, King Papers.

23. Clark 1986, pp. 63–65.

24. Document 5/28/59, Series D:XIII, Box:129.1, SCLC Papers, Martin Luther King Center.

25. SCLC Newsletter, November 1959, Series D:IX, Box:120:19, and Document May 28, 1959, Series D:XIII, Box 129.1, SCLC Papers, Martin Luther King Center.

26. SCLC Executive Staff Meeting, August 26–28, 1965, AI 3 37 #1 of 2, SCLC Papers; Seventh Annual Convention, September 24–27, 1963, Series D:XIII, Box 130:2 SCLC Papers; Staff Meeting September 16, 1964, EI Box 137 #4 SCLC Papers; SCLC Conference, November 10–12, 1964, Box 2 #22, Erna Dungee Papers; Annual SCLC Meeting, September 27–29, 1961, DXIII 129:12, SCLC Papers; SCLC Conference, September 25–28, 1962, DXIII 129:31, SCLC Papers; SCLC Convention 1963, D:XIII 130:2 SCLC Papers; Letter from King, February 3, 1962, Box 29: 1, King Papers; SCLC Board Meeting Minutes, May 16, 1962, also 1960, 1961, Box 29:1, King Papers; Board Meeting Minutes, September 24–25, 1963, Box 29:2, King Papers; Board Meeting Minutes, August 9, 1965, Box 29:5, King Papers; Martin Luther King Center.

27. Baker, interview transcript, p. 34.

28. Septima Clark, Transcript #17, p. 39, Oral History Project, Martin Luther King Center.

29. Ibid.

30. See sources listed in note 26. For the years 1958, 1960–1966, there is only one press release from the SCLC that mentions a woman, Dorothy Cotton (Series IX Box 120:6). She is mentioned several times in newsletters. Some women are recognized as graduating from the Citizenship Education classes and going back to start schools in their communities; see SCLC newsletters, D:IX Box 120:20, 120: 21, and 122:19, Martin Luther King Center, Atlanta.

31. King letter to Associate Editor, E.P. Dutton & Co., July 2, 1962, Box 29: 18, King Papers, Martin Luther King Center.

32. Box 3, Folder 5, Reverend H.J. Palmer Papers, Martin Luther King Center.

33. Letters from Carole Hoover to Dr. King, Box 34:4 and 34:5, King Papers, Martin Luther King Center.

34. Minutes of SCLC Executive Staff Meeting, August 26–28, 1964, A I 3 37 #1 of 2, SCLC Papers. The view that Dr. King was ambivalent toward women is presented throughout Coretta Scott King's My Life With Martin Luther King Jr. (1969).

35. Dorothy Cotton, interview by author, January 20, 1990.

36. Memorandum from Andrew Young, December 17, 1963, Box 29:13, King Papers, Martin Luther King Center.

37. Alabama Staff List, December 2, 1965, Box 28:6, King Papers, Martin Luther King Center.

38. SCLC newsletter, November–December 1963, vol. 2 (3), D:IX Box 122:24, King Papers, Martin Luther King Center.

39. Golden A. Frinks, Field Secretary Report, August 9, 1963, EI Box 142:2, SCLC Papers, Martin Luther King Center.

40. Cotton, interview.

CHAPTER SIX

1. As quoted in Dallard 1990, p. 81.

2. Ibid., pp. 82–83.

3. News release, A VI Box 34 #3, 5 of 20, SNCC Papers, Martin Luther King Center.

4. Ibid.

5. Subgroup A, Series I Box 1 #4, SNCC Papers, Martin Luther King Center.

6. Subgroup A Series I, Box 1 #1–4, 8, 10, 11, 19, 21, 23, SNCC Papers, Martin Luther King Center; Diane Nash, interview by author, January 26, 1990; Subgroup A Series IV, Box 7 #1, SNCC Papers, Martin Luther King Center.

7. As quoted in Dallard 1990, p. 32.

8. Dallard 1990, pp. 33–38.

9. Ella Baker, Transcript, p. 58, Spingarn Center, Howard University.

10. Mueller 1990, pp. 51–52.

11. Fay Bellamy, interview by author, February 7, 1990.

12. Diane Nash, interview by author, January 26, 1990.

13. Subgroup A Series I Box 1 #11, SNCC Papers, Martin Luther King Center.

14. Nash, interview.

15. Anonymous SNCC member, interviewed by author, March 16, 1989.

16. Letter from Marion Michaels, June 5, 1962, to James Forman, A IV Box 16:221, SNCC Papers, Martin Luther King Center.

17. Response to Marion Michaels from Julian Bond, June 16, 1962, A IV Box 16:221, SNCC Papers, Martin Luther King Center.

18. Zinn 1964, p. 38.

19. As quoted in Zinn 1964, p. 44.

20. Branch 1988, p. 430; Also quoted in Morris 1984, p. 232.

21. Jo Ann Grant, interview by author, August 25–26, 1992.

22. As quoted in Forman 1972, p. 151.

23. As quoted in Carson 1981, p. 34.

24. Garrow 1986, p. 202.

25. Forman 1972, p. 148.

26. As quoted in Zinn 1964, p. 52.

27. Zinn 1964, p. 54.

28. Garrow 1986, pp. 187–202; Also quoted in Zinn 1964, p. 80; Evans 1979, p. 40.

29. Garrow 1986, pp. 202–203.

30. Mary King 1987, p. 437.

31. SNCC minutes undated, Box A 3 6 #3; Executive Committee Minutes, 1964 and 1965, A 3 6 #3; April 10, 1964, March 29, 1964, March 5, 1965, September 4, 1964, April 12–14, undated; Executive Committee minutes, December 27–31, 1963, May 10, 1964; Staff Committee Minutes, June 9–12, 1964, October 11, 1964, A 4 7 #1 8 of 14, SNCC Papers, Martin Luther King Center.

32. Anonymous SNCC member, interview.

33. Bellamy, interview.

34. Persons Working out of the Atlanta Office, A:VI Box 28 #21, SNCC Papers, Martin Luther King Center.

35. Bellamy, interview.

36. Persons Working, SNCC Papers.

37. Job Description, A:IV Box 28#17, SNCC Papers, Martin Luther King Center.

38. Office Staff Meeting Minutes, February 16, 1964, A 4 7 #! 5 of 14, SNCC Papers, Martin Luther King Center.

39. Executive Committee Minutes, September 4, 1964, A 3 6 #4 2 of 3, SNCC Papers, Martin Luther King Center.

40. Anonymous SNCC member, interview.

41. Persons Working, SNCC Papers.

42. Muriel Tillinghast, interview by author, July 19, 1992.

43. Prathia Hall Wynn, interview by author, November 9, 1992.

44. Ibid.

45. Anonymous SNCC member, interview.

46. Ibid.

47. Gloria Richardson, interview by author, August 8, 1992.

48. Jones 1985, p. 21; Davis 1981, pp. 20–22.

49. As quoted in Davis 1981, . 20.

50. As quoted in Bennett 1968, p. 135.

51. Bennett 1968, pp. 137–140.

52. Ibid, pp. 142–143.

53. Anonymous SNCC member, interview.

CHAPTER SEVEN

1. See McAdam 1988; Evans 1979; Rothschild 1982.

2. Rothschild 1982, p. 139.

3. Giddings 1984, pp. 17–31.

4. Evans 1979, p. 81.

5. Ibid.

6. Ibid., p. 80.

7. Constancia (Dinky) Romilly, interview by author, June 5, 1992.

8. Casey Hayden, interview by author, January 12, 1990.

9. Ibid.

10. Washington 1977, pp. 14–15.

11. For example, McAdam 1988, pp. 93–111, 125, 144; Evans 1979; Rothschild 1982, pp. 127–154.

12. See McAdam 1988, p. 111; Evans 1979.

13. Mary King 1987, p. 459.

14. Hayden, interview.

15. Hayden 1989, p. 14.

16. Hayden, interview.

17. Hayden 1989, p. 14.

18. Mary Lane, Transcript. p. 12, Spingarn Center, Howard University.

19. Ibid.

20. Hayden, interview; Mary King 1987.

21. Ibid.

22. Alvin Poussaint, 1966 report, MFDP Microfilm Reel 70, Frame #0158.

23. Constance Curry, interview by author, August 22–23, 1992.

24. Romilly, interview.
25. Dottie Zellner, interview by author, July 27, 1992.
26. Penny Patch, interview by author, August 10, 1992.
27. Prathia Hall Wynn, interview by author, November 9, 1992.
28. Ibid.
29. Patch, interview.
30. Ibid.
31. Zellner, interview.
32. Faith Holsaert, interview by author, September 1, 1992.
33. Ibid.
34. Curry, interview.
35. Muriel Tillinghast, interview by author, July 19, 1992.
36. Zellner, interview.
37. Patch, interview.
38. Zellner, interview.
39. Jean Wheeler Smith Young, interview by author, August 9, 1992.
40. Ibid.
41. Ladner, interview by author, July 27, 1992.
42. Wynn, interview.
43. Joanne Grant, interview by author, August 25–26, 1992.
44. Tillinghast, interview.
45. Curry, interview.
46. Jean Wheeler Smith Young, interview by author, August 9, 1992.
47. Ibid.
48. Judy Richardson, interview by author, July 10, 1992.
49. Ladner, interview.
50. Tillinghast, interview.
51. Ibid.
52. Grant, interview.
53. Richardson, interview.
54. Ibid.
55. Bernice Johnson Reagon, interview by author, November 30, 1992.
56. Gloria Richardson, interview by author, August 8, 1992.
57. Reagon, interview.
58. Zellner, interview.
59. Ibid.
60. Ibid.
61. Richardson, interview.
62. Ibid.
63. Smith Young, interview.
64. Ibid.
65. Ladner, interview.
66. Richardson, interview.
67. Tillinghast, interview.
68. Reel 22, Frame #0218–0222, CORE Papers, Microfilming Corporation of America.
69. Ibid.
70. Ibid.
71. Southwest Georgia Project: Report and Proposals, December 27, 1963, pp. 3–12, A IV Box 21 341, SNCC Papers, Martin Luther King Center, Atlanta.

72. Ibid.

73. News release, 1962, A VI Box 34 #3, 2 of 20, SNCC Papers, Martin Luther King Center.

74. Jake Rosen, *Freedom* newsletter, April 18, 1964, Reel 67, Frame #0093, CORE Papers, Microfilming Corporation of America.

75. Lerner 1973, pp. 206–212.

76. As quoted in Lerner 1973, p. 158.

77. Ibid, p. 162.

78. Sellers 1973, pp. 101–105.

79. Ibid.

80. Ibid.

CHAPTER EIGHT

1. Zinn 1964, p. 60.

2. Muriel Tillinghast, interview by author, July 19, 1992.

3. Boynton 1979, p. 43. Also see Kelley (1990), pp. 111–112 and Kelley (1994), pp. 42), for a similar finding regarding the Black clergy and labor unions. Painter (1979, pp. 13, 129) offers a similar characterization of the Black clergy who refused to protest or speak out against the death sentence of the Scottsboro Nine, who were unjustly convicted of raping two White women on a train. Black clergy were often reluctant to join activist groups, whether labor unions or civil rights organizations.

4. Gloria Richardson, interview by author, August 8, 1992.

5. Boynton 1979, p. 45.

6. Moody 1968, pp. 253–254.

7. Press release, May 20, 1965, from McGraw-Hill Book Company for *Letters From Mississippi*, ed. Elizabeth Sutherland, Reel 23, Frames 0475–0476, CORE Papers, Boston University.

8. Joyce Brown, "The House of Liberty," COFO Report on Mississippi Freedom Schools, August 14, 1964, Box 16:19, King Papers, Martin Luther King Center, Atlanta.

9. Dottie Zellner, interview by author, July 27, 1992. Zellner recalls that many of Bob Moses initial contacts in rural Mississippi were friends of Ella Baker. They included many men who would later become bridges themselves between King's inner circle and the local movement groups, or because of a lack of education between the local movement group and the community. Such men included Aaron Henry, who would later become the chair of the Mississippi Freedom Democratic Party and bow to the pressures of the formal leaders. Others, such as Hartman Turnbow and E. W. Steptoe, uneducated farmers who owned their land, acted as indigenous bridge leaders facilitating the connection between COFO and the community.

10. From McGraw-Hill press release for *Letters from Mississippi*, ed. E. Sutherland.

11. Ibid.

12. Prathia Hall Wynn, interview by author, November 9, 1992.

13. Unita Blackwell, interview by author, January 30, 1990.

14. Ibid.

15. Lincoln County Voter Education Project, A 4 Box 15 #197; Peter Cummings, Report on Benton County, August 15, 1964, A 4 Box 14 #175; Larry Rubin, Report on Voter Registration, July 31, 1964, A 4 Box 14 #175; Cleve Sellers,

Final Report, Marshall County, A 4 Box 14 #175; SNCC Papers, Martin Luther King Center.

16. Moody 1968, pp. 303–305.

17. Ibid.

18. See Crawford (1987, p. 101) for similar findings.

19. Blackwell, interview.

20. Annelle Ponder, Greenwood, Mississippi, report, March 3, 1963, Box EI 141:7, King Papers, Martin Luther King Center.

21. Voter Registration Project A Box 15 #197, Lincoln County, SNCC Papers, Martin Luther King Center.

22. Voter Registration Report, Annie Raines Headquarters, Lee County, Georgia, June 1962, A 4 Box 15 #187, SNCC Papers, Martin Luther King Center.

23. Larry Rubin, Lee County Report, December 1962, A IV Box 19 #324, SNCC Papers, Martin Luther King Center.

24. As quoted in Crawford 1987, p. 86.

25. Crawford 1987, p. 101.

26. Victoria Gray, interview by author, February 6, 1990.

27. Blackwell, interview.

28. Charles McLaurin, Ruleville, Mississippi, report August 18, 1964, A 4 Box 15 #187, SNCC Papers, Martin Luther King Center.

29. Quoted in Mills 1993, pp. 23–24.

30. News release, A VI Box 34 #3 5 of 20, SNCC Papers, Martin Luther King Center.

31. As quoted in Mills 1993, p. 41.

32. Ibid.

33. Gray, interview.

34. Zinn 1964, p. 258.

35. COFO report, Proposed Community Centers, Box 5:19, MFDP Papers, Martin Luther King Center.

36. The Nation, "Tired of Being Sick and Tired," Jerry Delluth, June 1, 1964.

37. Data compiled from minutes of eighteen precinct meetings and list of six county delegates and alternatives, Box 4:15, MFDP Papers, Martin Luther King Center.

38. Gray, interview.

39. Ibid.

40. Constance Curry, interview by author, August 22–23, 1992.

41. See report of November 10, MFDP meeting in Washington, D.C., Box 3:4 6 of 6, MFDP Papers, Martin Luther King Center.

42. Newspaper clippings and press releases, Box 3:4 4 of 6; Minutes of Executive Committee Meeting, September 13, 1964, Box 20:20, MFDP Papers, Martin Luther King Center.

43. Minutes of FDP Statewide Convention, Box 20:21, MFDP Papers; Pinole Meeting, January 8, 1965, Box 20:19, MFDP Papers; Sunflower County Meeting, August 1, 1964, Box 20:19, MFDP Papers; Baker County Meeting, September 24, 1965, Box 3, File 2, Sherrod Papers, Martin Luther King Center.

44. Gray, interview.

45. Clay County Report, November 29, 1965, Reel 65, Frame #305, MFDP Microfilm, Microfilming Corporation of America.

46. Ada Holliday, Letter to the Department of Agriculture, November 26, 1965, Reel 65, Frame #324, MFDP Microfilm, Microfilming Corporation of America.

47. Annelle Ponder Report, Box 29:13 p. 5–7, King Papers, Martin Luther King Center.

48. Documents of Reprisals, Box EI 142:1, EI 141:7 and 29:13, King Papers, Martin Luther King Center.

49. Annelle Ponder, Greenwood, Mississippi Report, March 1963, EI 141:7, King Papers, Martin Luther King Center.

50. June Johnson as quoted in the "Fannie Hamer, Civil Rights Leader Dies," *Washington Post*, March 17, 1977.

51. Press Release sent to the *Delta Dem-Times*, April 15, 1964, Reel 68, Frame #'s 0892–0895, MFDP Microfilm.

52. Gray, interview.

53. Canton Project History, compiled by Debbie Bernstein, Southern Regional Office, February 28, 1965, Reel 10, Frame 334–344, CORE Papers, Microfilming Corporation of America.

54. Press release, July 1962, A:IV Box 34 #3 3 of 20, SNCC Papers.

55. Ibid.

56. Mary King, Letter to Mr. Marceo Hubbard, Department of Justice, September 25, 1963, A 4 15 #180, SNCC Papers, Martin Luther King Center.

57. August 15, 1964, A 4 Box 14 #175, Peter Cummings, Report on Benton County, SNCC Papers, Martin Luther King Center.

58. Bernice V. Robinson, Report from the Field, EIII, Box 155:30, SNCC Papers, Martin Luther King Center.

CHAPTER NINE

1. Ed King, as quoted in Mills 1993, p. 125.

2. As quoted in Mills 1993, pp. 127–128.

3. Ibid., p. 128.

4. Mills 1993, pp. 129–133.

5. Unita Blackwell, interview by author, January 30, 1990.

6. As quoted in Mills 1993, p. 129.

7. Ibid.

8. Blackwell, interview.

9. As quoted in Mills, 1993, p. 130.

10. Gloria Richardson, interview by author, August 8, 1992.

11. As quoted in Cook 1988, p. 52.

12. Ibid.

13. Foeman 1996, pp. 605–606.

14. Quoted in Brock 1990, p. 130.

15. Brock 1990, p. 130.

16. Ibid.

17. Cook 1988, p. 52

18. As quoted in Foeman 1996, pp. 608–609.

19. Foeman 1996.

20. As quoted in Foeman 1996.

21. Ibid., p. 609.

22. Ibid.

23. Foeman, pp. 612–613.

24. Ibid., pp. 611–612.

25. Ibid., p. 611.

26. Ibid., p. 610.
27. Evans and Boyte 1986.
28. Ella Baker, Transcript, p. 10, Spingarn Center, Howard University.
29. As quoted in Cantarow and O'Malley 1980, p. 54.
30. Baker, transcript.
31. Ibid.
32. Clark 1986, p. 78.
33. As quoted in Garrow 1986, p. 294.
34. Reel 22, Frame #0234, CORE Papers, Microfilming Corporation of America.
35. Reel 20, Frame #0947, CORE Papers, Microfilming Corporation of America.
36. Reel 11, Frame #0406; Reel 9, Frame #0494; Reel 21, Frame 051; Reel 9, Frame #0502; Reel 2, Frame #0634; Reel 21, Frame 1199, CORE Papers, Microfilming Corporation of America.
37. Meier and Rudwick 1973, p. 68.
38. Ibid., pp. 153–154.
39. Ibid., pp. 292, 310.
40. Ibid., p. 292.
41. Ibid., p. 153.
42. As quoted in Meier and Rudwick 1973, p. 18.
43. Meier and Rudwick 1973, p. 416.
44. Ibid., p. 113.
45. Reel 2, Frame # 0974, CORE Papers, Microfilming Corporation of America.
46. Reel 23, Frame #0339–0340, CORE Papers, Microfilming Corporation of America.
47. Reel 18, Frame #0309, CORE Papers, Microfilming Corporation of America.
48. Meier and Rudwick 1973, pp. 169–170.
49. Victoria Gray, interview by author, February 6, 1990.
50. Gusfield 1966, p. 141.

CHAPTER TEN

1. Sellers 1990, p. 111.
2. Dottie Zellner, interview by author, July 27, 1992.
3. As quoted in Mills 1993, pp. 142, 143.
4. Ibid., p. 141.
5. Ibid., p. 144.
6. Ibid., p. 170.
7. Ibid., p. 171.
8. Sellers 1973, pp. 117–118.
9. Garrow 1986, pp. 397–400.
10. Ibid., pp. 407–408.
11. As quoted in Garrow 1986, p. 413.
12. Ladner 1970, p. 139.
13. Ibid.
14. As quoted in Ladner 1940, p. 151. See also Sitkoff 1981, chaps. 6, 7.
15. Prathia Hall Wynn, interview by author, November 9, 1992.
16. Ibid.
17. Jean Wheeler Smith Young, interview by author, August 9, 1992.
18. Muriel Tillinghast, interview by author, July 19, 1992.
19. Gloria Richardson, interview by author, August 8, 1992.

20. Penny Patch, interview by author, August 10, 1992.
21. Bernice Reagon, interview by author, November 30, 1992.
22. As quoted in Giddings 1984, pp. 314–315.
23. As quoted in Giddings 1984, pp. 316–317.
24. Giddings 1984, p. 317.
25. Ella Baker, Transcript, p. 78, Spingarn Center, Howard University.
26. See, for example, Hippler 1974, p. 217; Moynihan 1965.
27. Brewer 1988; Cromwell and Cromwell 1978, pp. 754–756; Staples 1973, pp. 174–183; Barnes 1986; Davis 1971; Jackson 1972; Sizemore 1973.
28. Staples 1973, p. 109.
29. Dill 1983, p. 143.
30. Ladner, 1970, p. 135.
31. Ibid., pp. 144–145
32. Ibid., pp. 145–146.
33. Ibid., p. 148
34. Ibid., p. 150
35. Faye Bellamy, interview by author, February 7, 1990.
36. Ibid.
37. Ladner 1970, p. 136.
38. Ibid., p. 152
39. Ibid., p. 153.
40. Carson 1981, p. 229.
41. As quoted in Stoper 1989, p. 272.
42. Carson 1981, pp. 229–230.
43. As quoted in Carson 1981, p. 230.
44. Carson 1981.
45. Ibid., pp. 231, 232, 234–235.
46. "Today's Challenge: More Action and a New Direction," Fourteenth Annual Convention of Operation PUSH, Memphis, July 17, 1985, quoted in Hatch 1988, pp. 127–129.
47. Ibid.

CHAPTER ELEVEN

1. Payne 1990, p. 158.
2. Payne 1994.
3. Barnett 1993, p. 176.
4. Morris 1984, pp. 7–11.
5. Wasielewski 1985.
6. Charles Tilly 1978.
7. Bourdieu 1984, 1990; Swidler 1986.
8. Alexander 1990.
9. Zald 1996, p. 262; see also pp. 266–267.
10. Acker 1995, p. 141.
11. Penny Patch, interview by author, August 10, 1992.
12. Freeman 1973; Gilligan 1982; Chodorow 1978; Tronto 1989. Also see Whittier (1995) and Stobel (1995); both discuss feminist organizing efforts that begin with an emphasis on consensus and the collective, but over time move to a more hierarchical organizational structure. Along with this shift is a corresponding change from participatory democracy to individual representation. They discuss

at length the difficulties movements face in using nonhierarchical models when participants have diverse organizing skills and knowledge.

13. Freeman 1975; Cassell 1977; Buechler 1990; Martin 1990.
14. Clemens 1996, p. 211.
15. As quoted in Mills 1993, p. 84.
16. Ibid., p. 85.
17. McAdam 1996, pp. 25–26.
18. McAdam 1982, p. 41.
19. hooks 1990; Spelman 1988.
20. Jaggar and Rothenberg 1984.
21. Tom 1995, p. 166.
22. Meyer and Staggenborg 1996, p. 1634.
23. Gamson and Meyer 1996, p. 275.
24. Whittier 1995.
25. Taylor 1996, p. 177. Also see Lorber 1994.
26. Friedman and McAdam 1992; Fantasia 1988.
27. Mueller 1994.
28. See Klandermans (1994) for a discussion of how groups redefine themselves over time.
29. Haines 1988; Barkan 1979. Clearly, I disagree with Haines's view of SCLC as a part of the radical flank of the movement. Haines supports his view by claiming that the SCLC was most responsible for direct action—that is, the Freedom Rides, etc. I have already demonstrated the relationship between SNCC and SCLC regarding the Freedom Rides, as well as the interaction between King and the Kennedy administration. Even Haines (p. 159) points out that as early as 1963, King in his Birmingham jail letter warns that if Blacks don't gain government concessions soon, their frustrations will lead them to join Black nationalist groups. And he documents Attorney General Robert Kennedy's awareness of the threat.
30. See Garrow 1986, chaps. 8–11; Haines 1988, pp. 144–145. Additionally, Haines (1988, p. 84) makes a convincing argument that the SCLC, SNCC, and CORE all experienced dramatic drops in financial support in 1966. Yet the SCLC was still receiving financial support well above the peak years of movement mobilization.
31. See Clemens (1996, pp. 204–226) for a discussion of how organizational forms frame action and identity.
32. Taylor 1996. Also see Staggenborg 1995.
33. Freire 1970.

EPILOGUE

1. See Haines 1988. While I agree with Haines that a radical arm of the social movement sector gains state concessions for the organizations viewed as more moderate, I disagree with his conceptualization of the SCLC as a radical arm of the movement.
2. National Urban League 1995, p. 297.
3. Ibid., p. 298
4. Ibid., p. 162.
5. Ibid., p. 108.
6. Barbara Smith 1992, p. 38.
7. Jordan 1991, pp. 12–13.

8. Malveaux 1995.
9. Ibid.
10. Dyson 1995, p. 1100–1101.
11. Ibid.
12. As quoted in Marriot 1995.
13. Ibid.
14. The original title is "National Negro Anthem" or "Lift Ev'ry Voice."
15. James Weldon Johnson, "Lift Every Voice," 1993.

Bibliography

Acker, Joan. 1988. "Class, Gender and the relations of Distribution." *Signs* 13:473–497.

———. 1990. "Hierarchies, Jobs, Bodies: A Theory of Gendered Organizations." *Gender and Society* 4(2):139–158.

———. 1995. "Feminist Goals and Organizing Processes." In *Feminist Organizations: Harvest of the New Women's Movement*, ed. Myra Marx Ferree and Patricia Martin Yancey. Philadelphia: Temple University Press, pp. 137–144.

Adams, Frank. 1972. "Our Lives Were Filled with Action." In *Martin Luther King Jr*, ed. C. Eric Lincoln. New York: Hill, pp. 219–227.

Alexander, Jeffrey C. 1990. "Analytic Debates: Understanding the Relative Autonomy of Culture." In *Culture and Society*, ed. Jeffrey Alexander and Steven Seidman. Cambridge: University Press, pp. 1–30.

Angelou, Maya. 1969. *I Know Why the Caged Bird Sings*. New York: Random House.

———. 1978. "Still I Rise" in *And Still I Rise*. New York, N.Y.: Random House, pp. 41–42.

Anonymous SNCC Member. Interview by author. March 16, 1989.

Baker, Ella. Transcript. Spingarn Center. Howard University.

Barkan, Steven E. 1979. "Strategic, Tactical, and Organizational Dilemmas of the Protest Movement against Nuclear Power." *Social Problems* 27:19–37.

Barnett, Bernice McNair. 1993. "Invisible Southern Black Women Leaders in the Civil Rights Movement: The Triple Constraints of Gender, Race and Class." *Signs* 7(2): 162–182.

Barnes, Annie S. 1986. *Black Women: Interpersonal Relationships in Profile*. Bristol, Ind.: Wyndham Hall.

Bates, Daisy. 1962. *The Long Shadow of Little Rock*. New York: Van Rees.

Bellamy, Fay. Interview by author. February 7, 1990. Bendix, Reinhard. 1977. *Max Weber: An Intellectual Portrait*. Los Angeles: University of California Press.

Bennett, Lerone Jr. 1968. *Pioneers in Protest*. Chicago: Johnson Publishing.

Berk, R. A. 1974. *Collective Behavior*. Dubuque: Brown.

Blackwell, Unita. Interview by author. January 30, 1990.

Blumer, Herbert. 1969. "Collective Behavior." In *The Principles of Sociology*, ed. A. M. Lee. New York: Barnes & Noble, pp. 65–121.

Bookman, Ann, and Sandra Morgen. 1988. *Women and the Politics of Empowerment*. Philadelphia: Temple University Press.

Bourdieu, Pierre. 1984. *Distinction: A Social Critique of the Judgment of Taste*. Translated by R. Nice. Cambridge, Mass.: Harvard University Press.

———. 1990. *The Logic of Practice*. Stanford, Calif.: Stanford University Press.

Boynton, Amelia. 1979. *Bridge Across Jordan*. New York: Carlton Press.

Branch, Taylor. 1988. *Parting the Waters*. New York: Simon and Schuster.

Breines, Wini. 1982. *Community and Organization in the New Left, 1962-68*. New York: Praeger.

Brewer, Rose. 1988. "Black Women in Poverty: Some Comments on Female-Headed Families." *Signs* 13(2):331–339.

———. 1989. "Black Women and Feminist Sociology: The Emerging Perspective." In *American Sociologist* 20(1): 57–70.

———. 1993. "Theorizing Race, Class and Gender: The New Scholarship of Black Feminist Intellectuals and Black Women's Labor." In *Theorizing Black Feminisms: The Visionary Pragmatism of Black Women*, ed. Stanlie M. James and Abena P. A. Busia. New York: Routledge, pp. 13–30.

Brock, Annette K. 1990. "Gloria Richardson and the Cambridge Movement." In *Women in the Civil Rights Movement: Trailblazers and Torchbearers, 1941-1965*, ed. Vicki Crawford, Jacqueline Rouse, and Barbara Woods. Brooklyn: Carlson Publishing. pp. 121–144.

Brooks, Evelyn. 1983. "The Feminist Theology of the Black Baptist Church, 1880-1900." In *Class, Race, and Sex: The Dynamics of Control*, ed. Amy Swerdlow and Hanna Lessinger. Boston: G. K. Hall, pp. 31–59.

Brown, Elaine. 1992. *A Taste of Power*. New York: Pantheon Books.

Brown, Elsa. 1989. "Womanist Consciousness: Maggie Lena Walker and the Independent Order of Saint Luke." In *Black Women in United States History*. ed. Darlene Hine ed. New York: A Carlson Publishing Series pp. 169–192.

Buechler, Steven M. 1990. *Women's Movements in the United States*. New Brunswick, N.J.: Rutgers University Press.

Burks, Mary Fair. Interview by the author. January 22, 1990.

Calhoun, Craig. 1994. "Social Theory and the Politics of Identity." In *Social Theory and the Politics of Identity*, ed. Craig Calhoun. Oxford: Blackwell, pp. 9–36.

Calloway-Thomas, Carolyn and Thurmon Garner. 1996. "Daisy Bates and the Little Rock Crisis: Forging the Way" In *Journal of Black Studies*, 26(5): 616–628.

Cantarow, Ellen, and Susan O'Malley. 1980. *Moving the Mountain*. N.Y.: Feminist Press.

Carr, Johnnie. Interview by author. January 26, 1990.

———. Interview by Stephen M. Millner. 1989. In *The Walking City: The Montgomery Bus Boycott*, ed. David J. Garrow. Brooklyn: Carlson.

————. Transcript. Oral History Project #60. Martin Luther King Center, Atlanta.

Carson, Clayborne. 1981. *In Struggle:* SNCC *and the Black Awakening of the 1960s.* Cambridge: Harvard University Press.

Cassell, Joan. 1977. *A Group Called Women: Sisterhood and the Symbolism in the Feminist Movement.* New York: David McKay.

Chafetz, Janet Salzman, and Anthony Gary Dworkin. 1986. *Female Revolt: Women's Movements in World and Historical Perspective.* Totowa, N.J.: Rowman and Allanheld.

Chodorow, Nancy. 1978. *The Reproduction of Mothering: Psychoanalysis and the Sociology of Gender.* Berkeley: University of California Press.

Clark, Septima. 1986. *Ready From Within.* Edited by Cynthia Stokes Brown. Navarro, Calif: Wild Tree Press.

————. Trancscript #17. Oral History Project. Martin Luther King Center, Atlanta.

Clemens, Elisabeth S. 1996. "Organizational Form as Frame: Collective Identity and Political Strategy in the American Labor Movement, 1880-1920. In *Comparative Perspectives On Social Movements: Political Opportunities, Mobilizing Structures, and Cultural Frames,* ed. Doug McAdam, John McCarthy, and Mayer Zald. New York: Cambridge University Press, pp. 205-226.

Cockburn, Cynthia. 1983. *Brothers: Male Dominance and Technological Change.* London: Pluto Press.

————. 1985. *Machinery and Dominance.* London: Pluto Press.

Cohen, Jean L. 1985. "Strategy or Identity: New Theoretical Paradigms and Contemporary Social Movements." *Social Research* 52:663-716.

Coleman, Willi. 1990. "Black Women and Segregated Public Transportation: Ninety Years of Resistance." In *Black Women in United States History,* ed. Darlene Hine. Brooklyn, NY: Carlson Publihing Inc., pp. 295-302.

Collins, Patricia Hill. 1986. "Learning from the Outsider Within: The Sociological Significance of Black Feminist Thought." *Social Problems* 33(6):14-32.

————. 1990. *Black Feminist Thought: Knowledge, Consciousness and the Politics of Empowerment.* Boston: Unwin Hyman.

Collins, Patricia Hill, and Margaret L. Andersen. 1995. *Race, Class and Gender.* Belmont, Calif.: Wadsworth.

Collins, Randall. 1990. "Stratification, Emotional Energy and the Transient Emotions. In *Research Agendas,* ed. Theodore O. Kemper. Albany: State University of New York Press.

Congressional Quarterly. 1970.

Congress of Racial Equality (CORE) Papers. 1944-1968. Microfilm. Sanford, N.C.: Microfilming Corporation of America.

Connell, R. W. 1987. *Gender and Power.* Stanford, Calif.: Stanford University Press.

Cook, Melanie B. 1988. "Gloria Richardson: Her Life and Work in SNCC." *Sage: A Scholarly Journal on Black Women,* Student Supplement, pp. 51-53.

Cotton, Dorothy. Interview by author. January 20, 1990.

Couch, C. J. 1970. "Dimensions of Association in Collective Behavior Episodes." *Sociometry* 33: 457-460.

Couto, Richard A. 1991. *Ain't Gonna Let Nobody Turn Me Round.* Philadelphia: Temple University Press.

Crawford, Vicki Lynn. 1987. "We Shall Not Be Moved: Black Female Activists in the Mississippi Civil Rights Movement, 1960-1965." Ph.D. Diss., Emory University.

Crawford, Vicki, Jacqueline Rouse, and Barbara Woods. 1990. *Women in the Civil Rights Movement.* Brooklyn: Carlson Publishing.

Cromwell, Vicky, and Ronald Cromwell. 1978. "Perceived Dominance in Decision-Making and Conflict Resolution among Anglo, Black and Chicano Couples." *Journal of Marriage and the Family* 40: 749–759.

Curry, Constance. Interview by author. August 22–29, 1992.

Dallard, Shyrlee. 1990. *Ella Baker: A Leader Behind the Scenes.* Englewood Cliffs, N.J.: Silver Burdett.

Daniels, Arlene. 1987. "Invisible Work." *Social Problems* 34: 403–415.

Davis, Angela. 1971. "Reflections on Black Women's Role in the Community of Slaves." *Black Scholar* 3(4): 2–15.

———. 1981. *Women, Race and Class.* New York: Random House.

Dill, Bonnie Thornton. 1979. "The Dialectics of Black Womanhood." *Signs* 4(3): 543–555.

———. 1983. "Race, Class, and Gender: Prospects for an All-Inclusive Sisterhood." In *Feminist Studies* 9(1): 131–150.

Drake, St. Clair, and Horace Cayton. 1970. *Black Metropolis.* Chicago: University of Chicago Press.

Dungee (Allen), Erna. Interview by Stephen M. Millner. 1989. In *The Walking City: The Montgomery Bus Boycott,* ed. David. J. Garrow. Brooklyn: Carlson.

———. Papers. Martin Luther King Center, Atlanta.

Durr, Virginia. Interview by author. February 1, 1990.

———. Transcript. Oral History Project #66. Martin Luther King Center, Atlanta.

Dyson, Michael. 1993. *Reflecting Black: African American Cultural Criticism.* Minneapolis: University of Minnesota Press.

———. 1995. "African American Women and the Million Man March." *Christian Century* 112(34), column 3, pp. 1100–1101.

Ellis, Richard J. 1986. "A Theory of Charismatic Leadership in Organizations." Berkeley, Calif.: *Institute of Governmental Studies in Public Organization,* University of California, Working Paper No. 86–2.

England, Paula. 1989. "A Feminist Critique of Rational-Choice Theories: Implications for Sociology." *American Sociologist* 20:14–28.

Etzioni, Amitai. 1961. *A Comparative Analysis of Complex Organizations.* New York: Free Press.

Evans, Sara. 1979. *Personal Politics.* New York: Vintage Books.

Evans, Sara, and Harry Boyte. 1986. *Free Spaces.* New York: Harper and Row.

Fantasia, Rick. 1988. *Cultures of Solidarity.* Los Angeles, Calif.: University of California Press.

Ferguson, Kathy E. 1984. *The Feminist Case Against Bureaucracy.* Philadelphia: Temple University Press.

Ferree, Myra Marx. 1991–1992. "Institutionalizing Gender Equality: Feminist Politics and Equality Offices." *German Politics and Society* 24(Winter):53–67.

———. 1992. "The Political Context of Rationality: Rational Choice Theory and Resource Mobilization." In *Frontiers of Social Movement Theory,* ed. Aldon Morris and Carol Mueller. New Haven: Yale University Press, pp. 29–52.

Ferree, Myra Marx, and Beth Hess. 1985. *Controversy and Coalition: The New Feminist Movement.* Boston: Twayne.

Ferree, Myra Marx, and Frederick Miller. 1985. "Mobilization and Meaning: Toward an Integration of Social Psychological Resource Perspectives on Social Movements." *Sociological Inquiry* 55(1):38–61.

Fireman and Gamson. 1979. "Utilitarian Logic in the Resource Mobilization Perspective." In *The Dynamics of Social Movements,* ed. Mayer Zald and John McCarthy. Cambridge, Mass.: Winthrop, pp. 8–44.

Foeman, Anita K. 1996. "Gloria Richardson: Breaking the Mold." *Journal of Black Studies* 26(5) 604–615.

Forman, James. 1972. *The Making of Black Revolutionaries.* New York: Macmillan Company.

Fraser, Nancy. 1989. *Unruly Practices: Power, Discourse and Gender in Contemporary Social Theory.* Minneapolis: University of Minnesota Press.

Freeman, Jo. 1973. "The Origins of the Women's Liberation Movement." *American Journal of Sociology* 78(4):792–811.

———. 1975. *The Politics of Women's Liberation.* New York: David McKay.

———. 1979. "Resource Mobilization and Strategy: A Model for Analyzing Social Movement Organization Action." In *The Dynamics of Social Movements*, ed. Mayer Zald and John McCarthy. Cambridge, Mass.: Winthrop, pp. 167–189.

Freire, Paulo. 1970. *Pedagogy of the Oppressed.* New York: Seabury Press.

Friedman, Debra, and Doug McAdam. 1992. "Collective Identity and Activism: Networks, Choices, and the Life of a Social Movement." In *Frontiers in Social Movement Theory*, ed. Aldon Morris and Carol Mueller. New Haven, Conn.: Yale University Press, pp. 156–173.

Fromm, Erich. 1941. *Escape From Freedom.* New York: Rinehart.

Game, Ann, and Rosemary Pringle. 1984. *Gender at Work.* London: Pluto Press.

Gamson, Joshua. 1995. "Must Identity Movements Self-Destruct? A Queer Dilemma." *Social Problems* 42: 390–407.

Gamson, William. 1975. *The Strategy of Social Protest.* Homewood, Ill.: Dorsey Press.

———. 1992. "The Social Psychology of Collective Action." In *Frontiers in Social Movement Theory*, ed. A. Morris and C. Mueller. New Haven, Conn.: Yale University Press, pp. 53–76.

Gamson, William, and David Meyer. 1996. "Framing Political Opportunity." In *Comparative Perspectives on Social Movements: Political Opportunities, Mobilizing Structures, and Cultural Framings*, ed. Doug McAdam, John McCarthy and Mayer Zald. pp. 275–290.

Garrow, David J. 1986. *Bearing the Cross.* New York: Vintage Books.

Garrow, David J., ed. 1989. *The Walking City: The Montgomery Bus Boycott.* Brooklyn: Carlson.

Gates, Henry Louis Jr., ed. 1988. *Six Women's Slave Narratives.* New York: Oxford University Press.

Giddings, Paula. 1984. *When and Where I Enter.* New York: Bantam Books.

Gilkes, Cheryl Townsend. 1985. "Together and in Harness: Women's Traditions in the Sanctified Church." *Signs* 10(4):679.

Gilligan, Carol. 1982. *In a Different Voice: Psychological Theory and Women's Development.* Cambridge, Mass.: Harvard University Press.

Glass, Thelma. Interview by author. February 2, 1990.

Grant, Joanne. Interview by author. August 25–26, 1992.

Gray, Victoria. Interview by author. February 6, 1990.

Greenberg, Jack. 1994. *Crusaders in the Courts.* New York: Basic Books.

Gregory, Hazel. Interview by author. February 15, 1990.

———. Papers. Martin Luther King Center, Atlanta.

Gusfield, Joseph. 1966. "Functional Areas of Leadership in Social Movements." *Sociological Quarterly* 7:137–156.

Habermas, Jurgen. 1984. *The Theory of Communicative Action, Reason and the Rationalization of Society*, Vol. 1. Boston: Beacon Press.

———. 1987. *The Theory of Communicative Action, Lifeworld and System: A Critique of Functionalist Reason*, Vol. 2. Boston: Beacon Press.

Haines, Herbert. 1988. *Black Radicals and the Civil Rights Mainstream, 1954-1970.* Knoxville: University of Tennessee Press.

Hall, Jacquelyn Dowd. 1995. " 'The Mind that Burns in Each Body' ": Women, Rape and Racial Violence." In *Race, Class and Gender,* ed. Margaret L. Andersen and Patricia Hill Collins. Boston: Wadsworth, pp. 434–449.

Hall, Prathia Wynn. Interview by author. November 9, 1992.

Hall, Stuart. 1996. "New Ethnicities." In *Stuart Hall: Critical Dialogue in Cultural Studies,* eds. David Morley and Kuan-Hsing Chen. London: Routledge.

Hatch, Roger D. 1988. *Beyond Opportunity: Jesse Jackson's Vision for America.* Philadelphia: Fortress Press.

Hayden, Casey. 1989. "Women's Consciousness and the Non-Violent Movement Against Segregation, 1960-1965: A Personal History." Unpublished paper.

———. Interview by author. January 12, 1990.

Higgenbotham, Evelyn Brooks. 1992. "African-American Women's History and the Meta-language of Race." *Signs* 17(2):253–254.

Hippler, Arthur E. 1974. *Hunter's Point.* New York: Basic Books.

Hirsh, Marianne, and Evelyn Fox Keller. 1990. *Conflict in Feminism.* New York: Routledge.

Hochschild, Arlie Russell. 1975. "The Sociology of Feeling and Emotion: Selected Possibilities." In *Another Voice: Feminist Perspectives on Social Life and Social Science,* ed. Marcia Millman and Rosabeth Moss Kanter. Garden City, N.Y.: Anchor, pp. 280–307.

———. 1979. "Emotion Work, Feeling Rules, and Social Structure." *American Journal of Sociology* 8: 551–575.

Hoffer, Eric. 1951. *The True Believer: Thoughts on the Nature of Mass Movements.* New York: Mentor.

Holsaert, Faith. Interview by author. September 1, 1992.

hooks, bell. 1981. *Ain't I A Woman.* Boston: South End Press, chap. 3.

———. 1990. *Yearning: Race, Gender and Cultural Politics.* Boston: South End Press. Hull, Hull, Gloria T., Patricia Bell Scott, and Barbara Smith, eds. 1982. *But Some of Us Are Brave.* Old Westbury, N.Y.: Feminist Press.

Jackson, Jacqueline J. 1972. "But Where Are the Men?" *Black Scholar* 3(4): pp. 30–41.

Jaggar, Alison. 1989. "Love and Knowledge: Emotion in Feminist Epistemology." In *Gender/Body/Knowledge: Feminist Reconstructions of Being and Knowing,* ed. A. Jagger and S. Bordo. New Brunswick: Rutgers University Press, pp. 145–171.

Jagger, Alison, and Paula Rothenberg, eds. 1984. *Feminist Frameworks: Alternative Theoretical Accounts of the Relations between Women and Men.* 2nd. ed. New York: McGraw-Hill.

Jenkins, Craig. 1983. "Resource Mobilization Theory and the Study of Social Movements." *Annual Review of Sociology* 9: 527–553.

Jenkins, Craig, and Craig M. Eckert. 1986. "Channeling Black Insurgency: Elite Patronage and Professional Social Movement Organizations in the Development of the Black Movement." *American Sociological Review* 51:812–829.

Jonasdottir, Anna G. 1988. "On the Concept of Interest, Women's Interests and the Limitations of Interest Theory." In *The Political Interests of Gender,* ed. Kathleen B. Jones and Anna Jonasdottir. London: Sage, pp. 33–65.

Jones, Beverly Washington. 1990. *Quest for Equality.* New York: Carlson Publishing.

Jones, Jacqueline. 1985. *Labor of Love, Labor of Sorrow.* New York: Basic Books.

Jones, Kathleen, and Anna Jonasdottir. 1988. *The Political Interests of Gender.* London: Sage.

Jordan, June. 1991. "Can I Get a Witness?" *The Progressive* 55(12): 12–13.

Kanter, Rosabeth Moss. 1977. *Men and Women of the Corporation.* New York: Basic Books.

Kelley, Robin. 1990. *The Hammer and the Hoe: Alabama Communists during the Great Depression.* Chapel Hill: University of North Carolina Press.

———. 1994. *Race Rebels*. New York: The Free Press.

Killian, Lewis M. 1984. "Organization, Rationality and Spontaneity in the Civil Rights Movement." *American Sociological Review* 49(6):770.

King, Coretta Scott. 1969. *My Life with Martin Luther King, Jr.* New York: Holt, Rinehart and Winston.

King, Deborah. 1988. "Multiple Jeopardy, Multiple Consciousness: The Context of a Black Feminist Ideology." *Signs* 14(1):42–72.

King, Martin Luther Jr. 1958. *Stride Toward Freedom*. New York: Harper.

———. Papers. Boston University.

———. Papers. Martin Luther King Center, Atlanta.

King, Mary. 1987. *Freedom Song*. New York: William Morrow.

Klandermans, Bert. 1984. "Mobilization and Participation: Social-Psychological Expansions of Resource Mobilization Theory." *American Sociological Review* 49:583–600.

———. 1986. "New Social Movements and Resource Mobilization: The European and American Approach." *Journal of Mass Emergencies and Disasters* 4:13–37.

———. 1994. "Transient Identities?: Membership Patterns in the Dutch Peace Movement." In *New Social Movements: From Ideology to Identity*, ed. Enrique Larana, Hank Johnston, and Joseph Gusfield. Philadelphia: Temple University Press, pp. 168–184.

Klandermans, Bert, and Sidney Tarrow. 1988. "Mobilization into Social Movements: Synthesizing European and American Approaches." In *From Structure to Action: Comparing Social Movement Research Across Cultures*, International Social Movement Research, Volume 1, ed. Bert Klandermans, Hanspeter Kriesi, and Sidney Tarrow. Greenwich, Conn.: JAI Press, pp. 1–38.

Kornhauser, William. 1959. *The Politics of Mass Society*. Glencoe, Ill.: Free Press.

Ladner, Dorie. Interview by author. July 27, 1992.

Ladner, Joyce. 1970. "What Black Power Means to Negroes in Mississippi." In *The Transformation of Activism*. ed. August Meier. Aldine, pp. 131–154.

Lane, Mary. Transcript. Spingarn Center. Howard University.

Lang, Kurt, and Gladys Lang. 1961. *Collective Dynamics*. New York: Crowell.

Lawson, Ronald, and Stephen E. Barton. 1980. "Sex Roles in Social Movements: A Case Study of the Tenant Movement in New York City." *Signs* 6(2):230–247.

LeBon, G. 1960. *The Crowd: The Study of the Popular Mind*. New York: Viking Press.

Lerner, Gerder. 1973. *Black Women in White America*. New York: Vintage Books.

Lewis, Diane K. 1977. "A Response to Inequality: Black Women, Racism and Sexism." *Signs* 3(Winter): 341–342.

Lipsky, Michael. 1968. "Protest as a Political Resource." *American Political Science Review* 62:1144–1158.

Lofland, John. 1981. "Collective Behavior: Elementary Forms." In *Social Psychology Today: Sociological Perspectives*, ed. Morris Rosenberg and Ralph Turner. New York: Basic Books, pp. 413–446.

———. 1982. "Crowd Joys." *Urban Life* 10(4): 355–381.

Lofland, John. 1995. "Charting Degrees of Movement Culture: Tasks of the Cultural Cartographer." In *Social Movements and Culture*, eds. Hank Johnston and Bert Klandermans. Minneapolis: University of Minnesota Press.

Lorber, Judith. 1994. *Paradoxes of Gender*. New Haven: Yale University Press.

MacKinnon, Catherine. 1982. "Feminism, Marxism, Method and the State: An Agenda for Theory." *Signs* 7:515–544.

Malveaux, Julianne. 1995. "A Woman's Place Is in the March: Why Should I Stand by My Man, When He's Trying to Step Over Me?" *Washington Post*, October 8, p. C3.

Mansbridge, Jane. 1990. *Beyond Self-Interest*. Chicago: University of Chicago Press.

Marriot, Michael. 1995. "Black Women Are Split Over All-Man March on Washington." *New York Times*, October 14, p. D4.

Martin, Patricia Yancey. 1990. "Rethinking Feminist Organizations." *Gender and Society* 4: 182–206.

McAdam, Doug. 1982. *Political Process and the Development of Black Insurgency*. Chicago: University of Chicago Press.

———. 1983. "Tactical Innovation and the Pace of Insurgency." *American Sociological Review* 48:735–754.

———. 1988. *Freedom Summer*. New York: Oxford University Press.

———. 1992. "Gender as a Mediator of the Activist Experience: The Case of Freedom Summer." *American Journal of Sociology* 97:1211–1140.

———. 1996. "Conceptual Origins, Current Problems, Future Directions." In *Comparative Perspectives On Social Movements: Political Opportunities, Mobilizing Structures, and Cultural Framings*, ed. Doug McAdam, John D. McCarthy, and Mayer Zald. New York: Cambridge University Press, pp. 23–40.

McCarthy, John D., and Mayer N. Zald. 1973. *The Trend of Social Movements in America: Professionalism and Resource Mobilization*. Morristown, N.J.: General Learning Press.

———. 1977. "Resource Mobilization and Social Movements: A Partial Theory." *American Journal of Sociology* 82:1212–1239.

———, eds. 1979. *The Dynamics of Social Movements: Resource Mobilization, Social Control and Tactics*. Cambridge, Mass.: Winthrop.

Meier, August, and Elliot Rudwick. 1973. CORE: *A Study of the Civil Rights Movement: 1942-1968*. New York: Oxford University Press.

Melucci, Alberto. 1985. "The Symbolic Challenge of Contemporary Movements." *Social Research* 52:781–816.

———. 1988. "Getting Involved: Identity and Mobilization in Social Movements." In *From Structure to Action: Comparing Movement Participation Across Cultures*, International Social Movement Research, Vol. 1, ed. Bert Klandermans, Hanspeter Kriesi, and Sidney Tarrow. Greenwich, Conn.: JAI Press, pp. 329–348.

———. 1989. *Nomads of the Present: Social Movements and Individual Needs in Contemporary Society*. Philadelphia: Temple University Press.

———. 1995. "The Process of Collective Action." In *Social Movements and Culture*, ed. Hank Johnston and Bert Klandermans. Minneapolis,: University of Minnesota Press, pp. 41–63.

Meyer, David, and Suzanne Staggenborg. 1996. "Movements, Countermovements, and Political Opportunity." *American Journal of Sociology* 101(6):1628–1660.

Millner, Stephen M. 1989. "The Montgomery Bus Boycott: A Case Study in the Emergence and Career of a Social Movement." In *The Walking City: The Montgomery Bus Boycott*, ed. David Garrow. Brooklyn: Carlson, pp. 381–619.

Mills, Kay. 1993. *This Little Light of Mine: The Life of Fannie Lou Hamer*. New York: Dutton.

Mississippi Freedom Democratic Party (MFDP). Papers. Microfilm. Martin Luther King Center, Atlanta.

Montgomery Improvement Association (MIA). Papers. Martin Luther King Center, Atlanta.

Moody, Anne. 1968. *Coming of Age in Mississippi*. New York: Laurel Books.

Moraga, Cherrie, and Gloria Anzaldua. 1981. *This Bridge Called My Back*. New York: Kitchen Table Press.

Morris, Aldon. 1984. *The Origins of the Civil Rights Movement*. New York: Free Press.

Moynihan, Daniel P. 1965. *The Negro Family: The Case for National Action*. U.S. Department of Labor. Washington, D.C.: Government Printing Office.

Mueller, Carol. 1990. "Ella Baker and the Origins of Participatory Democracy." In *Women in the Civil Rights Movement*, Vicki Crawford, Jacqueline Rouse and Barbara Woods. New York: Carlson Publishing, pp. 51–70.

————.1994. "Conflict Networks and the Origins of Women's Literature." In *New Social Movements: From Ideology to Identity*, ed. Enrique Larana, Hank Johnston, and Joseph Gusfield. Philadelphia: Temple University Press, pp. 234–266.

Murray, Pauli. 1987. *Song in a Weary Throat*. New York: Harper and Row.

Nash, Diane Bevel. Interview by author. January 26, 1990.

National Urban League. 1995. *The State of Black America*. New York: The National Urban League

Nixon, E. D. Transcript. Spingarn Center. Howard University.

Oberschall, Anthony. 1973. *Social Conflict and Social Movements*. Englewood Cliffs, N.J.: Prentice Hall.

Ogunyemi, Chikwenye Okonjo. 1985. "Womanism: The Dynamics of the Contemporary Black Female Novel in English." *Signs* 11(1): 63–80.

Olson, Mancur. 1965. *The Logic of Collective Action*. Cambridge, Mass.: Harvard University Press.

Painter, Neil Irvin. 1979. *The Narrative of Hosea Hudson: His Life as a Negro Communist in the South*. Cambridge, Mass.: Harvard University Press.

Palmer, Reverend H. J. Papers. Martin Luther King Center, Atlanta.

Park, Robert E. 1967. *On Social Control and Collective Behavior*. Edited by Ralph H. Turner. Chicago: University of Chicago Press.

Parks, Rosa. Transcript. Spingarn Center. Howard University.

Patch, Penny. Interview by author. August 10, 1992.

Payne, Charles. 1989. "Ella Baker and Models of Social Change." *Signs* 14:885–889.

————.1990. "Men Led, but Women Organized: Movement Participation of Women in the Mississippi Delta." In *Women in the Civil Rights Movement*, ed. Vicki Crawford, Jacqueline Rouse and Barbara Woods, Brooklyn: Carlson Publishing, pp. 1–12.

————. 1994. *I've Got the Light of Freedom*. Berkeley: University of California Press.

Peare, Catherine Owens. 1951. *Mary McLeod Bethune*. New York: Vanguard Press.

Piven, Frances Fox, and Richard A. Cloward. 1979. *Poor People's Movements*. New York: Vintage.

Pizzorno, Alessandro. 1978. "Political Science and Collective Identity in Industrial Conflict." In *The Resurgence of Class Conflict in Western Europe Since 1968*, ed. C. Crouch and A. Pizzorno. New York: Holmes and Meier, pp. 277–298.

Raines, Howell. 1977. *My Soul is Rested*. New York: Penguin Books.

Reagon, Bernice Johnson. Interview by author. November 30, 1992.

Richardson, Gloria. Interview by author. August. 8, 1992.

Richardson, Judy. Interview by author. August 7, 1990, July 10, 1992.

Robinson, Jo Ann Gibson. 1987. *The Montgomery Bus Boycott and the Women Who Started It*. Knoxville: University of Tennessee Press.

————. Interview by Stephen M. Millner. 1989. In *The Walking City: The Montgomery Bus Boycott*, ed. David J. Garrow. Brooklyn: Carlson.

Robnett, Belinda. 1996. "African American Women in the Civil Rights Movement: Gender, Leadership and Micromobilization." *American Journal of Sociology*. 101(6):1661–1193.

Romilly, Constancia. Interview by author. June 5, 1992.

Rosenthal, Naomi, and Michael Schwartz. 1989. "Spontaneity and Democracy in Social Movements." In *Organizing for Change: Social Movement Organizations in Europe and the United States*, International Social Movement Research, Vol. 2, ed. Bert Klandermans. Greenwich, Conn.: JAI Press, pp. 33–59.

Rothschild, Mary Aickin. 1982. *A Case of Black and White: Northern Volunteers and the Southern Freedom Summers, 1964-1965.* Westport, Conn.: Greenwood Press.

Rupp, Leila, and Verta Taylor. 1987. *Survival in the Doldrums: The American Women's Rights Movement, 1945 to the 1960s.* New York: Oxford University Press.

Sacks, Karen. 1988. *Caring By the Hour.* Chicago: University of Illinois Press.

Salem, Dorothy. 1990. *To Better Our World.* New York: Carlson Publishing.

Scott, Joan. 1986. "Gender: A Useful Category of Historical Analysis." *American Historical Review* 91:1053–1075.

Seligman, Adam. 1994. *Innerworldly Individualism: Charismatic Community and its Institutionalization.* New Brunswick: Transaction Publishers.

Sellers, Cleve, with Robert Terrell. 1990. *The River of No Return: The Autobiography of a Black Militant and the Life and Death of* SNCC. New York: William Morrow and Co., Inc.

Siim, Birtie. 1988. "Towards a Feminist Rethinking of the Welfare State." In *The Political Interests of Gender,* ed. Kathleen B. Jones and Anna Jonasdottir. London: Sage.

Sitkoff, Harvard. 1981. *The Struggle for Black Equality, 1954–1980.* New York: Hill and Wang.

Sizemore, Barbara A. 1973. "Sexism and the Black Male." *Black Scholar* 4(6):2.

Smith, Barbara. 1992. "Ain't Gonna Let Nobody Turn Me Around." *Ms. Magazine,* January/February 1992, p. 38.

Smith, Dorothy. 1988. *The Everyday World as Problematic: A Feminist Sociology.* Boston: Northeastern University Press.

Snow, David A., Louis A. Zurcher Jr., and Sheldon Eckland- Olson. 1980. "Social Networks and Social Movements: A Microstructural Approach to Differential Recruitment." *American Sociological Review* 45(5):787–801.

Snow, David A., E. Burke Rochford Jr., Steven K. Worden, and Robert D. Benford. 1986. "Frame Alignment Processes, Micromobilization, and Movement Participation." *American Sociological Review* 51: 464–481.

Somers, Margaret, and Gloria Gibson. 1994. "Reclaiming the Epistemological "Other": Narrative and the Social Constitution of Identity." In *Social Theory and the Politics of Identity,* ed. Craig Calhoun. Oxford: Blackwell, pp. 37–99.

Southern Christian Leadership Conference (SCLC). Papers. Martin Luther King Center, Atlanta.

Spelman, Elizabeth. 1988. *Inessential Woman: Problems of Exclusion in Feminist Thought.* Boston: Beacon Press.

Spender, Dale. 1983. *There's Always Been a Women's Movement this Century.* London: Pandora Press.

Staggenborg, Suzanne. 1995. "Can Feminist Organizations Be Effective?" In *Feminist Organizations: Harvest of the New Women's Movement,* ed. Myra Marx Ferree and Patricia Yancey Martin. Philadelphia, Pa.: Temple University Press, pp. 339–355.

Staples, Robert. 1973. *The Black Woman in America: Sex, Marriage, and the Family.* Chicago: Nelson-Hall Publishers.

Stoper, Emily. 1989. *The Student Nonviolent Coordinating Committee: The Growth of Radicalism in a Civil Rights Organization.* Brooklyn: Carlson Publishing.

Strobel, Margaret. 1995. "The Chicago Women's Liberation Union." In *Feminist Organizations: Harvest of the New Women's Movement,* ed. Myra Marx Ferree and Patricia Martin Yancey. Philadelphia: Temple University Press, pp. 145-164.

Student Non-Violent Coordinating Committee (SNCC). Papers. Martin Luther King Center, Atlanta.

Sutherland, Elizabeth. ed. 1965. *Letters from Mississippi.* New York: McGraw-Hill.

Swidler, Ann. 1986. "Culture in Action: Symbols and Strategies." *American Sociological Review* 51:273–286.

Tarrow, Sidney. 1989. *Democracy and Disorder: Protest and Politics in Italy, 1965-1975.* Oxford: Oxford University Press.

Tarrow, Sidney. 1992. "Mentalities, Political Cultures and Collective Action Frames: Constructing Meanings Through Action." In *Frontiers in Social Movement Theory,* ed. A. Morris and C. Mueller. New Haven: Yale University Press, pp. 174–202.

———. 1994. Power in Movement: *Social Movements, Collective Action and Mass Politics in the Modern State.* Cambridge: Cambridge University Press.

Taylor, Verta. 1989. "Social Movement Continuity: The Women's Movement in Abeyance." *American Sociological Review* 54:761–775.

———. 1995. "Watching for Vibes: Bringing Emotions into the Study of Feminist Organizations." In *Feminist Organizations: Harvest of the New Women's Movement,* ed. Myra Marx Ferree and Patricia Yancey Martin. Philadelphia: Temple University Press, pp. 223–233.

———. 1996. *Rock-a-by-Baby: Feminism, Self-Help, and Postpartum Depression.* New York: Routledge.

Taylor, Verta, and Nancy Whittier. 1992. "Collective Identity in Social Movement Communities: Lesbian Feminist Mobilization." In *Frontiers in Social Movement Theory,* ed. A. Morris and C. Mueller. New Haven: Yale University Press, pp. 104–130.

Tierney, Kathleen J. 1982. "The Battered Women's Movement and the Creation of the Wife Beating Problem." *Social Problems* 29:207–220.

Tillinghast, Muriel. Interview by author. July 19, 1992.

Tilly, Charles. 1978. *From Mobilization to Revolution.* Reading, Mass.: Addison-Wesley.

———. 1986. *The Contentious French.* Cambridge: Harvard University Press.

Tom, Allison. 1995. "Children of Our Culture? Class, Power, and Learning in a Feminist Bank." In *Feminist Organizations: Harvest of the New Women's Movement,* ed. Myra Marx Ferree and Patricia Yancey Martin. Philadelphia: Temple University Press, pp. 165–179.

Toth, Michael. 1981. *The Theory of Two Charismas.* Washington, D.C.: University Press of America.

Touraine, Alain. 1981. *The Voice and the Eye: An Analysis of Social Movements.* New York: Cambridge University Press.

Traugott, Mark, ed. 1995. *Repertoires and Cycles of Collective Action.* Durham, N.C.: Duke University Press.

Tronto, Joan C. 1989. "Women and Caring: What Can Feminists Learn about Morality from Caring?" In *Gender/Body/Knowledge: Feminist Reconstructions of Being and Knowing,* ed. Alison M. Jaggar and Susan Bordo, New Brunswick: Rutgers University Press, pp. 172–187.

Turner, Ralph H. 1968. "Collective Behavior." In *Handbook of Modern Sociology,* ed. R. E. Farris. Chicago: Rand McNally, pp. 485–529.

Turner, Ralph H., and Lewis M. Killian. 1957. *Collective Behavior.* Englewood Cliffs, N.J.: Prentice-Hall.

Walker, Alice. 1983. *In Search of Our Mothers' Gardens.* New York: Harcourt Brace Jovanovich.

Washington, Cynthia. 1977. *Southern Exposure.* 4 (4):14–15.

Wasielewski, Patricia L. 1985. "The Emotional Basis of Charisma." In *Symbolic Interaction* 8(2):207–222.

Weber, Max. 1968. *Economy and Society: An Outline of Interpretive Sociology.* Berkeley: University of California Press.

West, Candace, and Don H. Zimmerman. 1987. "Doing Gender." *Gender and Society* 1: 125–151.

West, Guida, and Rhoda Lois Blumberg, eds. 1990. *Women and Social Protest*. New York: Oxford University Press.

White, Deborah Gray. 1985. *Ar'n't I A Woman? Female Slaves in the Plantation South*. New York: W.W. Norton.

Whittier, Nancy. 1995. "Turning it Over: Personnel Change in the Columbus, Ohio, Women's Movement, 1969-1984." In *Feminist Organizations: Harvest of the New Women's Movement*, ed. Myra Marx Ferree and Patricia Yancey Martin. Philadelphia: Temple University Press, pp. 180–198.

Young, Jean Wheeler Smith. Interview by author. August 9, 1992.

Zald, Mayer N. 1996. "Culture, ideology, and Strategic Framing." In *Comparative Perspectives on Social Movements: Political Opportunities, Mobilizing Structures, and Cultural Framings*, ed. Doug McAdam, John McCarthy, and Mayer Zald. New York: Cambridge University Press, pp. 261–274.

Zald, Mayer N., and Roberta Ash. 1966. "Social Movement Organizations: Growth, Decay and Change." *Social Forces* 44(3):327–341.

Zellner, Dottie. Interview by author. July 27, 1992.

Zinn, Howard. 1964. SNCC — *The New Abolitionists*. Boston: Beacon Press.

Zinn, Maxine Baca, and Bonnie Thornton Dill. 1994. *Women of Color in U.S. Society*. Philadelphia: Temple University Press.

Index